SUPRANATIONALISM
AND INTERNATIONAL
ADJUDICATION

**UNIVERSITY
OF ILLINOIS
PRESS**
URBANA
CHICAGO
LONDON
1969

SUPRANATIONALISM
AND INTERNATIONAL
ADJUDICATION

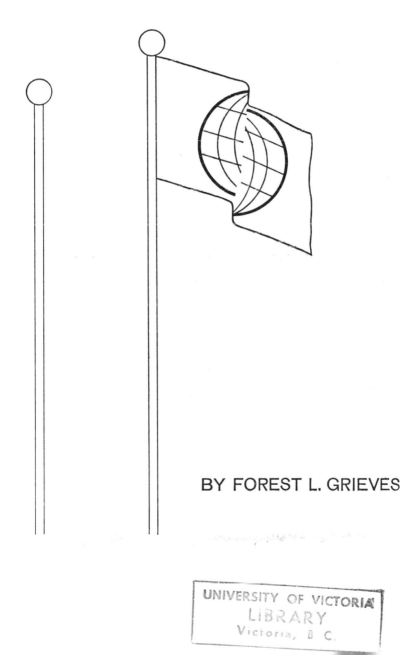

BY FOREST L. GRIEVES

To my mother,
who inspired this effort,
and to my wife Irmgard and son Kevin,
who helped me complete it

PREFACE

A relatively new word in the vocabulary of politics is the term "supranational." It conjures up grand visions of the exercise of political authority beyond the nation-state and suggests the imminence of a superstate capable of regulating sovereign states. While these visions are exaggerated, they highlight one of the major dilemmas of international relations: the existence of the traditional concept of national sovereignty, whereby independent states possess ultimate control over their actions, vis-à-vis the clear need to somehow regulate these actions, thus insuring international order.

There have always been, as Chapter 1 makes clear, certain restrictions of sovereignty. In the past 50 years a significant development has been for nations to submit voluntarily to restrictions of their sovereignty by allocating powers, often supranational powers, to international organizations. There is no precise definition of the term "supranational." It signifies generally, however, a level of international integration beyond mere intergovernmentalism yet still short of a federal system. One means of measuring the degree of supranationalism found in modern international organizations is by looking at international adjudication, for surely the development of an international "rule of law" represents one of the more advanced stages on the way to world order.

This political-legal study is intended to accomplish several things, which, when considered together, will hopefully reflect a worthwhile contribution to the study of international relations. First, the task of Chapter 1 is threefold: (1) to establish perspective for the study by briefly reviewing the nature of national sovereignty in modern international relations; (2) to survey the literature of the field in an effort to formulate a working concept of supranationalism (largely an uncharted area), which will be further defined on the basis of the actual record of five international adjudicative tribunals (the Central American Court of Justice, the Permanent Court of International Justice, the International Court of Justice, the Court of the European Communities, and the European Court of Human Rights); and (3) to set up a framework whereby these five tribunals can be meaningfully studied relative to the supranational characteristics they may or may not possess.

This latter goal requires some initial elaboration. A basic assumption of this study is the reasonable but unproven hypothesis that the level of supranational power possessed by an international court will generally reflect the limits of tolerance international society will accept regarding restrictions of sovereignty by the "rule of law." That is, one would expect the supranational power of an international court to indicate at least the minimum level of restrictions on sovereignty that nation-states are willing to accept.

While this hypothesis cannot be proven here, the object of this study is to examine it with a view toward defining this "minimum level." Each of the five tribunals will be studied on the basis of the following framework: (a) the supranational expectations of the statesmen who created the court, (b) the constitutional basis of the court (i.e., what restrictions of sovereignty did states actually commit themselves to in the treaty establishing the court?), and (c) the actual practice of the court (i.e., in its work, how does the court compare with the supranational powers suggested by the first two categories?). The general framework outlined by these three categories is refined further in Chapter 1.

A second goal of this study, the burden of Chapters 2 through 6, is to use the criteria outlined above to examine each court in detail. Finally, Chapter 7 attempts to define the position of national sovereignty in international courts and to evaluate the role of the international court in integration beyond the nation-state.

Much of the research for this study is based upon extensive use and translation of foreign source materials and compilation of previously untranslated data. This method, although tedious, has the twofold value of (1) allowing a greater field of research in original source materials most directly concerned with the tribunals under study, and of (2) providing new views and data to the English reader.

By way of acknowledgments, I am indebted to Professor Clifton E. Wilson of the Department of Government at the University of Arizona for guiding this research effort as a doctoral dissertation. I am also grateful to Professors Rosendo A. Gomez, Clifford M. Lytle, Currin V. Shields, and J. Richard Wagner, all of the Department of Government, University of Arizona, for reading the manuscript during its preparation.

The author is further indebted to Professor Kenneth S. Carlston of the College of Law at the University of Illinois for carefully reviewing the manuscript and making many valuable comments.

Finally, my special thanks go to my wife Irmgard for encouragement throughout and for bearing most of the typing burden.

CONTENTS

List of Tables

List of Figures

CHAPTER ONE

SOVEREIGNTY AND SUPRANATIONALISM

A. SOVEREIGNTY

Nation-State System

The springboard for any examination of international relations is the nation-state system. The rise of this system is usually linked with the Peace of Westphalia (1648). In the subsequent 300 years, the world has developed from a few essentially European states with limited contact to a high-pressure crowded system of over a hundred sovereign states with highly complex, intricate relations.

The dilemma of international relations is the seemingly impossible task of finding some middle ground between two opposite poles: a world of sovereign states (the logical consequence of which seems to be *Realpolitik*) vis-à-vis the need for ordered international relations (especially since the advent of atomic weapons). History is full of attempts to resolve this dilemma, ranging from loose cooperative efforts of international law and organization to outright federal integrative movements.

The basic political unit of world politics, and the barrier to the creation of world order, is of course the state. However one defines the state, a basic element is the concept of sovereignty. Unfortunately, as John Stoessinger so aptly notes in this regard, "it is very difficult, if not impossible, to discover where and in whom this sovereignty is actually vested."[1] The reason, of course, is because sover-

---

[1] John G. Stoessinger, *The Might of Nations: World Politics in Our Time* (rev. ed.; New York: Random House, 1965), p. 250.

eignty is basically an abstraction that defies precise definition.

A necessary prerequisite to understanding modern attempts at creating supranational organizations to regulate interstate conduct, and the role of the courts in these organizations, is a very brief survey of what sovereignty has generally meant—both in the past and today.

Nature of Sovereignty

Sovereignty as a social fact existed long before a legal concept of sovereignty was formulated. Defining "state" in loose terms, sovereignty really stems from that period in ancient history when more than one "state" existed. The rulers of such early "states" as Egypt, Greece, Persia, and Carthage possessed supreme power over a given territory and populace and were independent of any external power.

ROMANS   The term "sovereignty" did not really develop until the Middle Ages; however, a rather precise legal concept of the content of sovereignty had apparently been used already by the Romans. Marek Korowicz cites as an example the Roman legal concept of independence as stated by Proculus: "that nation is free which is not subject to any government of any other nation."[2]

MIDDLE AGES   The idea of sovereignty as the supreme power of the state was a product of the Middle Ages. De Jouvenel sees the growth of the concept of sovereignty as an answer to the "primordial character of the problem of who decides."[3] In the medieval period, it was the church which first solved this problem by its concentration of power in the spiritual realm. This plentitude of authority in a single office, de Jouvenel suggests, served as a model for the growth of sovereignty in the temporal realm.

The doctrine of sovereignty developed in the temporal realm as a principle of national unity. Kings sought to develop, during and following the decline of the church, strong national states and to bring under their centralized control the various elements of local authority.

Credit for the first systematic formulation of the doctrine of sovereignty belongs to Jean Bodin, who outlined the concept of the su-

---

[2] See Marek Korowicz, "Some Present Aspects of Sovereignty in International Law," *Recueil des Cours*, CII (1961), 7. He notes the terms *liber* and *libertas* which, although meaning "independent" and "independence," correspond exactly in meaning to "sovereign" and "sovereignty." He also notes that Hugo Grotius quotes this definition in *De Iure Belli ac Pacis* (1625).

[3] Bertrand de Jouvenel, *Sovereignty: An Enquiry into the Political Good* (Chicago: University of Chicago Press, 1957), p. 4.

preme power (*summa potestas, majestas,* or *suprema potestas*) of the state in his *Les Six Livres de la République* (1576) .[4] As France at this time was torn by a civil war, Bodin concluded that only a strong central authority could offer order. This strong central authority was the "principal foundation of every State"; there could be no state without sovereignty which is "the absolute and perpetual power of a State."[5]

Bodin was really concerned only with the concept of sovereignty *within* a state; however, since the sovereign is the single source from which all laws originate, a logical extrapolation is that the sovereign is not only above the law but independent of restrictions—internal or external. The Roman conception of sovereignty contained no limitations of the state's independence (*libertas*) . Bodin's seemingly absolute sovereign, however, was subject to very substantial limitations. Bodin's doctrine of sovereignty can be summarized in the following points:

1. sovereignty is the essence of the state;

2. the sovereign possesses supreme power over the territory and its inhabitants, unrestrained by any earthly law or power;

3. this supreme power is limited only by:

    a) divine law

    b) a sovereign's own obligations toward other sovereigns or toward individuals;

4. a sovereign should observe agreements made with other states.[6]

LATER VIEWS The foregoing summary shows that Bodin linked his idea of sovereignty with a broader idea of a world community ruled by natural law.[7] He made sovereignty essentially a

---

[4] Latin title: *De Republica Libri Six.*

[5] *De Republica,* L. I, IX, p. 125. Cited by Korowicz, *op. cit.,* p. 8.

[6] See Korowicz, *op. cit.,* pp. 8–9.

[7] A similar concept was formulated very clearly in 1609 by a great jurist, Charles L'Oyseau, who was contemporary with Henry IV; cf. "For sovereignty is the form which causes the state to exist; indeed, the state and sovereignty in the concrete are synonymous. Sovereignty is the summit of authority, by means of which the state is created and maintained. . . . However, as it is only God who can be all-powerful and the authority of men cannot be completely absolute, there are three sorts of laws which limit the authority of the sovereign, without affecting sovereignty. There are, the laws of God, because the prince is no less sovereign for being subject to God; the natural, as distinct from the positive, ordinances of justice, because, as we said above, it is right that the public seigniory should be exercised justly and not capriciously; and, finally, the fundamental laws of the state, because the prince should use sovereignty according to its own nature and under the powers and conditions on which it is established." C. L'Oyseau, *Traicté des Seigneuries* (Paris, 1609) , pp. 1–9. Cited by de Jouvenel, *op. cit.,* pp. 180–184.

principle of internal political order. Some subsequent writers, however, saw sovereignty rather as a principle of international disorder. The classic example is found in Hobbes's *Leviathan,* in which inter-state relationships are similar to men in the state of nature—characterized by war of every man against every man.[8] In modern terms, it must be noted that there are divergent views on the juridical meaning of sovereignty as well as on its location and consequences.[9] It is, however, true that in many respects Bodin's formulation of sovereignty is probably the predominant concept held today—although there have been and still are many divergent concepts.[10] For the

---

[8] See Thomas Hobbes, *Leviathan,* reprinted from the edition of 1651 (Oxford: Clarendon Press, 1958), p. 273 ff. Another classic example is Emerich de Vattel, *The Law of Nations* (London: new edition by Joseph Chitty, 1834), pp. I and V. He notes: "Nations being composed of men naturally free and independent, and who, before the establishment of civil society, lived together in the state of nature,—Nations, or sovereign states, are to be considered as so many free persons living together in the state of nature. But the body of the Nation, the State, remains absolutely free and independent with respect to all other men, and all 'other' Nations, as long as it has not voluntarily submitted to them."

[9] Oft-cited legal discussions of sovereignty are those by John Marshall in *The Schooner Exchange* v. *McFaddon,* 7 Cranch (U.S.), 116 (1812); the advisory opinion by the Permanent Court of International Justice of September 5, 1931, concerning the *Customs Regime Between Germany and Austria,* P.C.I.J., Series A/B, No. 41, pp. 45–46; and the "Report of Rapporteur of Committee 1 to Commission I," in United Nations Conference on International Organization, *Documents,* Vol. VI, Doc. 994 (English), I/1/34 (1).

Perhaps typical of the divergent view among leading publicists are the following. Quincy Wright and Georg Schwarzenberger, for example, see sovereignty as the cornerstone of international law and politics, while Charles Fenwick claims that "it is only by a fiction that sovereignty can be kept compatible with the numerous restrictions upon a state's freedom of conduct which arise as a direct consequence of the binding character of the rules of international law." See in this respect: Quincy Wright, *The Study of War,* II (Chicago: University of Chicago Press, 1944), 896, 898, 906, 907, 922; Georg Schwarzenberger, *International Law as Applied by International Courts and Tribunals* (London: Stevens & Sons Ltd., 1950), p. 53; and Charles Fenwick, *International Law* (4th ed.; New York: Appleton-Century-Crofts, Inc., 1965), p. 126. Another author even suggests that "most legal theorists today have avoided the use of the term [sovereignty] because of its inherent ambiguities. . . ." See William D. Coplin, *The Functions of International Law: An Introduction to the Role of International Law in the Contemporary World* (Chicago: Rand McNally and Company, 1966), p. 172.

[10] This point is well made by Professor Stephen S. Goodspeed in *The Nature and Function of International Organization* (New York: Oxford University Press, 1967), p. 10. He writes: "Jean Bodin in 1576 first introduced the term [sovereignty] into the literature of political science and defined it as 'the supreme power of the state over its citizens and subjects, unrestrained by law.' *The essential features of this definition have persisted down to the present with certain modifications and interpretations* [italics mine]. When one observes that a state is sovereign he usually means that the activities of the state are not legally subject to the control of any higher or external authority." The modern relevance of the Bodin view is also corroborated by the U.N. definition of

purposes of this study, sovereignty can be defined (following Bodin) simply as the supreme power of the state over its populace and territory, independent from any external authority.

The object here is not to establish a strict juridical definition of sovereignty or to explore its many shades of meaning in legal and political theory. Rather, a simple working definition of sovereignty (naturally, with due acknowledgment of the problems surrounding the use of the term) should be sufficient to give the perspective needed to understand what the concept has meant to the nation-state in the past and what potential supranational restrictions on sovereignty mean for the future.

Sovereignty then symbolizes one of the most basic assumptions of international relations—the authority of the state to act independently. This does not mean, however, that the sovereign state is free from obligations either to its citizens or to other states, or that the exercise of this sovereignty cannot be restricted. Korowicz uses the terms "qualitative" and "quantitative," which seem meaningful here to describe restrictions on sovereignty.[11] Unless a state is a dependent entity (such as occupied Germany), its sovereignty remains "qualitatively" unchanged. Yet every state is subject to certain "quantitative" limitations on its sovereignty, which do not destroy the basic sovereign character of that state. The nature of these latter restrictions is outlined below.

Limitations of Sovereignty

These "quantitative" restrictions come from two different but interrelated sources: the nature of world politics and voluntary submission to restrictions.

NATURE OF WORLD POLITICS A very significant limitation of state sovereignty has been effected by developments (perhaps inevitable and often quite unrelated to politics) in the past 300 years of world history. Some of these developments are:

1. Decline of the state. The real basis of sovereignty is the territorial state, which became the basic sovereign unit (i.e., the basic political unit) in international relations for a very practical reason. Sovereigns could hold only as much land as they could control and defend; conversely, people are only willing to recognize, in the long run, that authority which possesses the power of protection. Only the compact territorial state, following the breakdown of the feudal

---

sovereignty (presumably a condensation of major modern views) drafted by the International Law Commission in 1949. See *infra*, footnote 15.

[11] Korowicz, *op. cit.*, p. 108.

system, could provide such protection. There is much to suggest, however, that the concept of the territorial state is no longer meaningful. John Herz, for example, links the decline of the territorial state with the beginning of the nineteenth century.[12] This has come about because the hard outer shell of the state (i.e., its territorial limits) is no longer impenetrable—mostly because of technology, communications, industrialization, and weapons.

2. Proliferation of "sovereign" nations. The number of nations has increased so rapidly (particularly in recent years) that an increasingly larger number of "sovereign" states is forced to coexist within a limited arena of international action. The existence of a myriad of so-called "sovereign" states has simply meant the imposition of many practical limitations on sovereign prerogatives.[13]

3. Rising human demands. Not only does the fact that nation-states are "stumbling over" one another when they attempt various courses of action indicate some limitations of sovereignty, but the mere "closeness of quarters" creates common problems—problems which do not recognize sovereign territorial boundaries. Increases in population and advances in technology are forcing the interdependence of nations. There are rising human demands to meet such common problems as disease, economic depression, or mere ease of communications—demands which the state alone cannot meet. This has meant an increase in the importance of international organizations as well as of the individual person in international relations.[14]

---

[12] John Herz, "Rise and Demise of the Territorial State," *World Politics*, IX, 4 (July, 1957), 473–493. A broader discussion of the position of the state in world affairs is offered by John Herz, *International Politics in the Atomic Age* (New York: Columbia University Press, 1959). Consider also James N. Rosenau, "Compatibility, Consensus, and an Emerging Political Science of Adaptation," *American Political Science Review*, LXI, 4 (December, 1967), 983–988. Rosenau suggests the "convergence of national and international systems" whereby the old boundary lines separating them are becoming blurred.

[13] As far as the actual practice of states is concerned, Clyde Eagleton holds the following view: "No state since . . . [the Peace of Westphalia] has ever been wholly independent. Sovereignty presumed omnipotence, but there can only be one highest, and such a situation has not been found since the fall of the ancient universal empires. . . . States are only relatively independent [and] domestic law is constantly subordinated to international law. . . . Sovereignty has now been replaced by responsibility, and the word now means, in its external sense, nothing more than the sphere of relative external independence and exclusive jurisdiction reserved to it with the assent of the community, and limited by that community." Clyde Eagleton, *International Government* (rev. ed.; New York: The Ronald Press Company, 1948), pp. 25–26.

[14] This can be seen in a broad range of areas, from the U.N.'s trusteeship system and the functional organizations to the Nürnberg trials and the conventions on human rights.

4. Cooperation *v.* intervention. The interdependence of states has also brought with it many problems never envisaged by the seventeenth-century impenetrable sovereign states. Interdependence has meant the advent of the economic blockade and ideological-political penetration. But even where friendly interstate cooperation has been the goal, dependence (e.g., economic vassalage) and outright intervention have developed.[15] Many economic cooperation programs, even of the most general sort, often result in a greater degree of intervention into the affairs of the recipient state than even a loose interpretation of full sovereignty would allow. By way of brief example, in the well-known Point IV Program (Title IV of the Act for International Development, June 5, 1960, 64 *Stat.* 204 as amended) the granting of American funds was made conditional on American supervision and the observance, in the use of these funds, of certain American basic principles of fair labor standards, wages and working conditions, and management-labor relations.[16]

5. New concept of war. The *ius ad bellum* has always been a sovereign prerogative, an instrument of national policy. The main objective of war has always been the attainment of greater security, power, glory, or wealth. It still made sense for Prussia to make war on France in 1870, or for Japan to make war on Russia in 1904. General destructiveness aside, one might even argue that war still had some vestige of meaning as late as 1945, but the advent of atomic weapons has wrought a profound change. Total war, though not impossible, is for all purposes of *rational* national policy prohibited.

B. V. A. Rölling sees two major functions of war as being affected by its prohibition: (1) the function of war according to von Clausewitz (war as the continuation of politics by other means—i.e., war in order to promote national interests and to change the existing legal position) ; and (2) the function of war according to Hugo Grotius (i.e., war as the means of maintaining law) .[17] Rölling may be overstating his case, but one fact stands out clearly: although

---

[15] A restatement of international law principles by the International Law Commission of the U.N., in the "Draft Declaration of the Rights and Duties of States," inferred, *inter alia*, from the basic concept of sovereignty, the duty of non-intervention in the internal and external affairs of other states (Article 3). See United Nations, General Assembly, *Official Records* (4th Sess., Supp. No. 10, A/925, June 24, 1949) .

[16] For discussion see Karl Loewenstein, "Sovereignty and International Coöperation," *American Journal of International Law,* XLVIII, 2 (April, 1954), 232–233.

[17] B. V. A. Rölling, *International Law in an Expanded World* (Amsterdam: Djambatan, 1960) , pp. xix–xx.

states can and do use their atomic arsenals as "persuaders" in international politics, or use "limited wars" (with all the implications of possible escalation) as instruments of policy, the deadly seriousness of such action has a limiting effect on sovereignty that did not exist prior to 1945.[18] Because of this, the curious situation has resulted in which the smaller nations, due to their lack of "atomic responsibility," are often "more sovereign" than the larger nations.

6. New international actors. Partly because of many of the foregoing factors, new international actors have appeared in international relations, possessing some of the rights previously held exclusively by states. In classic international law states have been the only true international actors (and they still are the only *full* members of the international community), yet today a more important role for individuals and international organizations is emerging in international law. For example, there are two different ways to interpret the role of the sovereign state vis-à-vis the individual. In the words of Quincy Wright, one can

interpret the state as sovereign, protecting or punishing individuals in its own interest under such guidance as it chooses to accept from international law, but it is also possible to interpret the individual as a jural personality with rights under international law which he can only pursue through the agency of his state and with duties under international law which the society of nations can enforce only through the agency of the state with jurisdiction over him.

The state, in other words, may be construed not as a sovereign entity valuable in itself, but as an agent on the one hand of the individuals that compose it, and on the other of the universal society embracing all humanity.[19]

Wright further points out that the first interpretation was generally accepted during the nineteenth century, while the second interpretation reflects state principles adopted during the past generation. He attributes the transition to the many general treaties

---

[18] He even suggests that the recent national wars have modified the position of national sovereignty much as the wars of religion altered the position of religion. See *ibid.*, p. xxii.

[19] Quincy Wright, *Contemporary International Law: A Balance Sheet* (Garden City, N.Y.: Doubleday and Company, Inc., 1955), p. 21. One of the best-known arguments for recognizing the status of the individual is that discussed by Philip Jessup, who insists that "international law, like national law, must be directly applicable to the individual." Philip C. Jessup, *A Modern Law of Nations* (New York: The Macmillan Company, 1948), p. 2. A fuller review of the changing status of the individual in international law, along with bibliographical and case references, is offered by Fenwick, *op. cit.*, pp. 147–154, and by William Bishop, *International Law: Cases and Materials* (2nd ed.; Boston: Little, Brown and Company, 1962), Chap. 3, Sec. C.

specifying the rights of aborigines, minorities, workers, women, children, and other potentially oppressed classes.[20] The point is that individuals are slowly achieving increased importance in international affairs in relation to states.

In this same vein, the ever-increasing role of international organizations in regulating international relations has meant that many of them, in order to fulfill their role successfully, have assumed a juridical personality.[21] Although clearly not on an equal footing with states, international organizations have an enhanced status vis-à-vis states. As Chapter 5 of this study shows, this new status has developed to a point where an international organization (or an organ thereof) can even appear before an international court in contentious proceedings alongside a state. This shows a substantial degree of evolution from the situation in classic international law in which states were the sole legal subjects, unchallenged by "lesser" entities. This, combined with the factors noted on the preceding pages, means that state sovereignty is subject to very real limitations, stemming from the nature of the world itself.

VOLUNTARY SUBMISSION TO RESTRICTIONS   Although not always starkly delineated, the above restrictions on sovereignty have been largely the by-product of world developments. Closely linked (and perhaps inseparable) are those international agreements through which states have agreed to limit their sovereign preroga-

---

[20] Wright, *Contemporary International Law*, p. 21.

[21] See, for example, the Court's opinion in the famous Bernadotte Case, United Nations, I.C.J., *Reports of Judgments, Advisory Opinions and Orders*, 1949, p. 179, and Quincy Wright, "The Jural Personality of the United Nations," *American Journal of International Law*, XLIII, 3 (July, 1949), 509–516. See also Articles 19 and 20 of the ILO Constitution (as amended in 1946). Other examples are Article 19 of the WHO Constitution and Article 3 (b) of the Convention on IMCO. For a full discussion of this area, see Philip C. Jessup *et al., International Organization* (New York: Carnegie Endowment for International Peace, 1955), pp. 38–44. On private international organizations (e.g., Red Cross and Order of Malta) see H. B. Jacobini, *International Law* (Homewood, Ill.: The Dorsey Press, 1968), pp. 52–53, and Bishop, *op. cit.*, pp. 217–219.

For further discussion of the changing legal roles of international organizations vis-à-vis states see Bishop, *op. cit.*, Chap. 3, Secs. A and B, and (with particular reference to the legal status of the European communities) Peter Hay, *Federalism and Supranational Organizations: Patterns for New Legal Structures* (Urbana: University of Illinois Press, 1966), Chap. 2. Some discussion of the appearance and role of other legal entities (e.g., dependent states, the Vatican, tribal associations, and business enterprises) in international law is provided by Jacobini, *op. cit.*, pp. 45–55; Bishop, *op. cit.*, Chap. 3, *passim;* and Fenwick, *op. cit.*, Chap. 6, pp. 125–147. Some attention is devoted to the legal status of business enterprises in the European communities in Chapter 5 of the present study.

tives—partly because events have forced them to, partly because such agreements were convenient, and partly because of outright foresight. Beyond the pale of simple treaties one finds the most sophisticated restrictions on sovereignty in international integrative movements—ranging from the loosely confederative international organization on the one hand to the fully integrated federal state on the other. In the gray area in between, a new concept has achieved prominence in recent years—"supranationalism."

B. SUPRANATIONALISM
Definition

BACKGROUND OF THE TERM   The term "supranational" easily equals "sovereignty" in both abstractness and disagreement as to its exact meaning. This is in large measure true simply because the meaning of "supranational" hinges upon one's definition of "sovereignty"—as does indeed such a familiar concept as "federalism." In this context, Ernst Haas writes: "If the term 'federation' can boast an ancient and honourable lineage in the history of political thought, the same cannot be said of the kindred expression 'supranationality'. Yet this term, like political integration, is now current in discussions of regionalism and, like the notion of integration, is sadly in need of precise definition."[22]

The West German *Staatslexikon* notes that the term "supranational" appeared for the first time in positive law in the treaty establishing the European Coal and Steel Community (ECSC).[23] Article 9 of the Treaty reads:

The members of the High Authority shall exercise their functions in complete independence, in the general interest of the Community. In the fulfillment of their duties, they shall neither solicit nor accept instructions from any government or from any organization. They will abstain from all conduct incompatible with the *supranational character* of their functions.

Each member State agrees to respect this *supranational character* and to make no effort to influence the members of the High Authority in the execution of their duties [italics mine].[24]

---

[22] Ernst B. Haas, *The Uniting of Europe: Political, Social, and Economic Forces, 1950–1957* (Stanford, Calif.: Stanford University Press, 1958) , p. 32.

[23] Karl Zemanek, "Supranationale Institutionen," in *Staatslexikon: Recht, Wirtschaft, Gesellschaft* (Sechste, völlig neu bearbeitete und erweiterte Auflage. Bd. 7; Freiburg im Breisgau: Verlag Herder, 1962) , pp. 894–898.

[24] See "Treaty Between the Federal Republic of Germany, the Kingdom of Belgium, the French Republic, the Italian Republic, the Grand Duchy of Luxembourg and the Kingdom of the Netherlands Instituting the European Coal and Steel Community," Signed at Paris on 18 April 1951, *United Nations*

The Treaty does not define "supranational." Its meaning can only be gleaned from a careful study of the specific powers and practices of the organization—a subject for later chapters. By way of arriving at a working definition, however, it is of interest to note that the only occurrence of the term in the various European communities is in Article 9 of the ECSC Treaty. The term was used in the original version (1956) of the ECSC Personnel Statute (Articles 1 and 10), but was dropped when the Statute was amended in 1961. Further, it has not been used in the European Economic Community (EEC) or in the European Atomic Energy Community (Euratom) treaties. Werner Feld suggests that "the reason for this change may be that the term lacks legal clarity and has political rather than legal significance. From the political point of view the term is quite useful because it focuses attention on certain politically important aspects of the Communities."[25]

The term "supranational" apparently had very little currency in pre–European Community days. Edith Wynner and Georgia Lloyd, in a 1944 study of various peace plans, discussed the concept. They spoke of a "division of authority between member nations and the supra-national organization."[26] According to their view, "supranational" did not mean a giving up of sovereignty. Rather, nations retained full sovereignty over their national affairs, "transferring by common consent only that part of national jurisdiction which the authors believe will enable the supra-national organization to deal with problems that go beyond national interests and concern also other nations and peoples."[27]

Although later writers seem to accept the general framework of this view, disagreement over terms is so rampant as to leave nothing but a confusing tangle of words. A brief survey of some of the leading authors who have grappled with these terms is illustrative.[28] Au-

Treaty Series, CCLXI, 3229 (1957), 140–319. Various writers use the terms "supra-national," "supernational," or "super-national." "Supranational" is preferred here because it is the form used in the Treaty. The French text, which is the official language of the Treaty, reads *"le caractère supranational de leurs fonctions"* (italics mine).

[25] Werner Feld, *The Court of the European Communities: New Dimension in International Adjudication* (The Hague: Martinus Nijhoff, 1964), p. 2.

[26] Edith Wynner and Georgia Lloyd (eds.), *Searchlight on Peace Plans: Choose Your Road to World Government* (New York: E. P. Dutton and Company, Inc., 1944), p. 5.

[27] *Ibid.*

[28] The preponderance of European writers in this area is undoubtedly due to the immediacy of European integration. The views of selected other authors, however, are found elsewhere in this chapter.

thors find the essence of "supranational" in the "transfer of sovereignty" (Kunz) ; in the "transfers of sovereignty" and the "direct relations between the governed and the new institutions" (Reuter,
Schlochauer) ; in the transfer of "certain powers previously vested
in individual sovereign states" (Van Kleffens) ; in the "joint exercise
of sovereignty . . . by organs possessing the power to discharge their
task" (Nord) ; in the "autonomy of the [international] organs"
(Jaenicke) ; or in the exercise of powers previously held by national
governments, where "decisions of the governing body are binding
on the member governments and may be taken by majority vote"
(Stoessinger).[29]

Whether "supranational" implies a "limitation" on sovereignty
or an actual "transfer" is at this point immaterial, for the results,
when spelled out in specifics, are the same. In conformity with the
context outlined earlier in this chapter, this study will refer to "limitations" on the exercise of sovereignty and the "transfer" of jurisdiction. Before the details of these concepts in international courts
can be meaningfully examined, however, agreement on some con-
ceptual framework, however loose, must be reached. Paul Reuter,
Professor on the Faculty of Law at Paris, writing on the ECSC
Treaty negotiations, sets the tone for this need:

> During the course of negotiations on the Treaty one saw appear
> spontaneously, like a thing driven from within, the term "supranational".
> The success of this expression, rather new in the French language, was
> considerable.
>
> It would be perhaps premature and in any case futile to wish to present
> a too strict juridical theory on the meaning of this word; but the
> determination of its general sense is indispensable and it throws a bright
> light on the institutions of the Plan.[30]

---

[29] See Josef L. Kunz, "Supra-national Organs," *American Journal of Interna-
tional Law*, XLVI, 4 (October, 1952), 690–698; Paul Reuter, "Le Plan Schuman,"
Recueil des Cours, LXXXI, 2 (1952), 523–629; Hans-Jürgen Schlochauer,
"Rechtsformen der europäischen Ordnung," *Archiv des Völkerrechts*, V
(1955–56), 40 ff.; E. N. Van Kleffens, "The Case for European Integration:
Political Considerations," in C. Grove Haines (ed.), *European Integration*
(Baltimore: The Johns Hopkins Press, 1957), pp. 80–96; Hans Nord, "In Search
of a Political Framework for an Integrated Europe," also in Haines, pp. 215–228;
G. Jaenicke, "Die Sicherung des übernationalen Charakters der Organe internationaler Organisationen," *Zeitschrift für ausländisches öffentliches Recht und
Völkerrecht*, XIV, 1 (December–January, 1952–53), 46 ff.; and Stoessinger, *op.
cit.*, Chaps. 1, 11, and 13. A brief discussion of some of these views is offered by
Zemanek, *op. cit.*, pp. 896–897. A thorough survey of the differing views on the
political and legal meaning of "supranational" is offered by Hay, *op. cit.*,
especially Chap. 2.

[30] Reuter, *op. cit.*, p. 543 (my translation).

BASIC ASPECTS OF THE CONCEPT　The area in which "supranationality" is located is easily found. Nearly every writer on the subject agrees that it is "somewhere" between an intergovernmental organization and a federation. A notable example of this view is given by Ernst Haas, who notes, on the basis of his own survey, the following consensus: "The feature common to most of the jurists [this also holds true for scholars and statesmen] who were active in the drafting of ECSC is an admission that supranationality refers to a type of integration in which more power is given to the new central agency than is customary in the case of conventional international organizations, but less than is generally yielded to an emergent federal government."[31]

The exact limits of supranationality, or its relative position between international and federal, cannot be defined.[32] The area that is supranational merges with both ends of a spectrum of possible interstate organizations (*Staatenverbindungen*). Figure 1 shows this relationship.

INTERNATIONAL　　SUPRANATIONAL　　FEDERAL

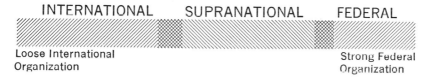

Loose International
Organization

Strong Federal
Organization

FIG. 1　Spectrum of Interstate Bonds (*Staatenverbindungen*)

Three points regarding Figure 1 should be made: (1) the fuzziness of the limits of suprantionalism should not lead to despair, for it is common, for example in federalism, to speak of "degrees of federalism"—i.e., strong or weak federal systems. The difference between a strong supranational bond and a weak federal one is bound to be unclear.[33] (2) Figure 1 is in part misleading, for rather than speak-

[31] Haas, *op. cit.*, p. 34.

[32] Interestingly, Robert Schuman, one of the principal sponsors of the ECSC Treaty, locates the supranational at an *equal distance* from both international individualism on one side and a federation of states on the other. See the Introduction to Paul Reuter's *La Communauté Européenne du Charbon et de l'Acier* (Paris: Librairie Générale de Droit et de Jurisprudence, 1953).

[33] Evidence of the confusion which exists here comes from such a venerable source as Jean Monnet himself. He once called the ECSC a "supranational, in other words a federal institution." Cited by Henry L. Mason, *The European Coal and Steel Community: Experiment in Supranationalism* (The Hague: Martinus Nijhoff, 1955), p. 123. Further, Albert Van Houtte, Registrar (*Greffier*) of the

ing of *supranational organizations,* one frequently speaks of international organizations or agencies with *supranational characteristics* (or with *elements of supranationality*). (3) The only way to set even relative limits of supranationalism is to examine the specific powers of specific organizations.

The working definition of supranationalism which will serve as the basis for this study is as follows: *The term "supranational" signifies that signatory states have transferred to an international institution certain limited decision-making powers normally exercised only by the governmental organs of a sovereign state, powers which include the capability of issuing, under certain specified conditions, binding norms to the states or to their inhabitants.*[34]

Pierre Pescatore, Minister Plenipotentiary and Political Director of the Luxembourg Ministry of Foreign Affairs, offers a valuable refinement to this definition: "By 'supranationality' we understand an institutional structure characterized by autonomous power placed at the service of the common interests of several states."[35] Three essential traits of this supranationalism are:

1. the existence of *common interests* (*intérêts communs*) among several states such that some common institutions will result;

2. the placement of *real powers* (*pouvoirs réels*) at the service of these institutions (the simple power of recommendation does not constitute supranationalism); and

3. the *autonomy of this power* (*autonomie de ce pouvoir*). An instance might be international majoritarianism or the independent exercise of power by an institution.[36]

OBJECTIONS TO THE TERM   Although most authors advocate care in the use of the term "supranational" (simply because the variety of interpretations as to its meaning can easily lead to confusion), a few have expressed outright opposition to the term. Two notable examples are Marek Korowicz and Ruth Lawson. The es-

---

Court of Justice of the ECSC, calls for the recognition of "le caractère fédéral de la Communauté." See Van Houtte, "La Cour de Justice de la Communauté du Charbon et de l'Acier," *Annuaire Européen,* II (1956), 190. Most scholars deny the federal character of the European communities. Mason, *op. cit.,* Chap. 6, offers a discussion of federalism vis-à-vis supranationalism in the European communities. For the general nature of federalism see K. C. Wheare, *Federal Government* (New York: Oxford University Press, 1964), especially Chaps. 1 and 2.

[34] Definition adapted from Feld, *op. cit.,* pp. 1–2.

[35] Pierre Pescatore, "Les Relations Extérieures des Communautés Européennes: Contribution à la Doctrine de la Personalité des Organisations Internationales," *Recueil des Cours,* CIII, 3 (1961), 27 (my translation).

[36] See *ibid.*

sence of their position is that since "supranational" organizations are really strong "international" organizations, why not refer to them as such?[37] Rather than introduce a new, confusing term, is it not more reasonable to speak of international organization in terms of degrees of strength or level of integration? The answer to this charge must be one of partial agreement with it. There are levels of integration, the delineation of which is both complex and confusing. Figure 1 has stressed both these points. It appears, however, that the differences between such a heretofore relatively strong regional organization as NATO and the much more highly integrated ECSC are real and profound. While the differences are clearly ones of degree the chasm separating them seems to justify the use of the term "supranational." "International" organizations such as the United Nations, the Council of Europe, or NATO are based on such concepts as the "sovereign equality" of the member states and the principle of "non-intervention" in internal affairs. A "supranational" organization clearly transcends this intergovernmental level, without constituting a federal state. Further, the term "supranational" has both academic and political utility. The scholar can employ the term, assuredly with caution, to describe the phenomena outlined by the foregoing definition (pp. 13–14). While the term may lack "scientific precision," the task of the scholar and part of the burden of the present study is to give "supranationalism" concreteness by examining its occurrence in the real world. The politician, on the other hand, finds that "supranational" has value as the basis for building myths—myths that are intended to replace the age-old bugaboo of nationalism. The nation-state itself was, after all, built on myths. If the dreams of Schuman, Monnet, Adenauer, Hallstein, and others indeed have meaning for the future, then the concept of "supranationalism" may become one of the most significant terms in the vocabulary of international organization.

---

[37] See Ruth Lawson (ed.), *International Regional Organizations: Constitutional Foundations* (New York: Frederick A. Praeger, 1962), pp. 62–69, and Marek Korowicz, *Introduction to International Law: Present Conceptions of International Law in Theory and Practice* (The Hague: Martinus Nijhoff, 1959), pp. 218–221. Korowicz notes that a supranational organ may only be an organ of a supranational law. "A body of rules, the creation, existence and abolition of which is fully independent of the will of the States upon which it is binding, would be a truly supranational law without, however, abolishing the sovereignty of States, and their independence of any other power inside or outside their territories" (pp. 218–219). The recent study by Hay, *op. cit.*, presents a compilation of the major scholars accepting and rejecting the term "supranational." See the appendices to Chap. 2 of his work, pp. 76–78.

The Supranational Judiciary

ELEMENTS WHICH GIVE AN INTERNATIONAL COURT A SUPRANATIONAL CHARACTER   In the prototype of an international court one would expect to find only sovereign nation-states as parties to litigation as well as national consent at the base of the court's jurisdiction. In areas where the court's power transcends this level supranational powers can be said to exist. Some courts may only have the slightest hint of such power, while others may exhibit strong supranational powers in several areas. The nature of a court's power can be examined on a threefold basis: (1) expectations of the statesmen who created the court; (2) the constitutional basis of the court; and (3) the practice of the court.

1. Expectations of statesmen. This element is not always a particularly reliable indicator of a court's power. The rhetoric of statesmen may vary from high-minded idealism to bitter condemnation regarding international adjudication. Yet when removed from the glare of the public spotlight, the same people may exhibit tough-minded realism. There is no way of measuring such variance. One can only survey the supranational views of leading statesmen during the *travaux préparatoires* and hope that they are relatively indicative of the milieu within which an international tribunal was founded.

2. Constitutional basis. The constitutional basis of a court (treaty, statute, etc.) is a much better indicator, although many provisions can clearly be ignored, circumvented, or modified in actual practice. Those constitutional elements of a court's structure (reflecting the criteria outlined on p. 14) to which one can look for supranational powers are:

    a) Composition of the court
        (1) national representation of judges
        (2) national control over selection of judges
        (3) national control over judges in office
    b) Access to the court
        (1) states
        (2) other international persons
    c) Jurisdiction
        (1) *ad hoc*
        (2) compulsory
    d) Judgments
        (1) binding character
        (2) means of enforcement

3. Practice of the court. On the basis of a case-by-case examination of a court's decisions in contentious cases,[38] one should be able to determine with reasonable accuracy the extent of supranational power (if any) that the court possesses in practice. The elements of a case most likely to reflect supranational characteristics are:

a) Jurisdiction

(1) accepted/contested by parties; result

(2) *compétence de la compétence:* international courts generally have some type of power in determining their own jurisdiction. The critical factor here is the pattern of outcomes in jurisdictional disputes. Did the court successfully impose the law on a state denying its jurisdiction?

b) Parties before the court

(1) states/international bodies/private organizations/individuals. The factor of interest here is the degree of variance from the traditional practice of states being the only parties before an international court.

c) Disposition

(1) for/against state. This criterion is intended as a measure of supranational power only for those tribunals which also accept other international persons as well as states as litigants before them. The central question is whether states ever lose, say to their citizens

d) Judicial impartiality

(1) judicial freedom. This point relates to national efforts to control the composition of the court as described above under "Constitutional basis."

(2) judges' vote. Although not always determinable, the object of interest here is the discovery of instances where a judge voted against his country when it was a party to a dispute.

e) Enforcement

The question here is simply whether the judgment was carried out.

The Problem Defined

History seems to record a dual development. On the one hand, national loyalty has held, and still holds, sway in the minds of men. Men cling to it for the security nothing else appears to offer. On the other hand, because experience has brought the realization

---

[38] Advisory opinions and separate opinions in contentious cases excluded.

that nationalism must be controlled, men have been attracted to political cooperation beyond the nation-state.

The apparent trend toward supranational integration since the turn of the century, but particularly since Robert Schuman's revolutionary proposal of May 9, 1950, for the integration of the French and German coal and steel industry, has created a great deal of excitement and interest among scholars and statesmen. Clearly the international adjudicative tribunal can only be separated academically from the over-all political process of which it has been a part during this period. Yet international courts are themselves important. As B. V. A. Rölling has noted, law is not a constant; rather, it is a function of society.[39] This holds true for international society. Traditionally the hallmark of stability and a basic definer of the legal norms which support social norms, the court should provide an ideal yardstick for measuring the limits of tolerance on behalf of the sovereign states vis-à-vis the supranational power accorded international organization. In the political arenas of the General Assembly or the European Parliament, states can bargain and haggle over their sovereign rights; in an international court of law the nebulous rights of sovereignty have to be clearly subjected to the "rule of law." The following study is intended to test to what extent the latter is indeed the case, or if the supranational court remains an idealistic hope. Five international courts will serve as the basis for this study: the Central American Court of Justice, the Permanent Court of International Justice, the International Court of Justice, the Court of the European Communities, and the European Court of Human Rights. These tribunals were chosen because they possess two qualities: (1) they are full-fledged international courts of law, and (2) they all have some elements (either real or potential) of supranationalism. Each of them will be examined on the basis of the supranational characteristics outlined in this chapter.

---

[39] Rölling, *op. cit.,* p. x.

CHAPTER TWO

CENTRAL AMERICAN COURT OF JUSTICE

A. EXPECTATIONS OF STATESMEN

In the words of Don Luis Anderson, Costa Rican Foreign Minister and President of the Washington Conference (1907) that drafted the Court's Statute, "the Court of Justice is the first tribunal of its class in the history of civilization."[1] A product of the "Hague spirit," the Central American Court of Justice was a full-fledged, permanent international court of law.[2] Undoubtedly the most supranational tribunal ever devised, the Central American Court, when compared with other international courts, possessed an incredibly broad jurisdiction. This fully independent tribunal, in addition to being the sole international mechanism for regulating Central American disputes, was competent not only to hear nation-states and individuals in contentious cases before it, but to decide certain domestic disputes as well.

Yet in spite of this apparently well-founded claim to recognition, the Central American Court of Justice is little remembered and little written about. The reasons for this neglect appear to be several-

---

[1] Luis Anderson, "The Peace Conference of Central America," *American Journal of International Law*, II, 1 (January, 1908) , 145.

[2] The "Hague spirit" reflected the rather widespread interest, if not the commitment, of the "civilized" nations in the prospects of international arbitration and disarmament. One of the best discussions of this commitment is provided by James Brown Scott (ed.) , *The Hague Conventions and Declarations of 1899 and 1907* (3rd ed.; New York: Oxford University Press, 1918) .

fold: (1) the Court was a dismal failure, and failures are generally readily forgotten; (2) the unbridgeable chasm between the ideals proclaimed by the Court and the reality of its operation discourages objective, serious assessment; (3) the Court kept poor records;[3] and finally, (4) it produced no significant jurisprudence.[4]

The mere fact that the Court existed, however, commands some attention. At least the supranational effort this tribunal represented (although a failure) could not have gone unnoticed by later international courts, or by the statesmen who created them.

Historical Setting

The Central American Court of Justice represented one of the highest points in international cooperation reached by the five Central American republics of Guatemala, El Salvador, Honduras, Nicaragua, and Costa Rica in their long struggle for unity—and if not for unity, at least for peaceful relations. Historian Thomas Karnes very appropriately sums up the nature of Central American politics in this paragraph:

> These five nations, whose chief importance to the world is their valued exports and strategic location, have a unique history that reveals much of man's tragic inability to get along with his neighbor. For 135 years these little states have tried to unite, federate, or confederate under numerous forms of government and have failed unconditionally, even though they apparently possess more bonds of similarity than any other small group of nations in the world. Their failure, in fact, should have a sobering effect upon those of us who expect such great accomplishments from Leagues of Nations, United Nations, or World Federation movements.[5]

Briefly told, the modern history of Central America began in 1820 with its separation from Spain. Independence was short-lived, for on September 15, 1821, Emperor Iturbide of Mexico annexed the

---

[3] The only major English-language study of the Court notes: "The decisions were not published in any uniform style; [although] some of the later decisions appear in the *Anales*." See Manley O. Hudson, *The Permanent Court of International Justice, 1920–1942: A Treatise* (New York: The Macmillan Company, 1943), p. 51 (hereinafter cited as *Treatise*). The *Anales de la Corte de Justicia Centroamericana* are not only sketchy, but are generally unavailable. Noted by a letter to the author from Chief of Public Services, Columbus Memorial Library, Pan American Union, Washington, D.C., August 1, 1966. Fortunately, the official U.S. publication *Papers Relating to the Foreign Relations of the United States* and the *American Journal of International Law (Document Supplement)* offer rather good coverage of the Court's work.

[4] The author has encountered no instance of the citation of the Court's jurisprudence by any of the remaining tribunals included in this study. This point is elaborated in Hudson, *Treatise*, pp. 69–70.

[5] Thomas L. Karnes, *The Failure of Union: Central America, 1824–1960* (Chapel Hill: University of North Carolina Press, 1961), p. 3.

area.[6] By July 1, 1823, however, this union was dissolved by a Central American National Assembly which promulgated a federal union at Guatemala City among the five states on November 22, 1824.[7] This union, which was also short-lived, represents the last time the area would be united. From 1838 to 1847 the various states declared their independence from the union, drew up national constitutions, and established separate state governments. Attempts at reconfederation, or at least adjustment of relations, have been so numerous that scholars disagree as to the major efforts. James Brown Scott, in a comprehensive survey, cites 15 separate, major attempts by the five republics of Central America to regulate their relations.[8]

Impetus for the Washington Conference

The prelude to establishing the Central American Court of Justice was 80 years of revolution and political instability since independence from Spain. The immediate impetus to establish a court seems to have come from two main sources—the "Roosevelt Corollary" of the Monroe Doctrine and a Central American "troublemaker," President José Santos Zelaya of Nicaragua.

In reaction to Latin American instability, President Theodore Roosevelt proclaimed in December, 1904: "Chronic wrongdoing . . . may in America, as elsewhere, ultimately require intervention by some civilized nation, and in the Western Hemisphere the adherence of the United States to the Monroe Doctrine may force the United States, however reluctantly, in flagrant cases of such wrongdoing or impotence, to the exercise of an international police power."[9]

The "Corollary" was tested in 1906 when President Roosevelt, with the support of President Porfirio Díaz of Mexico, intervened to bring about peace negotiations between warring Guatemala and El Salvador (Honduras was also partially involved). The outcome of this effort was a preliminary treaty signed between the belligerents aboard an American warship, the U.S.S. *Marblehead*, on July 20,

---

[6] James Brown Scott, "The Central American Peace Conference of 1907," *American Journal of International Law*, II, 1 (January, 1908), 121.

[7] *Ibid.*

[8] *Ibid.*, pp. 122–126. Scott notes that official attempts at confederation or an international regulation of relations occurred in 1842, 1845, 1847, 1849, 1852, 1862, 1876, 1886, 1887, 1889, 1895, 1898, 1902, 1906, and 1907. The latter two attempts were respectively the treaty of the *Marblehead* and the Washington Conference. Cf. Hudson, *Treatise*, p. 42.

[9] *Congressional Record*, 58th Cong., 3rd Sess., 1904, p. 19.

1906.[10] The significance of this treaty was the promise by the parties to submit future disputes to the presidents of the United States and Mexico for arbitration.[11]

The first use of this promise resulted in the calling of the 1907 Washington Conference and the drafting of the Central American Court. The situation was precipitated by Nicaraguan President José Zelaya, whom one historian labels "the greatest cause of disturbance on the Isthmus."[12] Engaged in varying degrees of warfare with all his neighbors except Guatemala, and on the brink of an all-out invasion of El Salvador, Zelaya's actions prompted Roosevelt and Díaz (following the *Marblehead* precedent) to call representatives of the five Central American republics together for a Washington peace conference.[13]

Establishing the Court

The Central American Court of Justice was surely more deeply grounded in optimism and idealism than any of the other courts in this study—even more than the League's Permanent Court of International Justice. A distinguished series of speakers inaugurated the Central American Peace Conference, which met in Washington, D.C., from November 14 to December 20, 1907.[14] Unfortunately, the *travaux préparatoires* of the conferees are not available; however, the speeches of the major statesmen involved seem to represent rather well the expectations of the delegates. U.S. Secretary of State Elihu Root (highly respected both as a statesman and as a scholar of international law) opened the Conference. Interestingly, he seemed to be one of the few to view realistically Central America's chances for international cooperation. He spoke in glowing terms of the delegates' common heritage: "You are one people in fact, your citizenship is interchangeable—your race, your religion,

---

[10] *Papers Relating to the Foreign Relations of the United States* (hereinafter cited as *U.S. Foreign Relations*), I (Washington, D.C.: Government Printing Office, 1906), 851. In addition to the three belligerents, the American and Mexican ministers to Central America and observers from Costa Rica and Nicaragua were present. A final peace treaty was signed on September 25, 1906. See *ibid.*, p. 857.

[11] See *ibid.*, p. 851.

[12] Samuel Crowther, *The Romance and Rise of the American Tropics* (Garden City, N.Y.: Doubleday, Doran and Company, Inc., 1929), p. 175.

[13] *U.S. Foreign Relations*, II (1907), 681.

[14] The "Minutes of the Central American Peace Conference" are reprinted as Inclosure 4 to the "Minutes of the Preliminary Central American Peace Conference," *U.S. Foreign Relations*, II (1907), 681–690. The preliminary conference met in Washington on September 11, 1907, to lay the groundwork for the main conference.

your customs, your laws, your lineage, your consanguinity and lineage, your social relations, your sympathies, your aspirations, and your hopes for the future are the same."[15]

Yet Root was apparently well aware of the lesson of Central America's history. This common heritage had not prevented, or even mitigated, 87 years of strife. Consequently, he cautioned the Conference: "We can not fail, gentlemen, to be admonished by the many failures which have been made by the people of Central America to establish agreement among themselves which would be lasting, that the task you have before you is no easy one. The trial has often been made and the agreements which have been elaborated, signed, ratified, seem to have been written in water."[16]

After noting that perhaps this was the "threshold of a happier day for Central America," Root went on to suggest that "the all-important thing . . . to accomplish is that . . . [the delegates] devise also some practical methods under which it will be possible to secure the performance of those agreements."[17] "The mere declaration of general principles," he said, would be of "little value" without "practical and definite methods provided by which the responsibility for failing to keep the agreement may be fixed upon some definite person, and the public sentiment of Central America brought to bear to prevent the violation."[18]

Following Root, Don Enrique Creel, the Mexican Ambassador to the United States, exhorted the delegates to follow the example of the Hague tribunal. "All sacrifices," he noted, "seem small when made to obtain a solid, unmolested, firm peace."[19] Then he stated, in what must have been either idealism or naîveté, "If my judgment of your affairs is not erroneous, your disputes turn upon issues which are simple and, above all, susceptible of pacific adjustment. *Boundary questions, questions of wrongs to citizens, territorial invasion, and many others, which can not be prevented between adjoining countries, may be easily and peaceably settled according to such general rules as you may adopt at this conference . . .*" (italics mine).[20]

---

[15] "Address of the Hon. Elihu Root, Secretary of State of the United States, when calling the Conference to order on November 14, 1907," *U.S. Foreign Relations*, II (1907), 688–689.

[16] *Ibid.*, p. 688.

[17] *Ibid.*

[18] *Ibid.*

[19] "Address of His Excellency the Mexican Ambassador, Don Enrique Creel, at the inaugural session of the conference," *U.S. Foreign Relations*, II (1907), 690.

[20] *Ibid.*

In light of the "Hague spirit," Creel's view is understandable. However, simple political experience, combined with the fact that the Hague delegates had reached so little agreement,[21] should have been a cue that Creel's judgment was quite "erroneous." As this and later chapters will show, Creel's "simple questions" have in fact been among the toughest, for they are closely linked to national sovereignty.

Luis Anderson, President of the Conference, echoed Creel's words. Writing after the Conference, he labeled the new tribunal "a high court of justice against whose decisions there can be no appeal."[22] It was no "mere commission of arbitration, but a genuine judicial tribunal, whose work shall be to sift evidence, consider arguments, and pronounce judgment in all questions that may be brought before it. . . ."[23]

The entire tenor of the Conference seems to have followed the lines laid out by these men. The expectation was that a high altar would be created to which all problems could be carried and which would serve as a step toward confederation. The creation of this altar, Anderson declared, would represent "the only royal road to the definite triumph of the generous and noble idea."[24] Attempting to view the Conference against the background of Central American history, one rather cynical—but probably quite accurate—summation of the proceedings reads as follows:

Typically the subject of confederation did not long lie neglected. During the second session the Honduran delegation presented a plan to unite the five republics. They repeated the familiar story that it was the dream of every Central American and that it was the only way to end the isthmian wars. The men said that they recognized the many past failures but believed that the new roles of the United States and Mexico would bring about success. They suggested ratifying whatever conventions emerged from the Washington conference and then holding a constituent assembly for the designing of a greater republic.[25]

Nothing less than a supranational court could have satisfied the expectations of the Central American delegates. In fact, as a result of the few realistic views expressed at the Conference, the supranational aspects of the Court emerge as an unsatisfactory substitute for a full union with a *federal* court. Yet if the Conference was idealis-

---

[21] The outstanding exception was of course the creation of the Permanent Court of Arbitration by the First Hague Conference.

[22] Anderson, *op. cit.*, p. 151.

[23] *Ibid.*, p. 144.

[24] *Ibid.*

[25] Karnes, *op. cit.*, p. 189.

tic, the Central American reaction to the news of the Court's creation approached the irrational. The official report of William I.
Buchanan, the U.S. High Commissioner representing the U.S. President at the inauguration of the Court in Cartago, Costa Rica, includes excerpts from all the leading Central American newspapers,
official statements by the five governments and by the Court itself, as
well as a full description of the ceremonies.[26] All of the republics declared holidays and the city of Cartago overflowed with delegates
and well-wishers—an interesting comparison with the inaugural
sessions of the more recent tribunals, which have had limited newspaper coverage. There is no need to present here all the jubilant
reactions. In essence the Washington Conference was reproduced *in
extremis*.[27] An ironic example, however, which suggested that Central America's problems might have been covered up but not solved,
was the telegram from that archtroublemaker, Nicaraguan President
José Zelaya, which proclaimed: "That the installation of the court
of justice for Central America is a glorious and transcendental occurrence, signifying the stability of peace and of close and of cordial
union between the five Republics, and that it is a debt of patriotism
to give public testimony of the jubilee with which Nicaragua asso-
ciates itself with the inauguration of that high tribunal. . . ."[28]

As a final note on statesmen's expectations regarding the Court,
Buchanan's own conclusions are particularly relevant. Representing
one of the few realistic views, he wrote to Secretary of State Root:

> It remains to be seen to what degree and the extent to which the new
> court at Cartago will act as a deterrent by preventing the appearance of
> disputes between the different Republics and the character of support that
> will be given its decisions.
> It will be no doubt difficult, on the part of the five Republics, for a time
> to harmonize that unity of purpose that must form the underlying neces-
> sary stratum upon which the success of the court depends, with the
> national individualism that has been the rule in Central America.[29]

He then went on to point out that the Court could not solve the
most basic political problem in Central America, namely, "how to

---

[26] "Report of William I. Buchanan, High Commissioner, Representing the
President of the United States to Attend the Inauguration of the Court of Justice
for Central America," *U.S. Foreign Relations* (1908), 217–247. As a point of
interest, Buchanan's report reads somewhat like an adventure story, relating his
travels overland and by sea through Mexico and Central America (picking up
officials along the route) and describing the gay pageantry of the inauguration.
[27] See especially *ibid.*, pp. 225–245.
[28] *Ibid.*, p. 239.
[29] *Ibid.*, p. 246.

avoid internal outbreaks against existing authority in the Republics."[30] The fact that such internal difficulties were usually aided by neighboring governments merely compounded tension, distrust, and instability. If political agents could not control these problems, there was no reason to believe a court could. Worse, politics before the Court could wreck it. Buchanan closed his report with this observation: "On this point I venture to express the belief that if the excellent work represented in the organization of this court is not to be jeopardized as to its future usefulness, the greatest prudence, tact, and statemanship [sic] must be shown by each of the five Republics in everything even remotely likely to reach the court. An entire absence of business for the court would be the highest justification for its creation."[31]

Unfortunately for the Court, Buchanan's fears turned out to be a fateful premonition of what was to come.

B. CONSTITUTIONAL BASIS

As a result of the deliberations of the Washington Conference, no less than eight conventions were agreed to. The conventions were:

Communications
General Treaty of Peace and Amity
Additional Conventions to the General Treaty
Establishing a Central American Court of Justice
Extradition
On Future Conferences (monetary)
Establishing an International Central American Bureau
Establishing a Pedagogical Institute[32]

Of interest here is the Convention establishing the Central American Court. First, it established concrete international machinery for handling disputes—the first true international court of continuing and compulsory jurisdiction. It is interesting to note that no other "peace-keeping" institutions were discussed by the Conference. Yet the Court alone was apparently regarded as a worthwhile experiment to cope with international strife. The most notable example of this regard was Andrew Carnegie's donation of $100,000 to build a Central American Peace Palace to house the Court in Car-

---

[30] *Ibid.*, p. 247.
[31] *Ibid.*
[32] These conventions are reprinted in *U.S. Foreign Relations*, II (1907), pp. 673–727.

tago, Costa Rica.[33] Second, the Convention provided the constitutional basis for the operation of the Court.[34]

Composition of the Court

NATIONAL REPRESENTATION OF JUDGES   Articles VI through XIII of the Convention establishing the Central American Court of Justice deal broadly with the composition of the Court. (Those articles of the Convention cited in this chapter are reprinted in full in Appendix A.) As one of the basic elements of a truly supranational tribunal, one would expect to find a situation in which each state, a party to the Court, need not necessarily be represented on the Court (although in realistic political terms such representation might not be suitable). In any event this was not the case with the Central American Court. Article VI specified that the Court would consist of "five Justices, one being appointed by each Republic and selected from among the jurists who possess the qualifications which the laws of each country prescribe for the exercise of high judicial office, and who enjoy the highest consideration, both because of their moral character and their professional ability."

NATIONAL CONTROL OVER THE SELECTION OF JUDGES   National control over the selection of justices was absolute. There was not even the room for "political maneuvering" that has characterized later international tribunals, in which judges are elected from some sort of list. Article VII provided that "the Legislative Power of each one of the five contracting Republics shall appoint *their* respective Justices" (italics mine). Whether this type of selection necessarily means that judges are "national representatives," the sad fact is that the way is clear for charges of this nature. The actual practice of the Court (discussed below) proved this factor to be a basic reason for its failure.

NATIONAL CONTROL OVER JUDGES IN OFFICE   Even a careful reading of the Convention does not reveal any suggestion that the judges were less than fully independent. Although Article VIII

---

[33] See "New Peace Palace of the Central American Court of Justice," *Bulletin of the Pan American Union*, XLIV (June 17, 1916), 734–739. Illustration included. The Palace was nearly completed in 1910 when a violent earthquake demolished the structure. Carnegie made another $100,000 grant, dependent upon changing the site. San José, Costa Rica, was agreed upon and the building was rebuilt.

[34] The Spanish text of the Convention (official text) is reprinted in the *American Journal of International Law Supplement: Official Documents*, II, 1 and 2 (January and April, 1908), 231–243. The English translation used here comes from *U.S. Foreign Relations*, II (1907), 697–701.

only provided for a term of five years, this should have been enough (in light of the standard for many subsequent tribunals at all levels of government) to insure independence. Article X provided that "in the country of their appointment" justices would "enjoy the personal immunity which the respective laws grant to the magistrates of the Supreme Court of Justice." According to the same article, judges "shall have the privileges and immunities of Diplomatic Agents" while in the "other contracting Republics."

The clause that was to become a significant element of national control over justices was the second part of Article VII relating to salaries. Although disputed in practice, the article read simply: "The salary of each Justice shall be eight thousand dollars, gold, per annum, *which shall be paid them by the Treasury of the Court"* (italics mine). Article VII further stated that each state would contribute periodically, and *in advance,* toward their estimated share of the Court's operating expenses. On paper, at least, there was no indication that national control was present here.

As a capstone to the recognition of judicial independence, Article XIII provided: "The Central American Court of Justice represents the national conscience of Central America, wherefore the Justices who compose the Tribunal shall not consider themselves barred from the discharge of their duties because of the interest which the Republics, to which they owe their appointment, may have in any case or question."

This article raises a point about the "truly impartial" international judge, and the implications for supranationalism are interesting. Nation-states apparently believe that judges of their own nationality are quite able to elevate themselves above national considerations and be objective (although the evidence discussed in this and subsequent chapters does not support this belief). On the other hand, this same confidence does not extend to judges of other states —at least not to the extent that a state feels "safe" if its own judge is not sitting on the Court.[35]

Access to the Court

The jurisdiction *ratione personae* and *ratione materiae* of the Central American Court has been unequaled in scope by any other international court. Allowed to appear as parties before the Court were: (a) nation-states, (b) individuals, and (c) domestic institutions.

---

[35] Cf. Article VI of the Convention establishing the Central American Court of Justice, *supra,* p. 27.

STATES   The Convention provided for two categories of state controversies to be heard by the Court:

1. Article I states that the high contracting parties agree to "bind themselves *to submit all controversies or questions which may arise among them, of whatsoever nature and no matter what their origin may be,* in case the respective Departments of Foreign Affairs should not have been able to reach an understanding" (italics mine).

2. Further, the Court "can likewise take cognizance of the international questions which by special agreement any one of the Central American Governments and a foreign Government may have determined to submit to it" (Article IV).

INDIVIDUALS   In a radical break from traditional nation-state monopoly of international relations, the Convention allowed the Court to "take cognizance of the questions which individuals of one Central American country may raise against any of the other contracting Governments" (Article II).[36] Jurisdiction covered violations of treaties or conventions as well as "other cases of an international character." In clear recognition of the individual's status before the Court, the Convention expressly provided that individual claims would be entertained, "no matter whether their own Government supports said claim or not" (Article II). The only qualification was that local remedies must have been exhausted and a denial of justice must have been shown (Article II). Finally, by the terms of Article XVII, both governments and individuals arguing in Court had "the right to be represented before it by a trustworthy person or persons, who shall present evidence, formulate arguments, and shall . . . do everything that in their judgment shall be beneficial to the defense of the rights they represent."

DOMESTIC INSTITUTIONS   An unusual breadth of jurisdiction was given to the Court, somewhat as an afterthought, through the correction of Article III by an annexed article.[37] According to this article, the Court "shall also have jurisdiction over the conflicts which may arise between the Legislative, Executive, and Judicial Powers, and when as a matter of fact the judicial decisions and reso-

---

[36] Interestingly, the concern of modern international tribunals that admit individuals (e.g., the European Court of Human Rights) has been to give the individual status for challenging *his own* government, not *other* governments. There is no available explanation as to why the Washington Conference did not include this facet of jurisdiction. Possibly it was simply because there was little acceptance at this time of the concept of international protection of human rights.

[37] Reprinted as Inclosure 8 in *U.S. Foreign Relations,* II (1907), 701.

lutions of the National Congress are not respected." The exact nature of the access to the Court created by this article is unclear. The article appears to allow warring domestic governmental institutions to drag one another into an international court—a most unusual supranational innovation. Possibly the intent was to add stability via international machinery to volatile internal situations resulting from such frequent occurrences as political squabbles, attempted coups, and military dictatorships. Unfortunately from the standpoint of clarification, this article was never used and has been virtually ignored by scholars.

Jurisdiction

The general aspects of the Court's jurisdiction have been outlined above. A further important area to which one can look for supranational aspects is the "compulsory" nature of the jurisdiction. Is jurisdiction on an *ad hoc* basis, requiring the agreement of contending states before a case can be submitted, or does the Court have the "real, autonomous" power described by Pescatore to allow states to sue other states against their will?[38]

Ad hoc jurisdiction between the high contracting parties and foreign governments was provided by Article IV discussed above. It must be said that the Central American Court of Justice indeed had compulsory jurisdiction. It was spelled out at two points in the Convention:

1. Article I, discussed above, proclaimed that the states bound themselves (in advance) "to submit all controversies or questions which may arise among them. . . ." While the force of Article I was clearly grounded in moral and legal obligation, the fact that the whole Convention largely revolved around this article gave it the entire strength the five republics were willing to give to their new creation. Also, the Court was competent to determine its own jurisdiction (Article XXII).

2. Articles XIV and XV, however, made compulsory jurisdiction a reality (on paper at least) by providing the specific means whereby the Court could assume jurisdiction regardless of national protest. Article XIV gave all parties against whom a complaint had been lodged 60 days in which to answer. Failing to receive an answer, the Court could, by the terms of Article XV, "require" the complainant(s) to present the case. After hearing the available evidence, the "Tribunal shall render its decision in the case, which decision shall

---

[38] *Supra,* p. 14.

be final" (Article XV). On this basis, the Court's jurisdiction was quite powerful. Unfortunately, the key to effective compulsory jurisdiction lies in the enforcement mechanism of judgments.

Judgments

By the terms of Article XXV the binding character of the Court's judgments was proclaimed: "the judgments of the Court shall be communicated to the five Governments of the contracting Republics. The interested parties solemnly bind themselves to submit to said judgments, and all agree to lend all moral support that may be necessary in order that they may be properly fulfilled, thereby constituting a real and positive guarantee of respect for this Convention and for the Central American Court of Justice."

Further, the Court was given rudimentary machinery for the implementation of its decisions. It could address itself "to the Governments or tribunals of justice of the contracting States . . . in order to have the measures that it may dictate within the scope of its jurisdiction carried out" (Article XIX). This would be done through the Ministry of Foreign Relations or the office of the Clerk of the Supreme Court of Justice. If compliance with judgments beyond this point were refused, the Court was helpless to take further action. There was no international enforcement agency with supranational power.

By way of review of what seem to be the supranational characteristics covered to this point, certain elements stand out. The drafters at the Washington Conference appeared to have had rather high supranational expectations, which presumably were reflected in the Convention. Indeed, the Convention was strongly supranational, particularly when viewed in light of the traditional role of the nation-state. The most striking example was the broad jurisdiction granted the Court, which was not only unlimited as to subject matter but also provided means for circumventing the state's dominant role as a subject of international law. An important adjunct was the compulsory nature of the Court's jurisdiction.

Although the judges were nominally independent of national ties, the Convention makes it quite clear that judges owed their position to their governments. Finally, while the Court's decisions were legally and morally binding on the parties, there was no supranational machinery for forcing compliance. It is surely one of those unanswerable questions whether obedience to the law depends ultimately upon the "will to obey" or upon a *force majeure*. Assuming a "will to obey," the Central American Court at least drew strength from the fact that it had direct access to domestic institutions for enforcement. Yet, in either case, enforcement of the Court's decisions did not go beyond the intergovernmental level.

C. PRACTICE OF THE COURT

There is bound to be a gap between the ideal and the real in the operation of any institution. The ideal, as represented in the Washington Conference and the Convention on the Court, was assessed in the following manner by one leading scholar: "On the whole, the representatives had no reason to feel ashamed of the results of their labors. Although the results were only on paper, and all looked towards the future, the ideas adopted were specific and practical, and they were grounded upon a solid basis of coöperation which alone was bound to be beneficial to all."[39]

Whether the reality of the Court's operation justified this view can of course only be determined by looking at Court practice. The Court operated from 1908 to 1918.[40] During this ten-year period the

Table 1   Work of the Central American Court of Justice[a]

Year	New Cases	Judgments	Cases Withdrawn, Denied, or Otherwise not Handled by Court
1908	2	1	—
1909	—	—	1
1910	1[b]	—	1
1911	1	—	1
1912	1[b]	—	1
1913	2	—	1
1914	1	1	1
1915	—	—	—
1916	2	1	—
1917	—	1	—
1918	—	—	—

[a] Data derived from *Papers Relating to the Foreign Relations of the United States* (Washington, D.C.: Government Printing Office, 1907–18) and the *American Journal of International Law*, including *Document Supplement* (1907–18).
[b] Action initiated by the Court in the 1910 and 1912 revolutions in Nicaragua. Offer to mediate declined by parties. The column heading "New Cases" is not being used in the strict juridical sense.

[39] Graham H. Stuart, *Latin America and the United States* (New York: D. Appleton-Century Company, Inc., 1943), p. 342.
[40] See Hudson, *Treatise*, p. 65, for a discussion of this time period. The official life of the Court (per Article XIX of the Convention) was from 1907 to 1917; however, the period in which it was actually "open for business" ran from May 25, 1908, to March 12, 1918. See also Buchanan's report, *op. cit.*, p. 222.

Court heard ten cases (see Table 1), from which only four full judicial decisions resulted.

No immediate peace flowed from the installation of the Court at Cartago in May, 1908. One report notes that "there could be no peace as long as Zelaya remained in power. . . . There was a strong disposition on the part of Guatemala and Salvador to get Zelaya out of the way at once."[41] The result was an invasion of Honduras by El Salvador in 1908 which rapidly involved Nicaragua and Guatemala in an unofficial general war. In a novel move, the Court took the initiative by sending telegrams to the presidents of the warring countries urging that they use the Court.[42] They complied, putting the Court "in business" hardly a month after it had been installed.

It is neither feasible nor desirable to review the history of each case. It is, however, reasonable to survey the case law of the Court on the basis of the potential supranational elements outlined in Chapter 1.[43] Through this means, either confirmation or variance with the supranational expectations reflected in the Convention should become apparent. Table 2 attempts to present the majority of these elements so that they may be seen in relation to one another.

Jurisdiction

In the case of *ad hoc* jurisdiction, the Court's role is clearly based on consent. On the other hand, when an international tribunal has been given a supranational aura by the introduction of compulsory jurisdiction (as the Central American Court had), the acid test of the reality of this power will come when this jurisdiction is contested. Possessing *compétence de la compétence* (Article XXII), as is true of all the tribunals examined in this study, the key was whether the Central American Court could (or would) implement this power.

Table 2 shows that the Court's jurisdiction was contested in nearly every case. In most instances there were no significant issues involved. In fact, in three cases defendant states apparently did not even bother to appear in Court.[44] The most important cases, from a jurisdictional standpoint as well as generally, were the first and the last two. The Court deserves credit for resolving the conflict repre-

---

[41] Crowther, *op. cit.*, p. 194.

[42] See "The First Decision of the Central American Court of Justice," *American Journal of International Law*, III, 2 (April, 1909), 434–436, which reprints the telegrams.

[43] *Supra*, p. 14.

[44] This occurred in the *Díaz*, *Cerda*, and *Larios* cases. Cf. Hudson, *Treatise*, pp. 52–62.

Table 2 Nature and Solution of Cases Before the Central American Court of Justice[a]

Case/Jurisdiction	Issue	Disposition	Judges' Vote
1. *Honduras & Nicaragua v. Guatemala & Salvador* (C/A);[b] Dec. 19, 1908[c]	Guatemala and El Salvador allegedly violated Honduran neutrality by protecting and encouraging a revolutionary movement there.	Decision acquitted Guatemala and El Salvador. Legal validity of decision unclear as it was signed by only three justices.	3 to 0; Honduran and Nicaraguan judges refused to sign award.
2. *Díaz v. Guatemala* (denied by Court); March 6, 1909	National of Nicaragua claimed false arrest and imprisonment by Guatemala.	Complaint inadmissible; failure to exhaust local remedies.	Unanimous.
3. *The 1910 Revolution in Nicaragua* (declined by parties); June 27, 1910	Mediation of Estrada revolution between leaders of contending parties in Nicaragua.	Mediation offers of Court declined.	————
4. *Cerda v. Costa Rica* (accepted); Oct. 14, 1911	Denial of the equal rights of a Nicaraguan national living in Costa Rica. Violation of Treaty of Washington and Costa Rican Constitution.	Complaint inadmissible; failure to exhaust local remedies.	4 to 1; Honduran judge dissenting.
5. *The 1912 Revolution in Nicaragua* (declined by government, accepted by rebels); Oct. 27, 1912	Mediation.	Mediation offers of Court declined.	————
6. *Felipe Molina Larios v. Honduras* (denied by Court); Dec. 10, 1913	Nicaraguan national claimed imprisonment, expulsion, and illegal search by Honduras.	Complaint inadmissible; failure to exhaust local remedies.	Unanimous.
7. *Alejandro Bermúdez y Nuñez v. Costa Rica* (C/A); April 7, 1914	Nicaraguan national expelled from Costa Rica.	Decision for Costa Rica. Resident of a country obliged to respect its neutrality. Expulsion legal.	3 to 2; judges from Salvador and Honduras dissenting.
8. *Election of Gonzàlez Flores as President of Costa Rica* (denied by Court); July 3, 1914	Five individuals (one from each republic) protested election of Costa Rican President by Congress.	Complaint inadmissible; internal matter.	Unanimous.

Case		Decision	Vote
9. *Costa Rica v. Nicaragua* (C/A); Sept. 30, 1916	Right of Nicaragua to negotiate and enter into agreements with United States concerning matters of direct or indirect interest to other republics of Central America (Bryan-Chamorro Treaty).	Decision for Costa Rica. Nicaragua refused to comply.	4 to 1; Nicaraguan judge dissenting.
10. *El Salvador v. Nicaragua* (C/A); March 9, 1917	Violation of El Salvador's rights of condominium with Honduras and Nicaragua in the Gulf of Fonseca.	Decision for El Salvador. Nicaragua refused to comply.	4 to 1; Nicaraguan judge dissenting.

ᵃ Material abstracted from *Papers Relating to the Foreign Relations of the United States* (Washington, D.C.: Government Printing Office, 1907–18); *American Journal of International Law*, including *Document Supplement* (1907–18); Manley O. Hudson, *The Permanent Court of International Justice, 1920–1942: A Treatise* (New York: The Macmillan Company, 1943), Chap. 3; and *Bulletin of the International Bureau of the American Republics*, XXVIII, 2 (February, 1909), 276–277.

ᵇ By way of explaining reactions to the Court's jurisdiction, the term "accepted" indicates the parties went before the Court on the basis of agreement stemming from the Convention. C (contested) shows that a party objected to the Court's jurisdiction. A (affirmative) indicates that the objection was overruled and that the Court found it had jurisdiction.

ᶜ Date of judgment, or other decision terminating the case.

sented in the first case.[45] Yet although the case itself was significant, the jurisdictional conflict (raised only by Guatemala) was of secondary importance.[46] Unfortunately, when a serious jurisdictional conflict developed in the last two cases, the Court collapsed—although it *unanimously* defended its *compétence de la compétence.*[47]

The significant jurisdictional question raised in these two cases (which were closely related) revolved around the right of Nicaragua to negotiate and enter into agreements with the United States regarding matters of direct or indirect interest to the other republics of Central America. In the first case, Costa Rica protested against the Bryan-Chamorro Treaty (U.S./Nicaragua) of August 5, 1914, which granted the United States, *inter alia,* an exclusive right to build an inter-oceanic canal across Nicaragua and to a naval base in the Gulf of Fonseca (see Fig. 2). Costa Rica's protest was based on a prior treaty which allowed her, as a co-riparian state on the San Juan River, to be consulted by Nicaragua in any negotiations affecting the river (e.g., for a canal).[48] Nicaragua's defense, and the resulting court battle, was a classic example of national interest versus attempts to create a supranational authority. Nicaragua's initial argument in denying the competence of the Court was: "As sole sovereign over the territory in which said canal was to be constructed, and as absolute owner of the benefits that she might derive in compensation for the favors and privileges to be conceded by her government, she would not permit them to be made the subject of judicial determination. . . ."[49]

This view, of course, meant that Nicaragua saw its legal position as the only valid one. The Nicaraguan government refused even to present its case in Court and ultimately refused to abide by the decision rendered. A flurry of correspondence ensued between the Court

---

[45] The most important action of the Court was undoubtedly the handing down of two interlocutory decrees on July 13, 1908, calling upon the warring parties to desist and respect the political status quo pending judicial action. See the *American Journal of International Law,* II, 4 (October, 1908), 838. The final decisions (English translation) appear in "The First Decision of the Central American Court of Justice," *American Journal of International Law,* III, 2 (April, 1909), 434–436, and in "*Honduras* v. *Salvador and Guatemala,*" *American Journal of International Law,* III, 3 (July, 1909), 729–736.

[46] See *ibid.,* as well as Hudson, *Treatise,* p. 53.

[47] English translations of the decisions (from Vols. V and VI, *Anales de la Corte de Justicia Centroamericana*) in *U.S. Foreign Relations* (1916), pp. 862–886, and (1917), pp. 1101–04.

[48] Costa Rica's position resulted from the Cañas-Jerez Treaty of 1858 and from President Cleveland's arbitral award of 1888, interpreting the Treaty. A good legal discussion is offered by Philip Marshall Brown, "*Costa Rica* v. *Nicaragua,*" *American Journal of International Law,* XI, 1 (January, 1917), 156–160.

[49] Quoted in *ibid.*

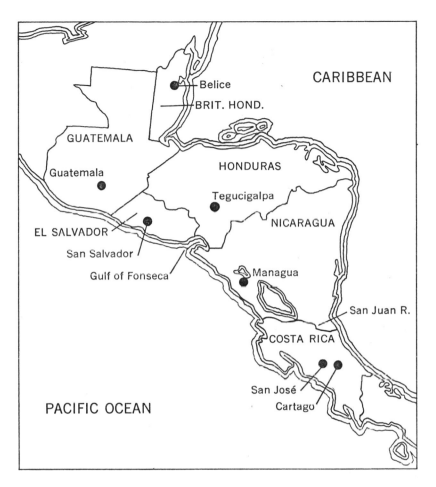

Fig. 2 Sketch Map of Central America

and the Nicaraguan government, throwing into sharp relief the national and international commitment.[50] Following Nicaragua's refusal to heed the decision, Manuel Echeveria, Secretary of the
Court, wrote the Nicaraguan Minister for Foreign Affairs, Diego
Chamorro, this note dated October 17, 1916:

> The Central American Court possesses *unrestricted power to take cogni-
> zance of all differences which may arise among the signatory States of the
> Washington Convention, whatever may be their origin and nature, and it
> has the exclusive right to determine its own competence.* In the case under

---

[50] Because of the obvious interest of the United States in the fate of the
Nicaraguan treaty, much of this diplomatic correspondence has been reprinted in
U.S. Foreign Relations (1916 and 1917) .

discussion that competence and jurisdiction were amply considered and determined by the tribunal after hearing and judging the allegations of the Government sued, and *the sentence issued is binding on the high litigant parties in respect due to the treaties. The Central American Court expects to guarantee with its authority, based on the honor of the States, the rights of each one of them in their reciprocal relations, and this high prerogative would become null, were it possible to protest against its sentences and disavow the moral and legal efficacy that they have* [italics mine].[51]

Failing the obvious support of Nicaragua and lacking the power to enforce its decision, the supranational venture that the Court represented was doomed. These facts made the foregoing sentences a hollow plea for support—capped by Echeveria's concluding note: "The tribunal is confident that these brief considerations will suffice in order that your excellency's Government, aware of the transcendency and gravity that its attitude involves, will respect the sentence issued as an homage due to honor and good faith pledged in the Washington International Pacts and due to the prestige of the noble institutions of Central America."[52]

Chamorro's answer to this note pointed out that the Court's "surprise" over Nicaragua's refusal to abide by the Court's decision was "inexplicable" because he himself had already decided on the "incompetency and total lack of jurisdiction of the Central American Court of Justice."[53] The tenor of these words stand in stark contrast to what both the spirit and the letter of the Convention clearly seemed to be. Worse than this, Nicaragua participated in the original proceedings before the Court, yet at that time declared "that in case of an adverse decision Nicaragua could not abide by it."[54] This interesting concept of the judicial process (i.e., that Nicaragua would participate on the condition that she would be allowed to win) was supplemented by Nicaragua's break with the tribunal. Chamorro's note is a prime example of the traditional position of the nation-state vis-à-vis attempts to build order in international relations. The tragic element is that Nicaragua categorically denied the very points to which she had earlier agreed. The note concluded:

---

[51] "Letter from the Secretary of the Court, Manuel Echeveria to the Nicaraguan Minister for Foreign Affairs (October 17, 1916)," *El Heraldo*, Managua, October 24, 1916. Reprinted in *U.S. Foreign Relations* (1916), p. 888.

[52] *Ibid.*

[53] "Note to Secretary of the Central American Court of Justice, San José, Costa Rica from Diego M. Chamorro, Nicaraguan Foreign Minister (Managua, October 22, 1916)," *U.S. Foreign Relations* (1916), p. 888.

[54] *Ibid.*

My Government does not admit nor could it admit the pretended unrestricted power of the Court to judge all differences arising between the Central American States.[55] The Treaty of Peace and Amity of 1907[56] as well as the Convention which created the same Court determine the true nature and the limit of the functions of this last, when it declares that its object is to establish the basis which should fix the general relations of the countries and insure among them unalterable peace and harmony, there efficiently guaranteeing their rights.

Nothing that touches on the sovereignty and the local integrity of the five Republics enters in the purposes of the agreement. By agreement they keep their full autonomy and equality, coming together only to maintain and insure their internal and pacific relations. And it could not be otherwise, for no nation in the world could possibly submit for the decision of a foreign nation its security and preservation and leave to the approbation of another country its own progress and development.[57]

The Nicaraguan position most directly challenged Article I of the Convention conferring jurisdiction over "all controversies" on the Court. In fact, the Court had based its decision on this article.[58] The Court's decision had concluded: "There is nothing to limit the jurisdiction of the Court by reason of the subject-matter, and it is consequently obvious that no Central American Nation can exempt itself from its obligation to answer before this Court any complaints which the other nations signing the said convention may lodge against it, under the pretext that the injuries alleged arise from acts performed in the exercise of its own sovereignty."[59]

The subsequent and final case before the Court, *El Salvador* v. *Nicaragua,* was a repeat of the one just examined.[60] The basic political situation that prompted both these cases was the fact that the United States and Nicaragua had made a mutually beneficial deal in the Bryan-Chamorro Treaty and neither was willing to back

---

[55] Cf. Article I of the Convention: the high contracting parties "bind themselves to submit all controversies or questions which may arise among them, of whatsoever nature and no matter what their origin may be. . . ."

[56] One of the eight conventions signed in Washington at the culmination of the Conference.

[57] Chamorro, "Note to Secretary of the Central American Court of Justice . . . ," *op. cit.,* pp. 888–889.

[58] *Costa Rica* v. *Nicaragua.* English translation of decision in *U.S. Foreign Relations* (1916), p. 877. Original from *Anales de la Corte de Justicia Centro-americana,* Vol. V.

[59] *Ibid.*

[60] *The Republic of El Salvador* v. *the Republic of Nicaragua, Anales de la Corte de Justicia Centroamericana,* Vol. VI. Official translation published by the Legation of El Salvador, Washington, D.C. Reprinted in "Judicial Decisions Involving Questions of International Law," *American Journal of International Law,* XL, 3 (July, 1917), 674–730. See also *U.S. Foreign Relations* (1917), pp. 1101–04.

down, regardless of legal considerations. The other republics (namely Costa Rica, El Salvador, and Honduras), for their part, were stirred to action by Nicaragua's bartering away of certain rights which they regarded as partially theirs. That the Court decided in favor of these republics was of little consequence in the face of Nicaragua's determination to disregard its legal obligations —a determination bolstered by the backing of a strong outside power.[61]

The one basic legal source of these problems, if any single one can be isolated, was Article I itself. It provided only poorly defined and ambiguous limits to the Court's jurisdiction. Even if the political situation had been relatively stable, Article I represented such a radical step in the direction of supranational power that problems surely would have arisen anyway. If states are to submit suddenly "all controversies or questions" to an incipient supranational authority—particularly when enforcement measures are lacking—the will to make the system succeed must be there. There was no evidence that Central America truly possessed this will. Such a will suggests a matter of value importance in having a dispute decided by the application of legal norms. When an international court has jurisdiction over all disputes of whatever character, this appears simply as an instance of nation-states using an inappropriate process for conflict resolution.[62]

Parties Before the Court and Disposition

The most (and probably only) significant feature of this aspect of the Court's practice was the fact that individuals, under the terms of Article II of the Convention,[63] did indeed bring cases before the Court. Of the ten cases handled by the Court, five of

---

[61] The generally held view of scholars is that the United States, as a dominant outside power, was both responsible for the creation of the Court and, unfortunately, instrumental in its demise. See Thomas A. Bailey, "Interest in a Nicaraguan Canal, 1903–1931," *Hispanic American Historical Review*, XVI (February, 1936), 2–28; Thomas A. Bailey, *A Diplomatic History of the American People* (6th ed.; New York: Appleton-Century-Crofts, Inc., 1958), pp. 551–553; and Karnes, *op. cit.*, pp. 199–202. A documentary of the U.S. role in this affair can be found in *supra*, footnote 50.

[62] An extensive discussion of the limits of arbitration and adjudication as means of conflict resolution is offered by Kenneth S. Carlston, *The Process of International Arbitration* (New York: Columbia University Press, 1946). See particularly his discussion of nullity. Also of relevance to the material discussed in this chapter is his treatment of the legal aspects of the cases handled by the Central American Court. See also Kenneth S. Carlston, "Development and Limits of International Adjudication," *Proceedings of the American Society of International Law* (1965), pp. 182–189.

[63] *Supra*, p. 29.

them dealt with claims by individuals (see Cases 2, 4, 6, 7, and 8 in Table 2). To this extent a significant supranational innovation was realized. On the other hand, one of the leading scholars on the Court notes: "None of the five cases in which individuals were parties was a case of great practical importance, and the fact that all of them were dismissed or declared to be inadmissible robs them of any great significance in the development of the court's jurisprudence."[64] This view is bolstered by the notation already made above that in several cases (all involving individuals, incidentally) defendant states did not bother to come to Court.[65] It would have been an interesting test of the states' willingness to support the innovation of individual access had a state lost one of these cases.

Judicial Impartiality

Judicial impartiality is a difficult factor to attempt to measure. Assuming a judge's vote in an international tribunal is discoverable, one can never be certain any particular connection exists between a judge's vote and his nationality. Since this would seem to be a key element if an international tribunal is to be truly supranational (i.e., whether judges can be found who can rise above their nationality), the vote cannot be disregarded.

The method employed here to produce rough generalizations about voting patterns (and this is all that can be done regardless of method) is simply to observe the votes of individual judges when their countries were parties before the court. In individual cases this method is not necessarily valid; but if over a period of time a correlation appears between nationality and vote, substantial questions can be raised about the impartiality of the tribunal.

An extreme charge that has been leveled against the Central American Court is: "The disinterestedness of the court was never demonstrated for in every case brought before it each judge voted for his own country."[66] Table 2 reveals that this assessment is not quite accurate. It is true that in the three important cases (Cases 1, 9, and 10), voting behavior followed "strict national lines."[67] This voting pattern clearly hurt the Court, especially in the politically sensitive cases following the Bryan-Chamorro Treaty.

On the other hand, voting in all the remaining cases did not follow any discernible nationalistic pattern. While one can argue that

---

[64] Hudson, *Treatise,* p. 70.

[65] *Supra,* footnote 44.

[66] Crowther, *op. cit.,* p. 194. Hudson, *Treatise,* pp. 42–70, and Karnes, *op. cit.,* pp. 187–202, are more moderate in their assessment.

[67] Phrase used by Karnes, *op. cit.,* p. 196.

because these cases were of little significance judges would be more prone to vote according to higher principles rather than national interest, this does not prove the claim that the judges were solely national representatives. That the judges functioned *substantially* as national representatives (and further, were regarded as such), however, is evidenced by several factors:

First, the correlation between nationality and judges' voting records in Cases 1, 9, and 10 is strong coincidence. Since Nicaragua refused to appear for the last two cases, the national representative character of the judges was bolstered by the fact that Judge Navas (Nicaraguan member of the tribunal) presented his government's case.[68]

Second, state control over justices in office was re-enforced by the fact that salaries were paid by the appointing state.[69] Article VII implied that judges' salaries would be paid *by the Court* out of contributions by the states. If one state failed to contribute, the rule should have been to dock each judge's salary proportionately. In practice, however, the precedent was set that if a state was in arrears, only the national judge of that state would lose his salary. This precedent developed when Justice Paniagua Prado was forced to return home in 1911 after a new regime in Nicaragua, desiring to replace him, refused to pay his salary.[70] Such a development could make the justices nothing but national representatives.

Finally, it seems to have been Nicaragua's somewhat justified position that the Court was *politically* stacked against her. While Nicaragua is normally acknowledged as the "villain" (along with the United States) responsible for the Court's demise, one journalistic account of the event notes that there are perhaps two sides to the story:

We cannot blame Nicaragua for being unwilling to submit the treaty to the Central American Court, for the Court was packed against her in advance. Nicaragua's northern neighbors, Salvador and Honduras, are just as much opposed to the treaty as her southern neighbor, Costa Rica, for they also claim rights in the territory covered by the proposed canal or its terminal harbors. Guatemala sympathizes with them, so as we might expect the Court stands four to one against Nicaragua.[71]

---

[68] Brown, *op. cit.*, p. 158.

[69] For discussion see Manley O. Hudson, *International Tribunals: Past and Future* (Washington, D.C.: Carnegie Endowment for International Peace and Brookings Institution, 1944), pp. 24–25.

[70] For the shaping of this precedent see Hudson, *Treatise*, pp. 51–52; Karnes, *op. cit.*, p. 202; and Roscoe R. Hill in A. Curtis Wilgus (ed.), *The Caribbean Area* (Washington, D.C.: George Washington University Press, 1934), p. 280.

[71] "Nicaragua Case," *Independent*, XC, 3571 (May 12, 1917), 274.

A note from the Nicaraguan Chargé d'Affaires (Nicaraguan Legation, Washington, D.C., April 14, 1917) to the U.S. Secretary of State lends credence to this view. It reads:

My Government wishes to impress your excellency with the assurance that Nicaragua is not in any way opposed to arbitration as the method par excellence recommended by civilization for the peaceful settlement of disputes among States. . . .

Nicaragua regards it as a matter of regret to put on record here the deplorable truth, that the Central American Court of Justice, far from responding to the lofty purposes of its creation, degenerated plainly . . . into a center of lively intrigues of the Central American Governments incited against Nicaragua in connection with the signing of the Chamorro-Weitzel Treaty which was not carried into effect, and more particularly the Bryan-Chamorro Convention of 1914.[72]

The note went on to point out how the court cases began "after a well known crusade for the preparation of the minds for concerted action by the capitals of the Isthmian Republics, the consequence being that both awards of the Court [were] invariably adverse. . . ."[73]

The only conclusion that can result from this evidence is that while the Court displayed impartiality in the minor cases, it clearly failed to rise above national considerations in terms of its over-all operation. In no sense did it become the "national conscience of Central America" proclaimed by Article XIII of the Convention.

Enforcement

There is little that can be said about enforcement. The Convention provided no means of enforcing decisions beyond moral suasion. All of the Court's decisions were complied with except for the last two, at which time the Court floundered.

The only major attempt to revive the Court was made at the Conference on Central American Affairs held in Washington from December 4, 1922, to February 7, 1923. One of the resulting conventions provided for an International Central American Tribunal.[74] Unfortunately, it never progressed beyond the ratification stage.[75]

---

[72] "Central America," *U.S. Foreign Relations* (1917) , p. 35.

[73] *Ibid.*

[74] For the text of the Convention see Manley O. Hudson, *International Legislation*, II (New York: Carnegie Endowment for International Peace, 1922–24) , 908–923. A comparison between the 1907 and 1923 conventions is offered by Jean Eyma, *La Cour de Justice Centre-Américaine* (Paris: Ernest Sagot & Cie., 1928) , pp. 171–177. He cites the placing of limits on the Court's jurisdiction as the major innovation.

[75] See Hudson, *Treatise*, pp. 66–69.

While the Central American Court was quite supranational both in letter and expectations, in spirit and practice it was not. Beyond the reality of allowing individuals to appear, national politics, jurisdictional problems, and lack of impartiality seem to have been the major elements preventing the Court from attaining its ideal.

CHAPTER THREE

PERMANENT COURT
OF INTERNATIONAL JUSTICE

A. EXPECTATIONS OF STATESMEN

The League of Nations and the United Nations were not created as supranational organizations, although as the following chapters show (particularly with the United Nations), some potential in this direction exists. Both the Covenant and the Charter (and the same holds true for the respective statutes of the courts) are intergovernmental. Further, the nation-states, if not in word at least in deed, have generally guarded very carefully against the introduction of supranational powers of the nature outlined in Chapter 1.

Two particular areas of these international organizations have received great attention because they represent, in a sense, the meeting ground between opposing views on supranational power vis-à-vis intergovernmental power. They are: (1) the "peace-keeping power" of the organization (only of indirect concern to this study),[1] and (2) the so-called "Optional Clause" relating to the voluntary acceptance of the Court's compulsory jurisdiction.[2]

The "Optional Clause" provides a basic focal point for this and the following chapter, not because these two courts are supranational, but because the drafting and implementation of the clause

---

[1] Articles 10, 11, and 16 of the League Covenant; Article 24 of the United Nations Charter.

[2] Article 36 of the Statute of the Permanent Court of International Justice (PCIJ); Article 36 of the Statute of the International Court of Justice (ICJ).

epitomizes the supranational expectations and fears that nations hold regarding a universal international tribunal. Rather than attempting to be historically comprehensive, this section is devoted to an examination of the major views advanced on the proper role for the Permanent Court of International Justice (PCIJ). The object of this examination is to highlight the supranational and intergovernmental proposals that were considered during the drafting of the Court. Research is greatly aided in this effort because the preliminary work preceding both the League and the United Nations has been extremely well documented and is available to the scholar.

American Beginnings

There were early stirrings among private groups in several countries for some type of international organization. In America a significant private group was sponsored by Theodore Marburg, who brought together historians, political scientists, and important statesmen at the Century Club in New York on January 25, 1915, for a series of discussions.[3] A brief examination of this group is worthwhile for several reasons: (1) it was "the first to undertake a serious consideration of the problem of the constitution and organization of a League";[4] (2) it considered many of the questions relevant to an international court; and (3) its work was made available to President Wilson.[5]

An interesting facet of the first meeting at the Century Club was the discussion of the role the Latin American countries should play in an international organization and of the fate met by the Central American Court of Justice.[6] Marburg's sketched notes read:

---

[3] See John Latané's Introduction to Theodore Marburg, *Development of the League of Nations Idea: Documents and Correspondence of Theodore Marburg,* ed. John H. Latané, I (New York: The Macmillan Company, 1932), vi. Marburg had been Ambassador to Belgium under President Taft and had an impressive number of important international acquaintances.

[4] *Ibid.*

[5] Latané notes that his compilation of Marburg's correspondence is of value for three reasons: (1) it shows conclusively that the League was not hastily improvised at Paris, but was rather the result of years of serious discussion; (2) it shows how groups of intellectuals thrashed out, on their own initiative, most of the preliminary problems and made their conclusions available to the statesmen who founded the League; (3) it contains some ideas, not in the Covenant, that may be of value for future development.

[6] Present at this and most of the following meetings were: Franklin H. Giddings, William J. Hull, W. W. Willoughby, Irving Fisher, Theodore S. Woolsey, George A. Plimpton, James L. Tryon, William H. Short, Frank Crane, Harold J. Howland, John B. Clark, Theodore Marburg, John A. Stewart, Hamilton Holt, and William B. Howland. Ex-President William H. Taft attended later meetings. Marburg, *op. cit.,* II, 703.

The idea was advanced that all Latin-American countries should be included in a League of Peace and it was reported that President Wilson was particularly sympathetic toward forming an American League of Peace. As against this view objection was raised to the presence of any backward countries in the League. It was pointed out that three arbitral awards had been rejected by Latin American countries in the last few years after an unbroken record of a century's acceptance of such awards.

The Court at Cartago instance of danger of setting up institutions among people not qualified to practice them. Failure of such institution often cited as failure of the principle whereas it is due to the character of the people who ought never to have been expected successfully to conduct it.[7]

In support of this view was Andrew D. White's statement that the presence of the Latin American countries at the Second Hague Conference was a mistake and that "Europe was loath to call the Third Conference by reason of their prospective presence."[8]

The Permanent Court of International Justice was an American though non-Wilsonian idea. This idea, formulated by the Marburg group, was first given public expression by former President Taft in an address before the World Court Congress, at Cleveland, Ohio, on May 12, 1915. The Taft conception of the "League of Peace" noted:

First: It ought to provide for the formation of a court, which would then be given jurisdiction by the consent of all the members of the League, to consider and decide justiciable questions between them or any of them, which have not yielded to negotiation, according to the principles of international law and equity, and that the court should be vested with power, upon the application of any member of the League, to decide the issue as to whether the question arising is justiciable.[9]

Taft's formulation, altered somewhat, became the first plank in the four-point program promulgated by the League to Enforce Peace at Independence Hall, Philadelphia, on June 17, 1915: "First: All justiciable questions arising between the signatory powers, not settled by negotiation, shall, subject to the limitations of treaties, be submitted to a judicial tribunal for hearing and judgment, both upon the merits and upon any issue as to its jurisdiction of the question."[10]

These proposals, which eventually found fulfillment in the Per-

---

[7] *Ibid.* One cannot help wondering to what extent these same charges might be easily applicable to the "advanced" countries in the League.

[8] *Ibid.* White had been president of the American delegation at the Hague Peace Conference.

[9] All of the Taft proposals are reprinted by Felix Morley, *The Society of Nations: Its Organization and Constitutional Development* (Washington, D.C.: Brookings Institution, 1932), p. 9.

[10] The entire program is reprinted in Marburg, *op. cit.*, I, viii–ix.

manent Court of International Justice (Articles 13 (3) and 14 of the Covenant, which are reprinted in Appendix B), differed in one major respect from the Central American Court. Jurisdiction was, although perhaps somewhat nebulously, limited to "justiciable questions" and by consent expressed through treaties.

These proposals later found a hearing by President Wilson. Lord Bryce, in a letter to Marburg dated May 1, 1918, suggested he make the organization's (League to Enforce Peace) plans available to Wilson. Marburg forwarded this suggestion to President Wilson, and his reply of May 6, 1918, indicated he was interested.[11] Wilson's interest in the movement had already been shown when he addressed their meeting in Washington on May 27, 1916.[12]

The final draft "Convention for an International Court" drawn up by the League to Enforce Peace, which was available to official policy makers, is reprinted in toto in Marburg's documents and correspondence.[13] Among those articles which seemed to have supranational implications were the following. Article 25 gave the court broad jurisdiction over "all disputes of a justiciable nature," while Article 27 gave the court power to "determine for itself whether disputes are justiciable." Article 26 gave the proposed court competence

to decide not only disputes of a justiciable nature arising between contracting Powers, but also disputes of a justiciable nature arising between a contracting Power and a non-contracting Power, or between non-contracting Powers, or between corporations or individuals on the one side and a contracting or non-contracting Power on the other, or wholly between corporations or individuals; but if there not be at least one Power on each side, there must be a certificate from the Foreign Office of a contracting Power to the effect that the dispute is of international consequence, with the exception, however, that no such certificate shall be required regarding a dispute arising in consequence of national courts involving foreigners.

Finally, Article 32 disqualified a judge if his country was a party, or if he might otherwise have a personal interest in the case. The only exception was by special agreement of the parties.

While these suggestions did not become part of the Statute of the League Court, they are nevertheless of value because of the progress beyond intergovernmentalism they embody. Especially interesting is Article 26. That they did not become part of the Statute is not surprising, however, for the PCIJ itself barely became part of the League framework, as the following section shows.

---

11 *Ibid.*, p. ix.
12 *Ibid.*
13 *Ibid.*, II, 737–740.

Paris Plans for an International Court

A survey of the plans put forth immediately prior and during the Paris Peace Conference of 1919 reveals three main themes: (1) the question of whether there should even be an international court, (2) the relation of the court to the League, and (3) the ever-present battle between those who wanted an intergovernmental organization and those who wanted to give it supranational powers.

PHILLIMORE PLAN   The first plan to be presented (March 20, 1918) was a British plan, which Morley links to the influence of the League to Enforce Peace.[14] The most interesting aspect of this plan is that it did not even mention a court.[15]

FRENCH PLAN   Chronologically, the next plan for an international organization was a French report (dated June 8, 1918) presented by the Commission Ministeriélle Française de la Société des Nations. Perhaps with an eye to controlling the Germans, the plan had strong supranational overtones.

It advocated a world court, with jurisdiction defined only as "au cas où le reglement amiable est impossible."[16] Further, the League as a whole had strong enforcement power. It was to "assure l'exécution de ses decisions et de celles du tribunal international; sur sa requisition, chaque nation est tenue d'user, d'un commun accord avec les autres, de sa puissance économique, maritime et militaire contre toute nation contrevenante."[17]

HOUSE AND WILSON DRAFTS   On July 8, 1918, President Wilson asked Colonel House to rewrite the Phillimore proposal.[18] The House Draft of a constitution for the League was submitted on July 16, 1918.[19] Interestingly, it was quite similar to the French formulation. Article 10 provided for a world court with "jurisdiction to determine any difference between nations which has not been settled by diplomacy, arbitration or otherwise. . . ." Although not very specific, Article 14 provided as a sanction that a nation not complying with the decision of the court would "lose and be de-

---

[14] See Morely, *op. cit.,* p. 10.

[15] The text of the Phillimore Plan is reprinted as Document 1 in David Hunter Miller, *The Drafting of the Covenant,* II (New York: G. P. Putnam's Sons, 1928) , 3–6.

[16] Article IV (3) . The full text of the plan is reprinted as Document 20 in *ibid.,* pp. 403–411. Annexe II of this proposal deals with the Court.

[17] Article IV (4) . Sections II and III of Annexe II outline in detail the nature of the available "Sanctions diplomatiques, juridiques, économiques et militaires."

[18] Morley, *op. cit.,* p. 15.

[19] The full text appears as Document 2 in Miller, *op. cit.,* pp. 7–11.

prived of all rights of commerce and intercourse with the contracting parties."

Certainly an unexpected surprise to most scholars was President Wilson's attitude toward a court (in view of his well-known commitment to internationalism), which he maintained throughout most of the Conference. He appeared indifferent, if not outright hostile, to the idea of a court. In his First Draft of the League (essentially a new edition of the House Draft), one of his most significant changes was the omission of any reference to an international court.[20] As a matter of fact, he did not include a court in any of his four drafts.

SMUTS PLAN   The next plan to achieve prominence was apparently a draft prepared by General Jan C. Smuts.[21] Essentially a call for some sort of arbitral tribunal, this long, oft-rambling document devotes only the closing two articles (Articles 20 and 21) to the judicial function. If not particularly helpful, at least this draft was candid. Smuts highlighted one of the basic problems of building a supranational tribunal—that of finding supranational judges. He notes that

the real difficulty . . . is to secure impartial arbitrators. The proposal has been made to create a permanent international tribunal or court, to which all justiciable cases may be referred by the council of the league. But the objection to this is that, as the judges on such a tribunal will be nationals of states, a state who appears as a litigant before the tribunal may feel aggrieved because a national of the opposing state may happen to be sitting in the case, and may be suspected of bias. On the whole, the most workable procedure seems to be to have a panel of arbitrators, to be prepared periodically by the council of the league, from which the litigants will select their respective arbitrators.[22]

Although veering from the supranational ideal, this view found expression in the statutes of both the PCIJ and the ICJ in the provisions for *ad hoc* judges.

ANGLO-AMERICAN SYNTHESIS   Other plans were presented, but the above were the most significant.[23] All of these plans were available to English and American statesmen, who drafted a large part of the Covenant. The essence of Anglo-American accord

---

[20] The text of Wilson's First Draft is reprinted as Document 3 in *ibid.*, pp. 12–15.

[21] *Ibid.*, Document 5, pp. 23–60.

[22] *Ibid.*, pp. 56–57.

[23] One other plan which deserves mention, but which had no significance beyond the prestige of its author, was the Cecil Plan. Submitted by Lord Robert Cecil to the British government on December 17, 1918, this draft was revised and presented to the Paris Conference on January 14, 1919. It was apparently intended to supplement the Phillimore Plan. See *ibid.*, Document 6, pp. 61–64.

was the Hurst-Miller Draft of February 2, 1919, which eventually became the heart of the Draft Covenant. Mr. David Hunter Miller, U.S. legal adviser, and Sir Cecil Hurst, British legal adviser, agreed upon this draft at the tenth meeting of the Commission of the League of Nations (February 13, 1919),[24] which was presented at the Plenary Session of the Peace Conference on February 14, 1919.[25]

Closely related were two other major steps taken in drafting the final Covenant: (1) a conference between President Wilson and Lord Robert Cecil produced agreement on several important changes (also Wilson's first agreement to a court),[26] and (2) changes were made by the final drafting committee, which was appointed at the close of the thirteenth meeting of the Commission for the purpose of redrafting the Covenant in accord with the changes agreed upon in the sessions of March 22, 24, and 26, 1919.[27]

We are here concerned only with Article 14, which seems (after examination of the minutes of the Commission's meetings) to have been the basic product of Anglo-American views. Great care was taken not only to avoid creating an international court with supranational power, but also to avoid creating even a very strong international court. President Wilson was apparently a key figure in these moves, although no explanation for such action is evident.[28] Table 3 presents the successive drafts of Article 14, which shows the status and general jurisdiction of the Court. Work to this point established agreement on three major elements: (1) there would be a permanent court, (2) it would be separate from the League,[29] and (3) compulsory jurisdiction seemed ruled out.

Looking at the three changes made in the final draft (see Table

---

[24] See *ibid.*, Document 19, pp. 316–335, for the minutes of the meeting and the annexed Draft Covenant.

[25] *Ibid.*, Document 23, pp. 557–579.

[26] For the text of the agreement see *ibid.*, Document 24, pp. 580–591.

[27] See Morely, *op. cit.*, p. 176.

[28] There is some evidence that President Wilson favored rather cumbersome arbitration provisions. See Article V of his Second Draft, dated January 10, 1919 (called also his First Paris Draft), which appears as Document 7 in Miller, *op. cit.*, pp. 65–93.

[29] The decision to keep the Court from becoming a supreme court for the League, in the words of Judge de Bustamente, "was simply a matter of preventing the Court from being turned into an auxiliary of the League, which would have been obliged to wait constantly for the Court's opinion before carrying out its work. Both needed to be, and became, separate organizations; they do not respond to the same impulse or to the same necessity; they can, and should, complete each other, without blending into each other." Antonio Sánchez de Bustamente y Sirven, *The World Court*, trans. Elizabeth F. Read (New York: The Macmillan Company, 1925), p. 91. Perhaps more of a "consideration" were the political views of the major powers, especially the United States.

Table 3   Development of Article 14 of the Covenant of the League of Nations[a]

February 14, 1919, Draft	Cecil-Wilson Agreement of March 18	Final Covenant
The Executive Council shall (1) *formulate plans for the establishment of a permanent court of international justice* and this court shall, when established, be competent to hear and determine (2) *any matter which the parties recognize as suitable for submission to it for arbitration* under the foregoing article.	The Executive Council shall (1) *formulate plans for the establishment of a permanent court of international justice* and this court shall, when established, be competent to hear and determine (2) *any matter which the parties recognize as suitable for submission to it for arbitration under the foregoing article, and also any issue referred to it by the Executive Council or Body of Delegates.*	The Council shall (1) *formulate and submit to the members of the League for adoption* plans for the establishment of a permanent court of international justice. The court shall be competent to hear and determine (2) *any dispute of an international character which the parties thereto submit to it.* (3) *The court may also give an advisory opinion upon any question referred to it by the Council or by the Assembly.*[b]

[a] The entire text of the first two drafts is reprinted in David Hunter Miller, *The Drafting of the Covenant*, Vol. II (New York: G. P. Putnam's Sons, 1928). They appear respectively as Documents 19 and 24.
[b] The italicized portions denote important changes made by the final drafting committee, which are discussed in the text.

3), Change 1 made it clear that the establishment of the court should be the subject of a separate treaty.[30] Change 2 arose because Cecil's wording of the article, as agreed to by President Wilson on March 18, 1919, was felt to "intimate a power of compulsory arbitration for the Court."[31] Change 3 was the inclusion of the famous world court advisory opinion clause, which would come to create such bitter debate and suspicion in the U.S. Senate. This clause was a Hurst-Miller innovation.[32] As it is beyond the basic focus of this study, it will not be considered further.

---

[30] See Morley, *op. cit.*, p. 185.
[31] *Ibid.*, p. 132.
[32] Many of the ideas put into the Covenant came from Hurst. Advisory jurisdiction was included at an informal meeting held between Hurst and Miller just prior to a meeting of the final drafting committee. See Miller's own account in Miller, *op. cit.*, I, 391. The so-called "neutral" states also had an important though not generally recognized role in contributing to changes in the various drafts of the Covenant. A particularly important informal meeting was called by Lord Cecil and Col. House (with Wilson's approval) on March 10, 1919, between the 14 members of the Commission (Belgium, Brazil, British Empire, China, Czechoslovakia, France, Greece, Italy, Japan, Poland, Portugal, Roumania, Serbia, U.S.A.) and the 13 "neutral" states (Argentina, Chile, Colombia, Denmark, Holland, Norway, Paraguay, Persia, Salvador, Spain, Sweden, Switzerland, and Venezuela). Prof. Philip Baker, who was himself at the proceedings, notes that the neutrals, *inter alia,* made it quite clear that "the real purpose of the

Advisory Committee of Jurists

After the League had been established, the Council on February 13, 1920 (in accordance with Article 14 of the Covenant), appointed an Advisory Committee of Jurists to report a scheme to it.[33] The Committee met from June 16 to July 24, 1920, to draft a statute for a court, which was approved by the Council on October 28, 1920, and submitted to the first session of the League Assembly.[34]

The work of the Advisory Committee of Jurists is of interest because it first dealt with the question of compulsory jurisdiction.[35] Article 34 (which, modified somewhat, eventually became Article 36 of the Statute) was the key element of the jurists' draft. It read:

Between States which are Members of the League of Nations, the Court shall have jurisdiction (and this without any special convention giving it jurisdiction) to hear and determine cases of a legal nature concerning:

(a) The interpretation of a treaty;

(b) Any question of international law;

(c) The existence of any fact which, if established, would constitute a breach of an international obligation;

(d) The nature or extent of reparation to be made for the breach of an international obligation;

(e) The interpretation of a sentence passed by the Court.

The Court shall also take cognizance of all disputes of any kind which may be submitted to it by a general or particular convention between the parties.

In the event of a dispute as to whether a certain case comes within any of the categories above mentioned, the matter shall be settled by the decision of the Court.[36]

Scott reports that "with but one dissenting voice, the Committee was of the opinion that a state belonging to the League of Nations

---

Commission was to secure the establishment of a true court of international justice." See Philip Baker, "The Making of the Covenant," in P. Munch (ed.), *Les Origines et l'Oeuvre de la Société des Nations* (Copenhagen: Rask-Örstedfonden, 1924), p. 50.

[33] U.S. Department of State, *The Treaty of Versailles and After: Annotations of the Text of the Treaty*, Publication No. 2724, Conference Series 92 (Washington, D.C.: Government Printing Office, 1947), p. 86.

[34] *Ibid.*

[35] The best report of the Committee's work is provided by James Brown Scott, who served as legal adviser to Elihu Root, the American member. The countries represented were: Argentina, Belgium, Brazil, England, France, Italy, Japan, Netherlands, Norway, Serbo-Croatia, Spain, and U.S.A. See James Brown Scott, *The Project of a Permanent Court of International Justice and Resolutions of the Advisory Committee of Jurists*, Pamphlet Series of the Carnegie Endowment for International Peace, Division of International Law, No. 35 (Washington, D.C.: Carnegie Endowment, 1920), pp. 2–3.

[36] The full text of this draft is presented as Annex A to Scott, *ibid.*, pp. 149–168. Article 35 dealt with the law to be applied (conventions, general principles of international law, teachings of publicists, etc.) and Article 36 concerned advisory opinions.

should, on its own initiative, be able to summon another state, also belonging to the League, before the Permanent Court of International Justice to litigate a judicial question concerning the subjects mentioned in Article 34."[37] The basis for this near unanimity was Article 13 of the Covenant, which implied that disputes would automatically be submitted to arbitration.[38] The only dissenting member of the Committee was Mr. Adatci of Japan, who felt that Article 14 of the Covenant clearly spelled out the voluntary nature of the Court's jurisdiction by giving it competence to hear international disputes "which the parties thereto submit to it."[39]

During the course of the Committee's meetings, both Root and Phillimore stood out as leaders for compulsory jurisdiction.[40] As Article 34 shows, their views carried the day, for the Draft Statute was reported back to the Council with this element included.

Mr. Bourgeois (President of the Assembly), speaking at the First Assembly, summarized Council action on the Draft Statute. He noted that the Council, realizing its members could not possess the technical judicial knowledge of the Committee of Jurists, had only made "certain modifications." "All it did," he said, "was to mark certain points which might give rise possibly to a general discussion and *to add certain finishing touches to the scheme, in particular that relating to the compulsory jurisdiction of the court*" (italics mine).[41] These "modifications" were in fact a series of amendments eliminating compulsory jurisdiction.[42]

Manley O. Hudson attributes a remark to Mr. Bourgeois (who had served as *Rapporteur* at the Council meetings considering the Draft Statute) to the effect that "the Council was not opposed to compulsory jurisdiction . . . and that the matter might be consid-

---

[37] *Ibid.*, p. 98.

[38] According to Article 13, the members of the League agreed "that whenever any dispute shall arise between them which they recognize to be suitable for submission to arbitration and which cannot be satisfactorily settled by diplomacy, *they will submit the whole subject-matter to arbitration*" (italics mine).

[39] Scott, *op. cit.*, pp. 98–99. Mr. Ricci-Busatti (Italy) also had voted against Articles 34 and 35 when first considered, as he preferred voluntary jurisdiction, but on the final vote (July 22, 1920), he voted for the draft proposals as a whole. See Scott, *op. cit.*, p. 99.

[40] *Ibid.*, p. 100.

[41] "The First Assembly of the League of Nations," in *A League of Nations,* World Peace Foundation Pamphlets, IV, 1 (Boston: World Peace Foundation, 1921), 104–105.

[42] See Hudson, *Treatise*, p. 191, and League of Nations, Secretariat, *Documents Concerning the Action Taken by the Council of the League of Nations Under Article 14 of the Covenant and the Adoption by the Assembly of the Statute of the Permanent Court* (Geneva, 1921), p. 44.

ered at a future date."[43] This may have been the case, but it does not explain the Council action. The record is not entirely clear, but if the record of the Assembly (where compulsory jurisdiction was hotly debated) is any indicator, the small powers on the Council emotionally, vigorously, and unanimously supported compulsory jurisdiction.[44] On the basis of the preceding comment by Bourgeois and this evidence, if both are true, one can only conclude that the Council—or more specifically the Great Powers—engaged in a "friendly" torpedoing of compulsory jurisdiction!

The significance of this action was enhanced by the fact that the Assembly's Third Committee (which considered the Draft) apparently considered the Council's action an important precedent. At the twentieth plenary meeting of the Assembly, Mr. Hagerup (Norway), *Rapporteur* of the Committee,[45] noted: "We thought that we should not radically modify the alteration introduced by the Council, which restricted the jurisdiction of the court to cases where it was accepted by both parties, thus excluding for the most part compulsory jurisdiction.[46] In an attempt to salvage something, the Committee made a notable contribution—the "Optional Clause." Mr. Hagerup, continuing his report before the Assembly, explained the innovation:

> We have slightly modified the article in order to make the idea clearer, but we have introduced no essential alterations, though we have made a very important addition to which I would draw special attention.
>
> If we were obliged to exclude a general compulsory jurisdiction, we thought we might leave open to such states as were inclined to accept such a system, the method of admitting a larger measure of compulsion in the jurisdiction of the court; and we therefore have adopted, on a proposal of the Brazilian Delegate, M. Fernandez, a scheme which was advocated by the Swiss delegate at the Hague in 1907.
>
> It consists in enumerating in the article concerning competence the cases to which compulsory jurisdiction may be applied. . . . It has not been possible thus to establish compulsory jurisdiction for all for the moment, but we have established compulsory jurisdiction for all those who are disposed to accept it.[47]

Compulsory jurisdiction was largely, and avidly, supported by the less powerful nations. Among those who spoke out strongly in the Assembly for compulsory jurisdiction were:

---

[43] Hudson, *Treatise,* p. 192.

[44] The small powers on the Council were Belgium, Brazil, Greece, and Spain (see *Covenant,* Article IV (1)). Their remarks in Assembly debate are summarized in "The First Assembly of the League of Nations," *op. cit.,* pp. 108–110.

[45] Mr. Hagerup had also served on the Committee of Jurists.

[46] "The First Assembly of the League of Nations," *op. cit.,* p. 107.

[47] *Ibid.*

Belgium	Panama
Brazil	Portugal
China	Roumania
Colombia	Serb-Croat-Slovene
Greece	State
Netherlands	Uruguay[48]

Typical of the view of this group was the statement by Raoul Fernandez (Brazil) indicating that "a satisfactory solution of the main problem involved in the establishment of the Court of Justice has not yet been reached, because compulsory jurisdiction has been denied the Court."[49] Seconding his remark was Dr. Blanco (Uruguay), who noted: "In South America we have an important tradition as far as compulsory arbitration is concerned, and I am in favor of a system of arbitration with no reservations. . . . I am sure that is the wish of South America as a whole."[50] He neglected to point out, however, that the capstone of the Latin American effort, the Central American Court of Justice, toppled.

The attitude that prevailed was that expressed by Mr. Balfour (England). Apparently speaking for the Great Powers, he noted that while compulsory jurisdiction was good and necessary, the time was not yet ripe for implementing it. Italy echoed this view.[51] Finally, the Draft Statute of the Permanent Court of International Justice, with the change outlined by Mr. Hagerup, was approved unanimously by a voice vote.[52] The Statute was then attached to a Protocol of Signature dated December 16, 1920, the ratification of which constituted adoption. The Statute entered into force in September of 1921. The first preliminary session of the Court was held on January 30, 1922.[53]

This brief survey of the proposals for an international court that were advanced prior to 1920 makes several points clear about the expectations of statesmen and the attitudes of nations toward an international court. First, from the earliest American beginnings of the League to Enforce Peace there was not only a rather constant desire to create an international tribunal but also an equally constant flirtation with supranationalism. Second, supranational ideas

---

[48] See *ibid.*, p. 108.

[49] *Ibid.*

[50] *Ibid.*

[51] Balfour's remarks are reprinted in *ibid.*, pp. 110–111; Mr. Schanzer's, the Italian delegate, on p. 110. For further remarks see C. Howard-Ellis, *The Origin, Structure and Working of the League of Nations* (Boston and New York: Houghton Mifflin Company, 1928), p. 367.

[52] "The First Assembly of the League of Nations," *op. cit.*, p. 112.

[53] U.S. Department of State, *The Treaty of Versailles*, p. 86.

were most strongly expressed in proposals for strong enforcement power of court decisions and compulsory jurisdiction, backed largely by the smaller nations. Finally, this impetus toward supranationalism notwithstanding, the resultant Permanent Court of International Justice was not a supranational tribunal because the big nations opposed the creation of such an institution.

B. CONSTITUTIONAL BASIS

While those statesmen who had favored building some supranational power into the Court had clearly been voted down, an examination of the Court's constitutional basis is nevertheless both interesting and profitable simply because the PCIJ had some well-developed potential supranational aspects.

It is true that the Central American Court had represented a spectacular stride forward in the area of supranational jurisdiction —but its fall backward was just as spectacular. Further, the Central American Court had made no progress at all away from the idea of judges as national representatives. The League Court represented a more balanced approach to the creation of judicial power. Presumably the resulting lesson is that attempts to create a strong international court, if they are to be successful, must be grounded in caution and evolutionary development, with awareness of the limits of the process of international adjudication.

Composition of the Court

Judge Manley O. Hudson summed up the nature of the Court's composition in one brief statement: "The Statute clearly excludes the idea of State representation on the Court."[54] The basis for such a remark can be found in the following articles of the Statute (articles of the Statute cited in this chapter are reprinted in Appendix C). The 15-member Court was to be a "body of independent judges, elected regardless of their nationality" (Article 2). Further, the court as a whole was to "represent the main forms of civilization and the principal legal systems of the world" (Article 9).

Also, members of the Court were not allowed to engage in any official or political activities outside the Court or to act as an agent or counsel in a case (Articles 16 and 17). Finally, there were provisions for diplomatic privileges and immunities (Article 19), and for an oath requiring every judge, before taking office, to "make a sol-

---

[54] Hudson, *Treatise*, p. 264.

emn declaration in open Court that he will exercise his powers impartially and conscientiously" (Article 20).

The Statute was most ambivalent regarding nationality, however, Judge Hudson's remark notwithstanding. Somewhat in contrast to the preceding articles was Article 10, which suggested that there was indeed something significant about nationality for it implied that no state should have more than one of its nationals elected to the Court. Further, the above articles contrast sharply with the tenor of Article 31 (2) and (3), which provides that a contesting party, when no judge of its nationality sits on the Court, may select an *ad hoc* judge for the duration of the case.[55]

Out of the confusion spawned by these seemingly conflicting statements, at least one point is clear. While Hudson's statement in the main is undoubtedly true, nationality did play a significant role in the *selection* of judges. "The results of elections held between 1921 and 1938," Hudson himself writes, "were largely determined by the nationality of the candidates."[56] Evidence is provided by the fact that the permanent members of the Council were always represented on the Court.[57] Also, it became somewhat of a practice to fill midterm vacancies by judges of the same nationality.[58] Although not in accord with the qualities one would expect to find in the ideal supranational court, the national representation of some judges is in accord with certain political realities—and hence probably unavoidable in any international court. At least the selection process for judges in the League Court had progressed beyond the strict concept of state representation found in the Central American Court.[59]

More important than the selection process is national control over judges in office. The only overt way this might be done is through some means of financial control, as was the case in the Central American Court. Great care was taken to make the Court's fi-

---

[55] The Statute does not mention the term *"ad hoc* judge," although it appears in various revisions of the Court's Rules. Cf. Article 4 of the 1922 Rules and in Articles 4 and 30 of the 1926 and 1931 Rules.

[56] Hudson, *Treatise,* p. 265.

[57] For lists of judges see League of Nations, P.C.I.J., *Reports,* Series E, Nos. 1–16. As a matter of fact, from 1921 to 1941 ten nations always had a representative on the Court (China, Cuba, England, France, Italy, Japan, Netherlands, Roumania, Spain, and U.S.A.).

[58] See the data presented by Hudson, *Treatise,* Appendix 10, pp. 776–777. In nine out of eleven positions filled in by-elections the practice was followed of electing judges of the same nationality as the one vacating the position.

[59] Articles 4–15 of the Statute outline the complex procedure whereby the Council and the Assembly separately vote on candidates for the Court.

nancial administration autonomous—not only in respect to the member states, but also to the Council and the Secretariat. According to the Financial Regulations of the League of Nations, adopted January 1, 1923, the provision was: "In the future, from each contribution paid by the members of the League of Nations into the general funds, the Court shall be granted a share corresponding to the proportion which its own budget bears to that of the League of Nations, it being understood that, when necessary, the Court may also be granted, in the same proportion, advances from the Working Capital Fund."[60]

Also, Part III of the League's annual budget (which is devoted to the Court) provided that, from member payments to the League treasurer at Geneva, the Court's percentage would be deposited to the credit of the Court in a bank at The Hague.[61]

To insure the independence of individual members of the Court, Assembly resolutions (of December 18, 1920, and September 25, 1930) further provided that judges' salaries would be tax free. In the event that fiscal laws of some countries could not be accommodated to the Assembly resolutions, provision was made to reimburse judges for any taxes they might be obliged to pay on their salaries.[62]

There was no direct way then for a country to control the Court or its members under the terms of either the Covenant or the Statute. It is true that certain practices became established in selecting judges, but there is no evidence to suggest that this impaired the independence of the tribunal. There was no way to exercise financial control over the Court except by jeopardizing League finances as a whole. As a matter of record, the Court was never without adequate funds and no difficulties arose in financing it.[63]

Jurisdiction and Access to the Court

The jurisdiction of the Permanent Court of International Justice can be divided into two basic types: (1) *ratione personae* and (2) *ratione materiae*. Article 34 of the Statute made clear that there was no supranational aspect to the first of these. It specified that "only States or Members of the League of Nations" could be parties before the Court. The *Sixteenth Report* of the Court recognized three types of states: (1) members of the League

[60] "How the World Court Is Financed," *Congressional Digest*, V, 2 (February, 1926) , 53.

[61] See Hudson, *Treatise*, p. 313.

[62] See League of Nations, *Records of the First Assembly*, Plenary, pp. 748, 766, and *Records of the Eleventh Assembly*, Plenary, p. 132.

[63] See Hudson, *Treatise*, p. 313.

as specified by Article 35 (1) of the Statute; (2) states mentioned in the Annex to the Covenant which do not belong to the League of Nations as specified by Article 35 (1) of the Statute; and (3) states in neither of the two above categories. Article 35 of the Statute provides that the conditions under which the Court will be open to such states are, subject to the special provisions of treaties in force, to be laid down by the Council. In no case, however, can such provisions place the parties in a position of inequality before the Court.[64]

The complete jurisdiction *ratione materiae* of the Permanent Court was provided by a complex "overlapping mosaic" of hundreds of documents conferring jurisdiction. As of December 31, 1945, ten basic instruments governed the Court's jursidiction:[65]

1. Covenant (Articles 12, 13, 14, and 15—as amended, September 26, 1924)

2. Resolution of the First Assembly of the League of Nations, Dated December 13, 1920,[66] Approving the Statute of the PCIJ[67]

3. Protocol of Signature of December 16, 1920[68]

4. Optional Clause[69]

5. Statute of the PCIJ (Articles 35, 36, 37, and 38)

6. Extract from the Report Presented to the Third Committee of the First Assembly of the League of Nations (by Mr. Hagerup) [70]

7. Resolution, Dated May 17, 1922, by Which the Council of the League of Nations at Its Eighteenth Session Drew up, in Conformity with Paragraph 2 of Article 35, the Conditions Under Which the Court Is Open to States Other Than Members of the League of Nations or Those Mentioned in the Annex to the Covenant[71]

8. Resolution, Dated September 21, 1922, by Which the Third Assembly of the League of Nations Has Recommended a Procedure To Be Followed in the Event of a Difference of Opinion Regarding the Treaties of Minorities[72]

9. Protocol of Signature of the Statute of the Court and Optional Clause (List of Signatories and Ratifications) [73]

---

[64] See League of Nations, P.C.I.J., *Sixteenth Report* (Series E, No. 16), pp. 55–57.

[65] See League of Nations, P.C.I.J., *Collection of Texts Governing the Jurisdiction of the Court* (Series D, No. 5), pp. 68–327.

[66] League of Nations, *Official Journal, Special Supplement* (January, 1921), p. 23.

[67] Cf. Article 35 of the Statute.

[68] League of Nations, *Treaty Series,* VI (1921), 380.

[69] *Ibid.,* p. 384. Cf. Article 36 (2) of the Statute.

[70] League of Nations, *Acts of the First Assembly, Plenary Meetings* (1920), p. 457.

[71] League of Nations, *Official Journal,* Third Year, No. 6 (June, 1922), p. 545.

[72] League of Nations, *Official Journal, Special Supplement,* No. 9 (October, 1922), p. 35.

[73] League of Nations, P.C.I.J., *Collection of Texts Governing the Jurisdiction of the Court* (Series D, No. 5), pp. 68–72.

10. Declarations of Acceptance of the Optional Clause Concerning the Court's Compulsory Jurisdiction (as Translated by the Secretariat of the League of Nations) [74]

In addition to these basic items, there are certain other instruments of jurisdiction, stemming essentially from treaties and other international agreements. As of December 31, 1945, there were 159 of these instruments registered with the Court. They can be grouped roughly into seven categories:

1. Peace treaties
2. Clauses relating to the protection of minorities
3. Mandates entrusted to certain members of the League of Nations by virtue of Article 22 of the Covenant
4. General international agreements (e.g., those concluded during the peace negotiations in 1919 or resulting from a conference held under the auspices of the League of Nations)
5. Political treaties (alliance, commerce, navigation, and others)
6. Various acts and conventions on transit, navigable waterways, and communications in general
7. Treaties on arbitration and conciliation[75]

One very important point should be gleaned from the foregoing maze of jurisdictional qualifications which is immediately relevant to this study. Nations, when realistically conferring jurisdiction on an international court which they intend to use, apparently can be expected to be quite specific and careful in the transfer of decision-making power to that tribunal. This point becomes more meaningful if one compares the unbelievable grant of power given the Central American Court of Justice in terms of its jurisdiction. Given the role of the nation-state in history, a clash between the idealistic expectations for the Court and cold, hard, political reality could not have been other than unavoidable. Presumably League members were avoiding this pitfall by grounding every conceivable facet of the Permanent Court's jursidiction in specific instruments of consent.

The most significant element of the Permanent Court's jurisdiction, however, in terms of a potential supranational transfer of decision-making power, was of course the famous "Optional Clause."

---

[74] *Ibid.*, pp. 73–79.

[75] Provided for by Article 36 (1) of the Statute. See *ibid.*, pp. 81–327. See also League of Nations, P.C.I.J., *Sixteenth Report* (Series E, No. 16), pp. 45–47. Likewise see Hudson, *Treatise*, pp. 380–385, for a discussion of "conventions and treaties in force." He notes that Article 36 (1) "has given encouragement to States to confer jurisdiction on the Court, and such action has resulted in a wide extension of its jurisdiction. The expression 'treaties and conventions' is general in its scope, and it applies to any form of international instrument in force when the Statute took effect or brought into force subsequently" (p. 380).

The legal elements of this clause included Article 36 (2) and (3) of the Statute and the Protocol of Signature of the Statute of December 16, 1920 (with ratifications).

By the terms of Article 36 (2) and (3):

The Members of the League of Nations and the States mentioned in the Annex to the Covenant may, either when signing or ratifying the Protocol to which the present Statute is adjoined, or at a later moment, declare that they recognize as compulsory *ipso facto* and without special agreement, in relation to any other Member or State accepting the same obligation, the jurisdiction of the Court in all or any of the classes of legal disputes concerning:
(a) the interpretation of a treaty;
(b) any question of international law;
(c) the existence of any fact which, if established, would constitute a breach of an international obligation;
(d) the nature or extent of the reparation to be made for the breach of an international obligation.
The declaration referred to above may be made unconditionally or on condition of reciprocity on the part of several or certain Members or States, or for a certain time.

For those member states subscribing to this clause a supranational feature had been added to the Court in the form of compulsory jurisdiction.[76] Before examining the operation of the clause in practice, however, one other constitutional element of the Court's jurisdiction deserves attention because of its supranational potential. Article 36 (4) provides that "in the event of a dispute as to whether the Court has jurisdiction, the matter shall be settled by the decision of the Court." Although in principle this holds true, from a constitutional standpoint there are several treaty provisions (then in force) which modify this article slightly.[77]

First, clauses of international conventions, referring to the terms of Article 36 (2) of the Statute (and thus determining the categories of disputes to be submitted to the Court), may *expressly mention* the special jurisdiction of the Court under Article 36 (4).[78]

Second, the principle in Article 36 (4) may be expressly *repeated*

---

[76] The Court defines "compulsory jurisdiction" as existing "when the Court may be made cognizant of a suit by *unilateral application* under an international agreement" (italics in original). See League of Nations, P.C.I.J., *Collection of Texts Governing the Jurisdiction of the Court* (Series D, No. 5), p. 13.

[77] See *ibid.*, pp. 39–40.

[78] See, for example, the Treaty of Conciliation and Compulsory Arbitration of April 6, 1925, between France and Switzerland. Article 14 provided that "it shall be for the Court to decide, as provided in Article 36, Paragraph 4, of the Statute, whether it has jurisdiction." See *ibid.*, Document No. 134, p. 277.

in treaty provisions which substitute special categories of disputes for the terminology of Article 36 (2) .[79]

Third, in some treaty clauses *dating from before* the preparation of the Statute the principle that the jurisdiction of the Permanent Court is to be determined by itself can be found, but the settlement of certain categories of disputes is reserved to other bodies.[80]

Finally, a related aspect is a series of clauses found especially in several conciliation conventions that provide for a *suspension of all pending proceedings before other bodies* when a question of jurisdiction is referred for consideration to the PCIJ.[81] None of these provisions offer any major modification of the general principle that the Court is competent to determine its own jurisdiction, nor is their occurrence in treaties widespread.[82] It is important, however, to be aware of their existence, for they further add to the complex of jurisdictional instruments delineating the Court's competence and make even more striking the contrast with the broad jurisdiction of the Central American Court.

Judgments

Regarding the execution of judgments, Judge Hudson has noted: "It is no part of the Court's task to see that its judgments are carried out, and except for the possibility of its interpreting or revising a judgment its competence with reference to a dispute is exhausted when it has delivered a judgment on the merits."[83]

Yet if an international court is to move beyond the intergovernmental level, it clearly must be able to give effect to its judgments. This implies some enforcement mechanism beyond the court itself. In this respect the institutional framework of the League represented a great advance from the days of the Central American Court.

---

[79] Cf. Article 13 of the Treaty of Conciliation and Judicial Settlement between Belgium and Switzerland, of February 13, 1925, *ibid.*, Document No. 129, p. 268.

[80] For instance, Article 37 of the Convention for the Regulation of Air Navigation, of October 13, 1919, *ibid.*, Document No. 18, p. 103.

[81] See, for example, Article 2 of the Convention of June 27, 1924, between Denmark and Sweden concerning the establishment of a conciliation commission, *ibid.*, Document No. 106, p. 228; Article 7 (3) of the Conciliation and Arbitration Convention of January 17, 1925, between Estonia, Finland, Latvia, and Poland, *ibid.*, Document No. 128, p. 265; Article 2 of the Conciliation Convention of March 28, 1925, between Latvia and Sweden, *ibid.*, Document No. 133, p. 275; and Article 2 of the Conciliation Treaty of May 29, 1925, between Estonia and Sweden, *ibid.*, Document No. 138, p. 282.

[82] See *ibid.*, pp. 83–327.

[83] Hudson, *Treatise*, p. 595.

First, parties before the Permanent Court of International Justice clearly had a legal obligation to execute a judgment. By the terms of Article 13 (4) of the Covenant, members of the League of Nations[84] bound themselves to "carry out in full good faith any award or decision that may be rendered" and also not to "resort to war against a Member of the League which complies therewith."

Although the nature of enforcement measures was not exactly clear, Article 13 of the Covenant provided that the Council could intervene to give effect to a Court decision. While there is no particular hint of coercion in Article 13 (4), which reads that "in the event of any failure to carry out such an award or decision, the Council *shall propose* what steps should be taken to give effect thereto," at least rudimentary enforcement machinery was there (italics mine). The clause was never used, so there is no way of telling whether a Court decision could in fact be imposed. Presumably, if the Council's "proposals" were not complied with, the sanctions of Article 16 would become applicable.[85]

By way of review at this point, at least two features of the Permanent Court of International Justice should be clear: (1) although various statesmen had had supranational expectations for the Court, its constitutional basis was intergovernmental, yet (2) the Court did have some supranational potential, particularly for those countries accepting compulsory jurisdiction. Only a survey of the practice of the Court can reveal the extent to which this potential was realized.

C. PRACTICE OF THE COURT
Jurisdiction

Sir Frederick Pollock had this to say about the new Court's jurisdiction: "At last we have a real jurisdiction; not yet compulsory, but according to the best judgment of historians all jurisdiction was voluntary to begin with."[86] This view gives rise to an interesting thesis about the supranational potential of an international court. Prof. de Lapradelle's (France) remark in the Committee of Jurists offers a positive formulation of this thesis: "There is an immutable law in the evolution of legal institutions which shows

---

[84] Non-members might be bound under Article 17 (1) of the Covenant.

[85] Article 16 included commercial, financial, and military sanctions.

[86] Sir Frederick Pollock, "The Permanent Court of International Justice," *British Yearbook of International Law* (1926), p. 135. The Greek international jurist M. Nicolas S. Politis makes a similar argument in *La Justice Internationale* (Paris: Librairie Hachette, 1924), p. 288.

that an optional jurisdiction has always, sooner or later, been followed by a compulsory jurisdiction."[87]

He did not explain the basis for this "law," and unfortunately the PCIJ and ICJ experiences do not prove the "immutability," or even the existence, of such a "law." There has been a general trend toward wider acceptance of the Optional Clause, although there is no reason to construe such a trend (which is only generally identifiable to begin with) as evidence of some inexorable process. On the other hand, however, the possibility that an "immutable law" might indeed be at work enhances the possible significance to be attached to acceptances of compulsory jurisdiction.

As of December 31, 1945, the Protocol of Signature of 1920 (indicating acceptance of the Statute), drawn up in accordance with the Resolution adopted by the Assembly on December 13, 1920,[88] had been signed by 59 states or members of the League of Nations.[89] As if to prove Prof. de Lapradelle's "law," by December 31, 1945, 54 of these states had signed the Optional Clause, thus taking a significant step toward supranationalism. They were:

Albania	Czechoslovakia	Haiti
Argentina	Denmark	Hungary
Australia	Dominican	India
Austria	Republic	Iran
Belgium	Egypt	Iraq
Bolivia	Estonia	Ireland
Brazil	Ethiopia	Italy
Bulgaria	Finland	Latvia
Canada	France	Liberia
China	Germany	Lithuania
Colombia	Greece	Luxembourg
Costa Rica	Guatemala	Netherlands

---

[87] Cited by Howard-Ellis, *op. cit.*, p. 388.

[88] According to this Resolution, the Protocol may be signed by members of the League or states mentioned in the Annex to the Covenant. As of December 31, 1945, the following members of this group had not signed: Afghanistan, Ecuador, Honduras, Mexico, and Saudi Arabia (Hedjaz). League of Nations, P.C.I.J., *Sixteenth Report* (Series E, No. 16), p. 37.

[89] They included: Albania, Argentina, Australia, Austria, Belgium, Bolivia, Brazil, Bulgaria, Canada, Chile, China, Colombia, Costa Rica, Cuba, Czechoslovakia, Denmark, Dominican Republic, Egypt, Estonia, Ethiopia, Finland, France, Germany, Greece, Guatemala, Haiti, Hungary, India, Iran, Iraq, Ireland, Italy, Japan, Latvia, Liberia, Lithuania, Luxembourg, Netherlands, New Zealand, Nicaragua, Norway, Panama, Paraguay, Peru, Poland, Portugal, Roumania, Salvador, Siam, Spain, Sweden, Switzerland, Turkey, Union of South Africa, United Kingdom of Great Britain and Northern Ireland, U.S.A., Uruguay, Venezuela, and Yugoslavia. Of these, the following never ratified the Protocol of 1920: Argentina, Costa Rica, Egypt, Guatemala, Iraq, Liberia, Nicaragua, Turkey, and U.S.A. *Ibid.*

New Zealand	Roumania	Union of South
Nicaragua	Salvador	Africa
Norway	Siam	United Kingdom
Panama	Spain	of Great Brit-
Paraguay	Sweden	tain and North-
Peru	Switzerland	ern Ireland
Poland	Turkey	Uruguay
Portugal		Yugoslavia[90]

The extent of this list is misleading, however, for several reasons. First, seven states signed subject to ratification, but never ratified:

Argentina	Iraq
Czechoslovakia	Liberia
Egypt	Poland[91]
Guatemala	

Second, three states signed without condition as to ratification but never ratified the Protocol of Signature of the Statute:

Costa Rica
Nicaragua
Turkey[92]

Finally, if one counts expirations, only 29 states were actually bound by the Optional Clause as of December 31, 1945:

Australia	Netherlands
Bolivia	New Zealand
Brazil	Norway
Bulgaria	Panama
Canada	Paraguay
Colombia	Portugal
Denmark	Salvador
Dominican Republic	Siam
Estonia	Sweden
Finland	Switzerland
Haiti	Union of South Africa
India	United Kingdom of Great
Iran	Britain and Northern
Ireland	Ireland
Latvia	Uruguay[93]
Luxembourg	

An interesting note indicated by this last list is that the only Great Power bound by the Optional Clause was the United Kingdom. The Italian, German, and French acceptances had all

---

[90] *Ibid.*, p. 49.
[91] *Ibid.*
[92] *Ibid.*, p. 50.
[93] *Ibid.* The question of reservations is explored *infra*, p. 69 ff.

expired.[94] Russia, Japan, and the United States never signed. The advent of instability in Europe and finally the war largely explains this situation.[95] The impact of instability in Europe after 1933 is also evident in the decline in business before the Court, which hitherto had been a relatively busy international tribunal (see Table 4). The war of course was not the only reason for the Great Power avoidance of compulsory jurisdiction. The United States' treatment not only of compulsory jurisdiction and the Court, but of the League as a whole, was a bizarre and tragic episode which offers a classic example of a nation's suspicions and fears of internationalism—of even the weakest efforts to organize beyond the nation-state. This subject has been examined in detail elsewhere.[96] It suffices here to quote a somewhat lengthy but illustrative excerpt from one senator's speech, which rather aptly summarizes the United States' view of compulsory jurisdiction. The senator notes:

One of two propositions is true: This court either has a jurisdiction or it does not have a jurisdiction. A court with jurisdiction may be dangerous, and that danger is to be measured by the degree of its jurisdiction. A court without jurisdiction is a court without power. A court without power is a vacuum; and when men are driven in defense of this proposition to the claim that the court has no power, they are driven to the contention that we propose a cipher and tell us that cipher represents value.

When you propose to make reservations to this court protocol and statute you certify your heart's belief that there is danger lurking there. When you say you will submit to no jurisdiction unless you consent in that particular case, you certify that you fear the decisions of the court. When you say that you will reserve the right to stay out on every question that you do not want to submit, you certify that the court is a doubtful court and that it might exercise its jurisdiction in such a manner as to imperil the rights and liberties of your country. So you fear it while you enter it.

It [the PCIJ] is a foreign court, named by the representatives of foreign nations, foreign in tongue, foreign in religion, foreign in basic thought,

---

[94] The respective dates are September 6, 1936; February 28, 1938; and April 24, 1941. See *ibid.* All expirations except China's (May 12, 1927) were in the 1930's and early 1940's.

[95] For an appraisal of the war's effect see Shabtai Rosenne, *The World Court: What It Is and How It Works* (Leyden: A. W. Sythoff, 1962), pp. 23–26.

[96] For a full description of the Senate's treatment of the League see D. F. Fleming, *The United States and World Organization: 1920–1933* (New York: Columbia University Press, 1938). A documentary report is provided by U.S. Department of State, *The United States and the Permanent Court of International Justice: Documents Relating to the Question of American Accession to the Court,* Publication No. 44 (Washington, D.C.: Government Printing Office, 1930). An incisive though somewhat impassioned discussion of "the Senate's technique of defeating peace treaties" is offered by D. F. Fleming, *The United States and the World Court* (Garden City, N.Y.: Doubleday, Doran and Company, Inc., 1945), especially p. 22 ff.

Table 4 Work of the Permanent Court of International Justice[a]

	New Cases Registered			Nature of Solution		
Year	Total	Contentious Cases	Req. for Adv. Opinions	Judgments Rend.	Advisory Opinions	Case Discontinued
1922	4	—	4	—	3	—
1923	5	1	4	2[b]	5	—
1924	6	2	2 + (1)[c]	2	1	—
1925	5	3	3	3	3	1
1926	3	1	2	1	1	—
1927	7	5	1 + (1)[c]	4	1	—
1928	6	5	1	2	2	—
1929	—	—	—	3	—	2
1930	2	—	2	—	2	—
1931	8	2	6	—	4	—
1932	11	10	1	3	3	—
1933	3	3	—	2	—	5
1934	1	1	—	2	—	—
1935	4	2	2	—	—	—
1936	6	6	—	1	—	1
1937	3	3	—	3	2	—
1938	4	4	—	1	—	1
1939	1	1	—	3	—	—
1940	—	—	—	—	—	—
1941	—	—	—	—	—	—
1942	—	—	—	—	—	—
1943	—	—	—	—	—	—
1944	—	—	—	—	—	—
1945	—	—	—	—	—	2
Total	79[d]	49	28 + (2)[c]	32	27	12

[a] Data derived from League of Nations, P.C.I.J., *Sixteenth Report* (Series E, No. 16), pp. 92–202.
[b] Includes an interlocutory judgment.
[c] Requests for interpretation of judgment.
[d] Manley O. Hudson's oft-cited figures from *The Permanent Court of International Justice: 1920–1942: A Treatise* (New York: The Macmillan Company, 1943), Appendix 12, list 65 new cases. This variance is explained by the fact that the above table lists *all* folios opened by the Court. Hudson excludes discontinued cases and requests for interpretation, a difference of 14, which if subtracted from the above total yields 65. The reason that the total of solutions presented in the last three columns do not equal the total number of new cases is due to the fact that Court orders joined several of the cases.

foreign in the principles of civilization, foreign in every way. Yet to this court we propose to consign the destinies of America.[97]

Assuming that the American position was extreme, perhaps the lesson to be drawn from national practice toward compulsory juris-

---

[97] Speech by Senator James H. Reed (D, Mo.) reprinted in "Senate Discusses U.S. Entry into World Court," *Congressional Digest*, V, 2 (February, 1926), 55–56. Speeches by the redoubtable Senators William E. Borah (R, Idaho) and Hiram W. Johnson (R, Calif.) against the Court are reprinted on pp. 57–62.

diction under the League Court is that, given general political stability, (1) acceptance of compulsory jurisdiction will spread, and (2) the Great Powers can and will submit. Quite possibly it has been the lack of general international political stability which has been the significant variable responsible for preventing the functioning of the "immutable law" from 1933 to the present. Unfortunately for an argument of this kind, however, there is no clear-cut definition of what constitutes "political instability."

A significant feature in accepting the Optional Clause was the nature of the reservations made by states. A survey of acceptances reveals that, contrary to practice under the U.N. Court, there were no significant reservations—having the effect of nullifying the original acceptance. Five categories of reservations were evident: (1) reciprocity; (2) time limit (usually five years, a few for ten years) ; (3) pending ratification; (4) "All future disputes except where the Parties may have agreed or may agree to some other method of pacific settlement"; (5) Brazil's unique reservation— "On condition that compulsory jurisdiction is accepted by at least two of the Powers permanently represented on the Council of the League of Nations."[98]

The first three types of reservations were made by nearly every country. In none of the five categories, however, was there any reservation that served to destroy the declaration of acceptance. State practice in this area at least should have been encouraging to those with supranational hopes.

National practice in actual jurisdictional disputes before the Permanent Court should have been equally encouraging, for in no case did a state challenge the very foundation of the Court as Nicaragua had done to the Central American Court. As noted above, jurisdiction was clearly grounded in an elaborate process of consent. Even for those states accepting a tinge of supranationalism in accepting compulsory jurisdiction, prior consent rather carefully delimited the nature and scope of cases the Court could hear. On this basis, then, one should be able to expect general compliance with the "spirit" of the League tribunal.

The first column of Table 5, "Case/Jurisdiction," lists all the judgments handed down by the Court and the jurisdictional issues raised, if any. In all, preliminary objections to the Court's jurisdiction were raised in 14 cases. Four of these were discontinued for var-

---

[98] See League of Nations, P.C.I.J., *Collection of Texts Governing the Jurisdiction of the Court* (Series D, No. 5) , pp. 68–72.

Table 5 Nature and Solution of Contentious Cases Before the Permanent Court of International Justice[a]

Case/Jurisdiction[b]	Issue	Disposition	Judges' Vote[c]
1. *S.S. Wimbledon (France, Great Britain, Italy, and Japan v. Germany)*; accepted; Ser. A/No. 1; 17 Aug. 1923[d]	Freedom of the Kiel Canal.	For applicants. Germany under obligation to keep canal open as "international waterway."	9 to 4. The Italian judge dissented against his government; the German *ad hoc* judge dissented.
2. *Mavrommatis Palestine Concessions* (jurisdiction) (*Greece v. Great Britain*); contested by Great Britain/A; Ser. A/2; 30 Aug. 1924	Objection to Court's jurisdiction. Negotiations a condition precedent to judicial proceedings.	Two parts: (1) British objection concerning Jaffa concessions upheld; (2) objection concerning Jerusalem concessions rejected.	6 to 4. The Greek *ad hoc* judge did not dissent; the British judge dissented to the holding on the Jerusalem concessions.
3. *Interpretation of Par. 4 of the Annex Following Art. 179 of the Treaty of Neuilly (Bulgaria v. Greece)*; accepted; Ser. A/3; 12 Sept. 1924 (summary procedure)	Bulgaria contended that the Treaty did not authorize certain classes of claims against her, especially for acts committed outside her territory.	For Greece.	Not determinable.
4. *Interpretation of Judgment No. 3 (Bulgaria v. Greece)*; accepted; Ser. A/4; 26 March 1925 (summary procedure)	Request by Greece for an interpretation under Art. 60 of the Statute.	Greek request refused.	Not determinable.

[a] Data derived from League of Nations, P.C.I.J., *Collection of Judgments and Orders* (Series A, Nos. 1–16) and *Collection of Judgments, Orders and Advisory Opinions* (Series A/B, Nos. 46–79); from Manley O. Hudson, *The World Court: 1921–1938* (Boston: World Peace Foundation, 1938); and from League of Nations, P.C.I.J., *Sixteenth Report* (Series E, No. 16).
[b] Under this heading, the term "accepted" indicates the parties went before the Court on the basis of agreement stemming from declarations accepting jurisdiction, *ad hoc* agreements, or treaties conferring jurisdiction. "Contested" shows that a party objected to the Court's jurisdiction. A (affirmative) indicates that the objection was overruled and that the Court found it had jurisdiction. N (negative) means that the objection was upheld. This column includes only cases where preliminary objections related to jurisdiction were invoked. Jurisdictional questions of one kind or another, however, were raised in nearly all other cases. The case citation and date of decision are also indicated.
[c] It is not possible in some cases to see how a particular judge voted because all of the dissenters were not identified.
[d] The interlocutory judgment in this case is not counted, giving a total of 31 judgments rather than 32 as shown in Table 4.

#	Case	Issue	Decision	Vote
5.	*Mavrommatis Palestine Concessions* (merits) (*Greece v. Great Britain*); accepted (see Judgment No. 2); Ser. A/5; 26 March 1925	Conditions for the validity of the Mavrommatis Jerusalem concessions.	For Greece, but claim for indemnity dismissed.	Unanimous. Neither the British nor the Greek *ad hoc* judge dissented.
6.	*German Interests in Polish Upper Silesia* (jurisdiction) (*Germany v. Poland*); contested by Poland/A; Ser. A/6; 25 Aug. 1925.	Does the Court have jurisdiction to determine, under the German/Polish Convention of 15 May 1922, the legality of certain expropriations made by Poland?	For Germany. Polish plea of lack of jurisdiction dismissed.	12 to 1. The Polish *ad hoc* judge was the lone dissenter.
7.	*German Interests in Polish Upper Silesia* (merits) (*Germany v. Poland*); accepted; Ser. A/7; 25 May 1926	Germany claimed a Polish law of expropriation would constitute a violation of Poland's obligations under the Geneva Convention relating to Upper Silesia.	For Germany.	9 to 3. The German *ad hoc* judge voted for Germany; the Polish *ad hoc* judge dissented.
8.	*Claim for Indemnity in Respect of the Factory at Chorzów* (jurisdiction) (*Germany v. Poland*); contested by Poland/A; Ser. A/9; 26 July 1927	Does the Court have the jurisdiction to determine the existence and extent of the obligation of Poland to make reparation for injuries inflicted as a result of the seizure of German nitrate factories at Chorzów?	For Germany. Polish plea of lack of jurisdiction dismissed.	10 to 3. The Polish *ad hoc* judge was one of the dissenters.
9.	*S.S. Lotus* (*France v. Turkey*); accepted; Ser. A/10; 7 Sept. 1927	Did Turkey act contrary to international law by prosecuting the responsible officers of French and Turkish vessels following a collision on the high seas?	For Turkey.	6 to 5 after the President (Swiss) voted to break a tie. The Turkish *ad hoc* judge voted with the majority; the French judge dissented.
10.	*Readaptation of the Mavrommatis Jerusalem Concessions* (merits) (*Greece v. Great Britain*); contested/N; Ser. A/11; 10 Oct. 1927	Great Britain claimed the Court had no jurisdiction under treaties in force *in re* readapted concessions.	For Great Britain.	7 to 4. The Greek *ad hoc* judge dissented.

Table 5 *Continued*

Case/Jurisdiction	Issue	Disposition	Judges' Vote
11. *Interpretation of Judgments Nos. 7 and 8 (Germany v. Poland)*; accepted; Ser. A/13; 16 Dec. 1927	Germany held the Polish government had no right to ask by process of law for any new determination of questions settled in Judgments 7 and 8.	Declaratory judgment for Germany.	8 to 3. The only identifiable dissent was by the Italian judge.
12. *Rights of Minorities in Upper Silesia (Minority Schools) (Germany v. Poland)*; accepted;[e] Ser. A/15; 26 April 1928	Germany claimed that under the Polish-German Convention (signed at Geneva 15 May 1922) minority groups should be able to choose the language of instruction in schools.	For Germany.	8 to 4. The German *ad hoc* judge voted for Germany; the Polish *ad hoc* judge dissented.
13. *Claim for Indemnities in Respect of the Factory at Chorzów* (merits) *(Germany v. Poland)*; accepted; Ser. A/17; 13 Sept. 1928	Nature of the reparation to be made by Poland for the seizure of factories.	For Germany.	9 to 3. The German *ad hoc* judge voted with the majority; the Polish *ad hoc* judge dissented.
14. *Serbian Loans Issued in France (France v. Serb-Croat-Slovene State)*; accepted; Ser. A/20; 12 July 1929	Holders of bonds and coupons of various Serbian loans demanded payment in gold, not paper, francs.	For France.	9 to 3. The French *ad hoc* judge voted for France; the Yugoslav *ad hoc* judge dissented.
15. *Brazilian Federal Loans Issued in France (Brazil v. France)*; accepted; Ser. A/21; 12 July 1929	Holders of bonds and coupons of various Brazilian loans in France demanded payment in gold, not paper, francs.	For France.	9 to 2. The French *ad hoc* judge voted with the majority; the Brazilian judge dissented.

[e] Poland objected to the Court's jurisdiction only in its rejoinder, after having filed its countercase without any objection or reservation related to jurisdiction. The Court ruled it could not admit this belated objection as it had already assumed jurisdiction.

16. *Territorial Jurisdiction of the International Commission of the River Oder (Great Britain, France, Germany, Czechoslovakia, Sweden, and Denmark v. Poland)*; accepted; Ser. A/23; 10 Sept. 1929	Whether the jurisdiction of the International Commission of the Oder extends, under the Versailles Treaty, to tributaries of the Oder.	For applicants.	9 to 2 against Poland, with the Polish *ad hoc* judge dissenting.
17. *Free Zones of Upper Savoy and the District of Gex (France v. Switzerland)*; accepted; Ser. A/B-47; 7 June 1932	Whether Art. 435, par. 2 of the Versailles Treaty abrogated existing treaty provisions establishing free zones around Geneva.	For Switzerland.	6 to 4. The Swiss judge voted for Switzerland; the French *ad hoc* judge dissented.
18. *Interpretation of the Statute of Memel (jurisdiction) (Great Britain, France, Italy, and Japan v. Lithuania)*; contested by Lithuania/A; Ser. A/B-47; 24 June 1932	Lithuania contested jurisdiction of the Court on the grounds that (under Art. 17 of the Convention of Paris) disputes had to be submitted first to the League Council.	For applicants.	13 to 3. All the judges of the plaintiff states voted for their governments; the Lithuanian *ad hoc* judge dissented.
19. *Interpretation of the Statute of Memel (merits) (Great Britain, France, Italy, and Japan v. Lithuania)*; accepted; Ser. A/B-49; 11 Aug. 1932	Whether the government of Lithuania violates the Statute by dismissing certain officials of the directorate of the Memel Territory.	The Court decided three questions in favor of Lithuania and three against it.	10 to 5. The British, Japanese, and French judges expressed no dissent; the Italian judge dissented on the grounds of inadmissibility; the Lithuanian *ad hoc* judge dissented on only one of the decisions unfavorable to Lithuania.
20. *Legal Status of Eastern Greenland (Denmark v. Norway)*; accepted; Ser. A/B-53; 5 April 1933	Denmark claimed that Norway's proclamation of 10 July 1931 (*re* police powers given to certain Norwegian nationals there) disrupted the existing legal situation in Greenland.	For Denmark.	12 to 2. The Danish *ad hoc* judge voted for Denmark; the Norwegian *ad hoc* judge dissented.

Table 5 *Continued*

Case/Jurisdiction	Issue	Disposition	Judges' Vote
21. *Appeal Against a Judgment of 3 Feb. 1933 by the Hungaro-Czechoslovak Mixed Arbitral Tribunal (Peter Pázmány University v. the State of Czechoslovakia)* (*Czechoslovakia v. Hungary*); accepted; Ser. A/B-61; 15 Dec. 1933	The M.A.T. had held that Czechoslovakia was bound to restore property to the Hungarian university taken at the time of the creation of the Czechoslovak state. Czechoslovakia appealed this decision.	For Hungary.	12 to 1. The Hungarian *ad hoc* judge voted for Hungary; the Czechoslovak *ad hoc* judge was the lone dissenter.
22. *Lighthouses Case (France v. Greece)*; accepted; Ser. A/B-62; 17 March 1934	Does a concessionary contract made in 1913 between the Ottoman government and a French firm (*re* the maintenance of lighthouses) bind the Greek government, which took over the territories after the Balkan wars?	For France.	10 to 2. The French judge voted for France; the Greek *ad hoc* judge was one of the dissenters.
23. *Oscar Chinn (Great Britain v. Belgium)*; accepted; Ser. A/B-63; 12 Dec. 1934	The Belgian government's virtual monopoly of Congo River traffic was forcing a British private firm out of business. The British government took up the case under "freedom of navigation" of the Convention of St. Germain (1919).	For Belgium.	6 to 5. The Belgian judge voted with the majority; the British judge dissented.
24. *Pajzs, Csáky, Esterhazy* (merits) (*Hungary v. Yugoslavia*); contested by Yugoslavia; objections joined to merits in A/B-66/N; Ser. A/B-68; 16 Dec. 1936	Whether an appeal to the Court can be entertained against decisions rendered by the Hungarian-Yugoslav M.A.T. established under the Treaty of Trianon (1920).	For Yugoslavia.	8 to 6. The Yugoslav *ad hoc* judge voted for Yugoslavia; the Hungarian *ad hoc* judge dissented.

No.	Case	Question	Holding	Vote
25.	*Diversion of Water of the Meuse* (*Netherlands v. Belgium*); accepted; Ser. A/B-70; 28 June 1937	Did either Belgium or Holland violate the provisions of a treaty of 12 May 1933 in building diversionary canals along the Meuse?	Both claims rejected.	10 to 3. The Netherlands judge dissented in the rejection of his country's claim. By the same vote the Court rejected the Belgian counterclaim, with the Belgian judge dissenting.
26.	*Lighthouses in Crete and Samos* (*France v. Greece*); accepted; Ser. A/B-71; 8 Oct. 1937	Does a concessionary contract made in 1913 between the Ottoman government and a French firm bind the Greek government which took over the territories after the Balkan wars?	For France.	10 to 3. The French judge voted with the majority; the Greek *ad hoc* judge dissented.
27.	*Borchgrave* (preliminary objections) (*Belgium v. Spain*); contested by Spain/A; Ser. A/B-72; 6 Nov. 1937	Belgium alleged failure of the Spanish government to use diligence in apprehending persons guilty in the death of Baron Jacques de Borchgrave. Spain raised preliminary objections on the jurisdiction because Belgium had not exhausted local remedies.	For Belgium. Case later discontinued.	Unanimous. No Spanish dissent.
28.	*Phosphates in Morocco* (preliminary objections) (*Italy v. France*); contested by France/N; Ser. A/B-74; 14 June 1938	France contested the jurisdiction on the basis of the *ratione temporis* limitation in her acceptance of the Optional Clause. Italy had contested the French phosphate monopoly in Morocco.	For France. Objection upheld.	11 to 1. The French judge voted with the majority; the Italian judge did not dissent.
29.	*Panevezys-Saldutiskis Railway* (merits) (*Estonia v. Lithuania*); contested by Lithuania; objections joined to merits in A/B-75; Ser. A/B-76; 28 Feb. 1939	An Estonian company purported to be the successor to the First Company of Secondary Railways in Russia and claimed compensation from the Lithuanian government for that part of the railway on Lithuanian soil.	For Lithuania. Objection upheld due to non-exhaustion of local remedies.	10 to 4. The Lithuanian *ad hoc* judge voted for Lithuania; the Estonian *ad hoc* judge did not dissent.

Table 5 *Continued*

Case/Jurisdiction	Issue	Disposition	Judges' Vote
30. *Electricity Company of Sofia and Bulgaria* (preliminary objection) (*Belgium v. Bulgaria*); contested by Bulgaria/A (in part); Ser. A/B-77; 4 April 1939	Belgium asked the Court to hold that Bulgaria had failed on three occasions to perform its international duties *re* power company concessions.	For Belgium (the Court took jurisdiction over two of the three counts).	9 to 5. The Belgian judge voted with the majority; the Bulgarian *ad hoc* judge dissented on those points unfavorable to Bulgaria.
31. "*Société Commerciale de Belgique*" (*Belgium v. Greece*); accepted; Ser. A/B-78; 15 June 1939	The Belgian government asked that the Greek government pay an award to a Belgian company for Greece's default in a railway contract.	Unclear. The Court admitted one of the submissions of each party, dismissed the rest, and declared that the 1936 arbitral award to Belgium was obligatory (which Greece admitted anyway).	13 to 2. Neither the Belgian judge nor the Greek *ad hoc* judge dissented.

ious reasons by orders of the Court.[99] Of the ten remaining cases (Judgments 2, 6, 8, 10, 18, 24, 27, 28, 29, and 30), the Court subsequently declared it lacked jurisdiction in four of them (Judgments 10, 24, 28, and 29). Of significance is the fact that all six of the judgments wherein the Court overruled a challenge to its jurisdiction were complied with. Two additional points stand out: the Court was able in all cases to make the final determination of its competence (*compétence de la compétence*) and also able to assume jurisdiction even over the protest of states.

The Court's jurisprudence regarding jurisdiction makes two further points clear. In respect to consent the Court noted in the *Rights of Minorities in Upper Silesia (Minority Schools)* Case: "The Court's jurisdiction depends on the will of the Parties. The Court is always competent once the latter have accepted its jurisdiction, since there is no dispute which States entitled to appear before the Court cannot refer to it."[100]

The significant feature of this case was the fact that the Court concluded it was competent to hear the merits simply because the respondent state had not raised a timely objection to its jurisdiction.[101] One author called this action testimony for the "conscious and liberal exercise of the *compétence de la compétence* with which the Permanent Court has honored Article 36 (4) of its Statute."[102]

Also, the Court indicated that the key factor in determining its *compétence de la compétence* was the establishment of original intent on the part of the litigants. In the *Chorzów Factory* (jurisdiction) Case the Court proclaimed:

It has been argued repeatedly in the course of the present proceedings that in case of doubt the Court should decline jurisdiction. It is true that the Court's jurisdiction is always a limited one, existing only insofar as States have accepted it; consequently, the Court will, in the event of an objection—or when it has automatically to consider the question—only affirm its jurisdiction provided that the force of the arguments militating in favour of it is preponderant. The fact that weighty arguments can be

---

[99] See League of Nations, P.C.I.J., *Sixteenth Report* (Series E, No. 16), p. 55. The cases were: (1) *Prince von Pless (Germany v. Poland)*, (2) *Appeal Against Two Judgments Delivered on Dec. 21, 1931, by the Hungaro-Czechoslovak M.A.T. (Czechoslovakia v. Hungary)*, (3) *Appeal Against a Judgment Delivered on April 13, 1932, by the Hungaro-Czechoslovak M.A.T. (Czechoslovakia v. Hungary)* and (4) *Losinger & Co. (Switzerland v. Yugoslavia)*.

[100] League of Nations, P.C.I.J., *Collection of Judgments and Orders* (Series A, No. 15), p. 32.

[101] See Table 5, footnote e.

[102] Ibrahim F. I. Shihata, *The Power of the International Court to Determine Its Own Jurisdiction: Compétence de la Compétence* (The Hague: Martinus Nijhoff, 1965), p. 35.

advanced to support the contention that it has no jurisdiction cannot of itself create a doubt calculated to upset its jurisdiction.

When considering whether it has jurisdiction or not, the Court's aim is always to ascertain whether an intention on the part of the Parties exists to confer jurisdiction upon it. The question as to the existence of a doubt nullifying its jurisdiction need not be considered when, as in the present case, this intention can be demonstrated in a manner convincing to the Court.[103]

Two basic rules emerge from these judgments that deserve restating. First, the Court's jurisdiction is wholly grounded in consent, a fact that is made amply clear by the instruments creating jurisdiction. Second, the mere fact that a state contests the Court's jurisdiction is not reason enough for the Court to decline jurisdiction. The Court, considering such contentions, will determine its own jurisdiction, basing its determination on its own interpretation of the states' original intent to confer jurisdiction.

Parties Before the Court

As noted earlier, the Permanent Court of International Justice followed the traditional practice of recognizing only states as international actors. The applications of individuals to be heard were invariably rejected.[104]

Judicial Impartiality

It has already been indicated that, in constitutional terms, there was no evidence of any national control over judges either in the selection process or after the assumption of office. On the basis of the data presented in the final column of Table 5, however, there appears to be a rather high correlation between judges' votes when their country was a party before the Court and their country's stand in the litigation. In 21 of the judgments there was evidence of possible correlation.[105] In only three judgments was there a clear lack of correlation.[106] The remaining seven cases defy categorization.[107]

---

[103] League of Nations, P.C.I.J., *Collection of Judgments and Orders* (Series A, No. 9) , p. 22.

[104] See League of Nations, P.C.I.J., *Sixteenth Report* (Series E, No. 16) , p. 66, which notes: "It often happens that private individuals apply to the Court with the object of laying before it matters at issue between them and some government. In response to such applications the registrar invariably states that, under the terms of Article 34 of the Statute of the Court, 'only States or Members of the League of Nations can be Parties in cases before the Court.'" Specific examples are noted in a footnote.

[105] Judgments 2, 6, 7, 8, 9, 10, 12, 13, 14, 15, 16, 17, 18, 20, 21, 22, 23, 24, 25, 26, and 30.

[106] Judgments 5, 27, and 31.

[107] Judgments 1, 3, 4, 11, 19, 28, and 29.

The discussion in Chapter 2 of judicial voting records has already cautioned against overestimating the significance of this type of tabulation. Judge Hudson's remarks in the context of such practice with the Permanent Court deserve mention. He warns:

The mere fact that a national judge is in a minority of one does not justify a conclusion that his views are attributable to national bias; such a conclusion could be reached only after a careful analysis of the substance of the views expressed by the majority and by the minority. Hence a statistical presentation of the positions taken by national judges in cases before the Court is almost certain to be misleading, and a conclusion that national judges are or are not disposed to follow the policies of their governments should not be based upon a mere tabulation of the votes which led to the adoption of the Court's judgments and opinions.[108]

This view is correct. However, Hudson is really raising a basic problem about the nature of judicial decision-making. Even assuming one has made "a careful analysis of the substance of the views expressed by the majority and by the minority," he is not likely to be any closer to discovering the real motivation behind a judge's vote. While *overreliance* on the results found in Table 5 is erroneous, so is *underestimation* of their significance. The rather high correlation of nationality and vote throughout 31 cases raises the specter of national bias among the judges—even if it does not prove it. This correlation, which looks suspiciously like something more than mere coincidence, is surely not lost on the nation-states.

Efforts by the United States to adhere to the protocols of the Permanent Court provide a case in point. During hearings before the Senate Committee on Foreign Relations in 1934, a large part of the ammunition used by opponents of the Court concerned alleged national bias on the part of the judges. The Court had just handed down an advisory opinion on the Austro-German Customs Union that reeked strongly of politics. Opponents of the Court were able to submit articles from respected newspapers all over the world, many friendly to the Court, which labeled the Court "political."

The highly regarded Swiss *Neue Zürcher Zeitung* claimed the "Court allowed itself to a large extent to be guided by political motives."[109] The English *New Statesman* wrote that the opinion was political rather than juridical in nature. . . . But even more serious is the nature of the national division in the Court. . . . The judges, in a word, hardly acted as an impartial body of jurists concerned with a scientific

---

[108] Hudson, *Treatise*, p. 355.

[109] U.S. Senate, Committee on Foreign Relations, *Hearings, Relative to the Protocols Concerning the Adherence of the United States to the Permanent Court of International Justice*, Part 2, 73rd Cong., 2nd Sess., May 16, 1934, p. 261.

problem of interpretation. Each had in his mind a political question and acted as though he were the representative of a government upon the tribunal. . . . [It] is not unfair to prophesy that *it will be a long time before one of the great powers is willing to seek the advice of the court upon so grave an issue. Yet it is precisely by such willingness that the prestige and power of the Court must hope to grow* [italics mine].[110]

Even the New York *Times* wrote that the opinion "shouts 'politics.' " Regarding American adherence, the same article continued:

A fear that the behavior of the World Court in the matter of the German-Austria customs alliance would be seized upon by American enemies of the court was justified last week. Washington dispatches related that Senators who have steadily opposed American adhesion to the Court . . . are prepared to fight the proposal again and believe that they at last have definite evidence to support their hitherto theoretical argument.

This evidence the Senators hold to has been supplied by these circumstances of the World Court's opinion—its political cast . . . and inferences to be gathered from the division among the judges. Realistic friends of the World Court are agreed that its prestige has been deeply injured.[111]

The main point raised by these newspaper views seems not so much to be whether the judges were *in fact* biased, but that observers *thought* they were. The kind of questions raised about judicial impartiality by the evidence presented in Table 5 cannot help but raise national fears, not only about supranationalism, but even about internationalism.

Enforcement

Most treaties that provided for the jurisdiction of the Court also had provisions for carrying out the judgment.[112] In any event, no case arose under the Permanent Court in which a state refused to carry out a judgment.[113] Apparently the only significant question in this regard was raised in the *Société Commerciale de Belgique* Case. In this last case to come before the Court the issue was not really Greece's refusal to abide by the decision. Rather, it was Greece's inability to comply with the decision (for financial reasons). This inability to pay, as well as the contending parties' desire to settle the affair amicably, were made known to the Court. The Court noted these submissions as follows:

---

[110] *Ibid.*, p. 256.

[111] *Ibid.*, p. 255. For a sampling of over 50 international newspapers see entire Appendix D, pp. 252–267. All agree generally with the above excerpts.

[112] See League of Nations, P.C.I.J., *Collection of Texts Governing the Jurisdiction of the Court* (Series D, No. 5) , pp. 44–46. Many also referred specifically to Article 13 of the Covenant.

[113] See Hudson, *Treatise*, p. 596.

Nevertheless, though the Court cannot admit the claims of the Greek Government, it can place on record a declaration which Counsel for the Belgian Government, speaking on behalf of the Agent for that Government who was present in Court, made at the end of the oral proceedings. This declaration was as follows: "If, after the legal situation had been determined, the Belgian Government should have to deal with the question of payments, it would have regard to the legitimate interests of the Company, to the ability of Greece to pay and to the traditional friendship between the two countries."

This declaration, made after the Greek Government had presented its final submissions, is in a general way in line with the Greek submissions. It enables the Court to declare that the two Governments are, in principle, agreed in contemplating the possibility of negotiations with a view to a friendly settlement, in which regard would be had, amongst other things, to Greece's capacity to pay. Such a settlement is highly desirable.[114]

Although the Permanent Court of International Justice had had a good deal of success, World War II effectively terminated its life. The twenty-first ordinary session of the Assembly adopted the following resolution: "That the Permanent Court of International Justice is for all purposes to be regarded as dissolved with effect from the day following the close of the present session of the Assembly [April 19, 1946], but without prejudice to such subsequent measures of liquidation as may be necessary."[115]

The "subsequent measures" dealt with the transfer of property and archives to the United Nations Court, the International Court of Justice.[116]

The League Court was, as has been seen, clearly not a supranational court. While it did have some supranational potential, any evaluation of this element cannot help but be ambivalent. On the one hand, supporters of a strong international tribunal could take heart at the broad acceptance of the Optional Clause and the fact that Court decisions were unfailingly implemented. Yet it cannot be overlooked that national consent and possible political overtones appeared at the base of the Court's work. In any case, the League Court is dead. The question of current interest concerns the status of the United Nations Court in terms of supranational development.

114 League of Nations, P.C.I.J., *Collection of Judgments, Orders and Advisory Opinions* (Series A/B, No. 78) , p. 178.

115 U.S. Department of State, *The Treaty of Versailles*, p. 86.

116 See League of Nations, P.C.I.J., *Sixteenth Report* (Series E, No. 16) , p. 12.

CHAPTER FOUR

INTERNATIONAL COURT OF JUSTICE

A. EXPECTATIONS OF STATESMEN

Much of what has been said about the Permanent Court of International Justice holds true for its successor, the International Court of Justice (ICJ). The latter inherited the archives, physical plant, and jurisprudence of the League Court. It also inherited many of its problems. The International Court of Justice, like the League Court, is not a supranational court, although some potential in this direction is present. Interesting in this respect is the fact that the statesmen who built the United Nations dredged up all the old arguments that had been used 20 years earlier in building the League. Needless to say, the argument of supranationalism versus intergovernmentalism again attracted a preponderance of attention.

The history of the ICJ prior to the San Francisco Conference requires only a brief description for present purposes. The novelty of a universal international organization had largely worn off through League experience, and many questions were already answered. These answers, as reflected in the Statute of the Permanent Court of International Justice, simply required modification and updating.[1]

---

[1] For an official report on the war years and the closing of the League see League of Nations, P.C.I.J., *Sixteenth Report* (Series E, No. 16), pp. 7–13. See also Manley O. Hudson, "The Twenty-fourth Year of the World Court," *American Journal of International Law*, XL, 1 (January, 1946), 1–52. Among

Initial Plans

INFORMAL INTER-ALLIED COMMITTEE   Called together by the British government in May, 1943, this informal committee of 12 leading international lawyers reviewed the status of the League Court in light of a possible new international organization. Their report, published early in 1944, constituted the first comprehensive re-examination of the Court since the outbreak of the war. Among the recommendations included in their report were these points: (a) the need for a Court was not questioned; (b) the Statute should remain the basic instrument with as few changes as possible; (c) the Court should continue to be independent of a world organization; (d) there should be no compulsory jurisdiction; rather, a better-defined optional clause should be retained.[2]

DUMBARTON OAKS AND THE COMMITTEE OF JURISTS   In October, 1944, the Dumbarton Oaks Proposals for the United Nations were published by the four sponsoring powers (the United States, Great Britain, China, and the Soviet Union). Chapter VII of these Proposals provided for "an international court of justice which should constitute the principal judicial organ of the Organization."[3]

In implementation of Chapter VII, a United Nations Committee of Jurists, convened by the sponsoring powers, met in Washington, D.C., from April 9 to April 20, 1945, to formulate a draft statute for the proposed court.[4] Forty-four states were represented, as was the Permanent Court of International Justice.[5]

---

other things, Hudson offers an excellent comparison of the texts of the two court statutes.

[2] See "Report of the Informal Inter-Allied Committee on the Future of the Permanent Court of International Justice," *American Journal of International Law Supplement: Official Documents,* XXXIX, 1 (January, 1945), 1–41. Reprinted from *British Parliamentary Papers,* Misc. No. 2 (1944), Cmd. 6531.

[3] Chapter VII of the Dumbarton Oaks Proposals is readily available in U.S. Department of State, *The International Court of Justice: Selected Documents Relating to the Drafting of the Statute,* Publication No. 2491, Conference Series 84 (Washington, D.C.: Government Printing Office, 1946), p. 14. For the full work of Dumbarton Oaks, see United Nations Conference on International Organization, *Documents* (hereinafter cited as *U.N.C.I.O.*), Vol. III (London and New York: United Nations Information Organizations, 1945).

[4] U.S. Department of State, *The International Court of Justice,* Preface.

[5] See *U.N.C.I.O.,* Vol. XIV. Judge Manley O. Hudson represented the PCIJ. The states were: Australia, Belgium, Bolivia, Brazil, Canada, Chile, China, Colombia, Costa Rica, Cuba, Czechoslovakia, Dominican Republic, Ecuador, Egypt, El Salvador, Ethiopia, France, Greece, Guatemala, Haiti, Honduras, Iran, Iraq, Lebanon, Liberia, Luxembourg, Mexico, Netherlands, New Zealand, Nicaragua, Norway, Panama, Paraguay, Peru, Philippine Commonwealth, Saudi Arabia, Syria, Turkey, United Kingdom, U.S.S.R., U.S.A., Uruguay, Venezuela, and Yugoslavia.

The supranational/intergovernmental dilemma was dealt with at length by the Committee. One author's summary of the proceedings notes: "The most important political issue concerning the Court in the new international system was that of its jurisdiction, which occupied the committee as much as all other questions combined. The problem before the jurists was whether to leave 'compulsory' jurisdiction on the basis of voluntary acceptance of the 'optional clause' as under Article 36 of the Statute, or to prescribe it as an obligation for all parties."[6]

The Committee decided to retain the Statute with slight amendment. Three major questions which were left unresolved, to be decided by the San Francisco Conference itself, were (1) the status of the Court in relation to the U.N.; (2) the nomination and election of judges; and (3) the jurisdiction of the Court.[7]

San Francisco Conference

The major question here concerns jurisdiction. The Committee of Jurists had prepared two alternative drafts on compulsory jurisdiction which they presented to the U.N. Conference (see Table 6). National debate on compulsory jurisdiction is interesting because not only were the old arguments from League days revived, but the national split between the large and small nations was again the same.[8]

In the Committee of Jurists the Soviet representative had even been opposed to the presentation of alternative drafts of Article 36 to the Conference. He declared that there was no need for an alternative text, as compulsory jurisdiction was "completely unacceptable to his government."[9] The United States was somewhat more conciliatory. The U.S. delegate in Committee IV/1 at the Conference noted that the purpose of the Committee was to define the Statute and establish a court which would be acceptable to the larg-

---

[6] Ruth B. Russell and Jeannette E. Muther, *A History of the United Nations Charter: The Role of the United States, 1940–1945* (Washington, D.C.: Brookings Institution, 1958), p. 868.

[7] See *U.N.C.I.O.*, Vol. XIV.

[8] This might be a good point at which to offer a more complete definition of "compulsory jurisdiction" than that provided in the foregoing chapter. Ruth Lawson, in "The Problem of the Compulsory Jurisdiction of the World Court," *American Journal of International Law*, XLVI, 2 (April, 1952), 219–238, gives this rather good definition: "compulsory jurisdiction means the power of a court to decide whether cases unilaterally referred, pursuant to a previous commitment and without the *ad hoc* consent of the respondent, come within its jurisdiction and, if so, to act upon such cases even over the objection of the respondent" (p. 221).

[9] *U.N.C.I.O.*, XIV, 166.

Table 6 Alternative Drafts of Article 36 of the Statute of the International Court of Justice[a]

The Committee submits two alternative texts of this Article since the opinion of the members of the Committee was divided on the selection of one or the other.[b]

(1) The jurisdiction of the Court comprises all cases which the parties refer to it and all matters specially provided for in the Charter of the United Nations or in treaties and conventions in force.

(2) The Members of the United Nations and the States parties to the present Statute may at any time declare that they recognize as compulsory *ipso facto* and without special agreement, in relation to any other Member or State accepting the same obligation, the jurisdiction of the Court in all or any of the classes of legal disputes concerning:

(a) the interpretation of a treaty;

(b) any question of international law;

(c) the existence of any fact which, if established, would constitute a breach of an international obligation;

(d) the nature or extent of the reparation to be made for the breach of an international obligation.

(3) The declaration referred to above may be made unconditionally or on condition of reciprocity on the part of several or certain Members or States, or for a certain time.

(4) In the event of a dispute as to whether the Court has jurisdiction, the matter shall be settled by decision of the Court.

(2) The Members of the United Nations and the States parties to the present Statute recognize as among themselves the jurisdiction of the Court as compulsory *ipso facto* and without special agreement in any legal dispute concerning:

(a) the interpretation of a treaty; or

(b) any question of international law; or

(c) the existence of any fact which, if established, would constitute a breach of an international obligation; or

(d) the nature or extent of the reparation to be made for the breach of an international obligation.

(3) In the event of a dispute as to whether the Court has jurisdiction, the matter shall be settled by decision of the Court.

[a] See U.S. Department of State, *The International Court of Justice: Selected Documents Relating to the Drafting of the Statute*, Publication No. 2491, Conference Series 84 (Washington, D.C.: Government Printing Office, 1946), pp. 106–107.

[b] The left-hand column adapted to the United Nations the language of Article 36 in the Statute of the Permanent Court of International Justice. The right-hand column presented compulsory jurisdiction as obligatory for the designated types of disputes.

est possible number of states.[10] "If the principle of compulsory jurisdiction is accepted," he went on, "certain states would not be able to ratify, which would deprive the solution of all practical advantages. The adoption of the optional clause would enable states in favor of compulsory jurisdiction to remain consistent with their principles and allow others to retain their views."[11]

[10] "Summary Report of the 14th Meeting of Committee IV/1," *U.N.C.I.O.*, Vol. XIII, Doc. 661 (English) IV/1/50 (May 29, 1945), p. 226.

[11] *Ibid.*

There is interestingly some indication that the United States was not entirely opposed to compulsory jurisdiction per se, but rather saw the Optional Clause as a temporary practical compromise pending further international developments. Ruth Russell credits President Truman with the statement: "If we are going to have a court, it ought to be a court that would work, with compulsory jurisdiction."[12] Undoubtedly mindful of the U.S. Senate, President Truman, however, instructed Secretary of State Stettinius "to strive for a formula that would make possible, at least eventually, compulsory jurisdiction of the International Court of Justice."[13] The Optional Clause, of course, provided the formula.

Francis Wilcox argues that the U.S. delegation at San Francisco spoke against the inclusion of compulsory jurisdiction in the Statute out of an honest fear that its inclusion might jeopardize the whole Charter. The delegation had a genuine desire to construct a document that the Senate (as well as the other states) could ratify, but it had no fundamental opposition to the principle of compulsory jurisdiction.[14]

This view seems substantiated by Senator A. H. Vandenberg (R, Mich.), who noted on the floor of the Senate on July 27, 1945:

It was the attitude of the American Delegation that in as much as each time this question has heretofore been submitted to the U.S. Senate the question of compulsory jurisdiction has always been a stumbling block, and there has always been a lack of willingness on the part of the Senate to go that far as yet, it would be unfortunate to write the court statute itself on a compulsory basis at the present time, but that rather we should leave its development to evolution in as much as the whole process of world peace itself is finally dependent upon evolution in the spirit and attitude of the peoples of the earth.

So we joined at San Francisco in maintaining the optional clause in order to be perfectly sure that at least this one needless hurdle would be removed from Senate consideration of the Charter.[15]

---

[12] See Russell and Muther, *op. cit.*, p. 878.

[13] *Ibid.*

[14] Francis O. Wilcox, "The United States Accepts Compulsory Jurisdiction," *American Journal of International Law*, XL, 4 (October, 1946), 700–701.

[15] *Congressional Record*, 79th Cong., 1st Sess., 1945, p. 8447. Some sense of the attitudes within the United States toward compulsory jurisdiction by the World Court can perhaps be gleaned by looking at the subcommittee hearings of the Senate Committee on Foreign Relations. In a total of about seven hours of hearings the subcommittee heard 17 witnesses. Noteworthy is the fact that not a single witness opposed U.S. acceptance. Furthermore, not a single letter or telegram was received which opposed U.S. acceptance. See U.S. Senate, Subcommittee of the Committee on Foreign Relations, *Hearings, on S. Res. 196, a Resolution Proposing Acceptance of Compulsory Jurisdiction of the Interna-*

The British delegate to Committee IV/1, although he was willing to accept compulsory jurisdiction for his own country, clearly saw the impending deadlock. He noted before the Committee: "Two countries, whose cooperation is essential, are not ready to accept compulsory jurisdiction. The same two countries had never acceded to the Statute of the Permanent Court of International Justice. They appear, however, ready to become members of the new Court. If the compulsory jurisdiction clause is introduced in the Statute, the Statute being a part of the Charter, the position of these two countries would be very difficult."[16]

He went on, in light of the inevitable, to recommend the Optional Clause as the only solution.[17] The widespread dissatisfaction among the smaller countries with the "inevitable" was manifested in the fact that 29 speakers took the floor to express their opinions after the Committee had heard the foregoing views. Nearly all of them favored compulsory jurisdiction (especially the Latin American group).

The Belgian position was that "Members of the Organization should recognize the obligatory jurisdiction of the Permanent Court of International Justice [*sic*] as regards any question of law for which they have not made use of another method of peaceful settlement."[18] Costa Rica, in a statement reminiscent of Central American Court days, called upon the members to take over the Permanent Court and recommended that "some thought might perhaps be given to the possibility of there being submitted to it not only questions of a juridical nature but *all questions, even those of a political character, that might affect the general security or peace*" (italics mine).[19] Cuba took a similar position. Further, the other Latin American countries generally agreed, although the views of Panama and Paraguay were probably even more extreme.[20]

The most moderate of the views favoring compulsory jurisdiction were expressed by the government of the Netherlands. It recommended a plan whereby all the member states could "recognise the Court as having compulsory jurisdiction in justiciable disputes to which they are a party and for the solution of which the parties do

---

tional Court of Justice by the United States Government, 79th Cong., 2nd Sess., 1946. See also the comment by Wilcox, *op. cit.,* p. 703.

[16] "Summary Report of the 14th Meeting of Committee IV/1," *op. cit.,* p. 227.

[17] *Ibid.*

[18] "Belgium, Memo of February 2, 1945," *U.N.C.I.O.,* XIV, 419.

[19] "Costa Rica, Memo of December 5, 1944," *ibid.,* p. 421.

[20] See *ibid.,* pp. 415–435.

not agree on another mode of settlement" as well as "recognise the Court's findings as binding."[21]

After a brief voting deadlock, any hopes for a move toward supranationalism (if any had seriously been entertained, in light of the power alignment) were quashed in a final vote. By a vote of 31 to 14 the text of Article 36 providing for optional jurisdiction was retained.[22] Ten of the fourteen negative votes were Latin American. Four countries, New Zealand, Australia, China, and Turkey, declared they voted merely to prevent a stalemate. The net result was that, after 20 years of experience with the League of Nations and six years of devastating war, the majority of nations were not willing to move any closer to transferring their decision-making prerogatives to an international body—at least not in the area of compulsory jurisdiction for an international court.

Another major question of supranational significance discussed at the San Francisco Conference was that of enforcement of the Court's decisions. There was apparently no opposition to the idea that each state had an obligation to comply with Court decisions. An Australian proposal giving effect to this idea was adopted unanimously in committee and became Article 94 (1) of the Charter.[23] (Articles of the U.N. Charter cited in this chapter are reprinted in Appendix D.) Beyond this point, however, disagreement began.

Norway and China both proposed a strong role for the Security Council. The Norwegian proposal, for example, read: "The Security Council is empowered to enforce by appropriate means the extension of any final decision in a dispute between States delivered either by the Permanent Court of International Justice or by any other tribunal whose jurisdiction in the matter has been recognized by the States parties to that dispute."[24]

A candid observation of the reaction to this proposal is provided by Ruth Russell. She notes that the United States, the Soviet Union,

---

[21] "The Netherlands, Memo of January, 1945," *ibid.*, p. 426.

[22] See *U.N.C.I.O.*, XIII, 251 and 266. The 31 affirmative votes included: Argentina, Australia, Belgium, Brazil, Byelorussia, Canada, Chile, China, Colombia, Czechoslovakia, Ethiopia, France, Honduras, India, Iraq, Netherlands, New Zealand, Nicaragua, Norway, Peru, Philippine Commonwealth, Saudi Arabia, Syria, South Africa, Turkey, Ukrainian S.S.R., United Kingdom, U.S.S.R., U.S.A., Venezuela, and Yugoslavia. The 14 negative votes were: Bolivia, Costa Rica, Cuba, Ecuador, Egypt, El Salvador, Greece, Guatemala, Iran, Liberia, Mexico, Panama, Paraguay, and Uruguay.

[23] See "Summary Report of the 20th Meeting of Committee IV/1," *U.N.C.I.O.*, Vol. XIII, Doc. 864 (English) IV/1/7 (June 8, 1945) , p. 297.

[24] See "Amendments and Observations on the Dumbarton Oaks Proposals, Submitted by the Norwegian Delegation, May 3, 1945," *U.N.C.I.O.*, Vol. III, Doc. 2 (English) G/7 (n) (May 4, 1945) , pp. 368–369.

and Great Britain all opposed the Norwegian plan (as well as a weaker but similar one), and suggests: "There may also have been in the background a more general objection in principle to the enforcement of Court decisions, which is one of the attributes of a sovereign government within its own jurisdiction. *To have made the Security Council an enforcement agency for the International Court, therefore, would have tended to give the Organization a certain supranational aspect*" (italics mine).[25]

Of course, it is this "supranational aspect" that nations have feared and avoided all along. Consequently, Committee IV/1 was only able to adopt a weaker Cuban proposal for Chapter VII of the Charter by a vote of 26 to 5. The proposal provided that "in the event of a state's failure to perform the obligations incumbent upon it under a judgment rendered by the Court, the other party may have recourse to the Security Council, which may make recommendations or decide measures to be taken to give effect to the judgment."[26]

While this proposal was weaker than previous ones, it created, nevertheless, an international executive agency for Court decisions —although with uncertain or even questionable strength. Apparently even this was too strong for the Soviet Union. At their insistence, a short phrase was added to remove the Security Council even further from the judicial realm. According to one report, the Soviet Union feared that the above wording "could be interpreted to require *positive* Security Council Action" (italics mine).[27] The Soviet addition provided that the Security Council "*may, if it deems necessary*, make recommendations" etc. "to give effect to the judgment" (italics mine).[28] The Coordinating Committee finally created Article 94 (2) of the Charter (with slight stylistic changes) out of the preceding compromises.

The full impact of the Soviet addition is not clear, as will be seen later in this chapter, simply because Article 94 (2) has never been really tested. Several points are clear, however. The authority of the Security Council in judicial matters was made "unquestionably discretionary." The Council has no positive role in enforcing judicial decisions per se. Rather, the implication seems to be that a failure to comply with a decision must be a threat to the peace before the Security Council will take action. At least this was the American

[25] Russell and Muther, *op. cit.*, p. 893.
[26] See *U.N.C.I.O.*, XIII, 298.
[27] See Russell and Muther, *op. cit.*, p. 895.
[28] *Ibid.*

view of Article 94 (2) as set forth by the U.S. State Department's legal adviser. "Presumably," he said, "the Security Council would not think it necessary to decide upon 'measures to be taken' unless it should feel that failure to respect the decision of the Court constituted a threat to the peace, in which event it might proceed under the provisions of Chapter VII of the Charter relating to threats to the peace, breaches of the peace, and acts of aggression."[29]

Simply stated then, the United Nations judicial system, with one possible exception, did not represent any supranational advance over the League. The possible exception would revolve around Article 24 and Chapter VII of the Charter, which appear to give the Security Council a rather positive role in international peacekeeping. As has been seen, Article 94 (2) provides for the possible implementation of this "positive role" in the judicial realm. A look at the practice of the Court at the close of this chapter will show the extent to which this "positive role" has materialized.

B. CONSTITUTIONAL BASIS

Most of what has been said about the constitutional basis of the Permanent Court of International Justice is, with stylistic modifications and updating, valid for the International Court of Justice. The constitutional basis for the latter will be only briefly outlined here.

Composition of the Court

NATIONAL RERESENTATION OF JUDGES   Articles 2 and 9 of the Statute (articles of the Statute cited in this chapter are reprinted in Appendix E) state that the Court will be composed of qualified "independent judges, elected regardless of their nationality," although the body as a whole should represent "the main forms of civilization and . . . the principal legal systems of the world. . . ."

As in the case of the League Court, this ideal was not strictly followed. Shabtai Rosenne, in a survey of the Court and its activities, presents tabulated evidence which clearly shows that the Americas and Europe have continually held a preponderance of seats on the Court. Needless to say, the traditions of these legal systems have also been dominant.[30] Further, as was true with the PCIJ, certain coun-

---

[29] Green H. Hackworth, "The International Court of Justice," *Department of State Bulletin*, XIII, 320 (August 12, 1945) , 216.

[30] See Shabtai Rosenne, *The World Court: What It Is and How It Works* (Leyden: A. W. Sythoff, 1962) , Tables II, III, and IV, pp. 51–53.

tries (e.g., the permanent members of the Security Council) have continually held seats, although there has been more turnover than under the League.[31]

Somewhat in conflict with the tenor of the above articles is Article 31, which makes provision for *ad hoc* judges and suggests that there is indeed something significant about nationality.

NATIONAL CONTROL OVER JUDGES There is no national control over the selection of judges in the sense that they are national representatives. Articles 4 through 15 of the Statute spell out in detail the same complicated election formula used by the League, whereby the Security Council and General Assembly proceed independently to elect judges. Unless there are certain unofficial understandings about candidates (e.g., as with the Big Five of the Security Council), however, the selection of candidates will ultimately rest on tests of political strength in the Assembly and the Council.

There is no direct national control over judges in office. Articles 2, 16, 17, 18, 19, and 20 of the Statute outline the independence of the judges (which parallels the League system). Article 20 provides that every member of the Court will "make a solemn declaration in open court that he will exercise his powers impartially and conscientiously." This declaration (Article 5 of the Rules of the Court) reads: "I solemnly declare that I will perform my duties and exercise my powers as judge honourably, faithfully, impartially and conscientiously."

Shabtai Rosenne insists that all of the above provisions have worked reasonably well in practice, and "no instance is known, whether from the history of the Permanent Court or in that of the present Court, in which doubt has been cast on the independence of the Court as a whole, or on any one of its members."[32]

If "worked reasonably well in practice" means that the Court's integrity has generally been accepted, then Rosenne's statement is probably valid. On the other hand, there are grounds for reasonable doubt about the judges' ability to rise above their national origins. To claim otherwise is to whitewash the obvious. This facet of the Court's activity will be examined later in this chapter.

Access to the Court

According to Article 34 (1) of the Statute, *only* states may be parties in cases before the Court. The Court recognizes three

[31] *Ibid.*, Table V, p. 54, and Appendix 3, pp. 213–216.
[32] *Ibid.*, p. 62.

categories of states: (1) all states members of the United Nations;[33] (2) states not members of the United Nations but parties to the Statute;[34] and (3) states not parties to the Statute to which the Court is open.[35]

Jurisdiction

Article 36 of the Statute, the central element of the Court's jurisdiction, provides two basic ways of conferring jurisdiction on the tribunal: (1) specific agreement between two or more states, and (2) unilateral declaration by a state deposited with the Secretary-General of the United Nations.

The Court's *Yearbook* outlines six major variations for the conferment of jurisdiction: (1) special agreement;[36] (2) cases provided for in treaties and conventions;[37] (3) compulsory jurisdiction in all legal disputes;[38] (4) the Court decides the question of its own

---

[33] Article 35 (1) of the Statute and Article 93 (1) of the Charter. There are currently 124 states in this category.

[34] Article 93 (2) of the Charter provides that states may become parties to the Statute of the Court on conditions to be determined in each case by the General Assembly upon the recommendation of the Security Council. The conditions, laid down for the first time as the result of a request by Switzerland, have been the same in each case since. On December 11, 1946, the General Assembly adopted Resolution 91 (I) which provides for the following conditions: (a) acceptance of the provisions of the Statute of the ICJ; (b) acceptance of all the obligations of a member of the U.N. under Article 94 of the Charter; (c) an undertaking to contribute to the expenses of the Court such equitable amount as the General Assembly shall assess from time to time after consultation with the Swiss government.

Currently, three states, not members of the U.N., are parties to the Statute under these provisions: Liechtenstein, San Marino, and Switzerland. See United Nations, I.C.J., *Yearbook: 1967–68* (No. 22) , p. 28. Before becoming a member of the U.N., Japan had been a party to the Statute from April 2, 1954, to December 18, 1956. See *ibid.*

[35] Article 35 (2) of the Statute. According to the Security Council resolution of October 15, 1946, states may make either general or particular declarations accepting the jurisdiction of the Court. Currently, two states have filed general declarations: the Federal Republic of Germany and the Republic of Viet Nam. Before their admission to the U.N., particular declarations had been filed by Albania and Italy and general declarations by Cambodia, Ceylon, Finland, Italy, Japan, and Laos. *Ibid.*, pp. 29–30.

[36] Articles 36 (1) and 40 (1) of the Statute.

[37] Article 36 (1) of the Statute. For a list of treaties and conventions governing the jurisdiction of the Court in contentious cases, see United Nations, I.C.J., *Yearbook: 1967–68* (No. 22) , Chap. IV, Sec. III. See also *supra,* Chapter 3, footnote 75.

[38] The conditions under which compulsory jurisdiction may be recognized are contained in paragraphs 2–5 of Article 36 of the Statute.

jurisdiction;[39] (5) interpretation of a judgment;[40] and (6) revision of a judgment.[41]

Judgments

As has already been indicated, the enforcement of judgments in the United Nations system was constitutionally stronger than under the League because of the Security Council's role under Article 94 (2). Beyond this, United Nations members have simply taken it upon themselves to comply with the Court's decisions.[42]

The observation to be made at this point is that, from a constitutional standpoint, the International Court of Justice represented little supranational advance beyond the League Court. Unfortunately, the same holds true for Court practice.

C. PRACTICE OF THE COURT

Jurisdiction

COMPULSORY JURISDICTION   The actions of the states at the San Francisco Conference made amply clear the fact that there was no widespread adherence to the concept of compulsory jurisdiction. As a consequence, only 43 states have submitted declarations accepting compulsory jurisdiction:

Australia	Honduras
Belgium	India
Cambodia	Israel
Canada	Japan
China	Kenya
Colombia	Liberia
Denmark	Liechtenstein
Dominican Republic	Luxembourg
El Salvador	Malawi
Finland	Malta
France	Mexico
Gambia	Netherlands
Haiti	New Zealand

---

[39] Article 36 (6) of the Statute provides that in the event of a dispute as to whether the Court has jurisdiction, the matter shall be settled by the decision of the Court. Article 62 of the Court's rules lays down the conditions which govern the filing of objections to the Court's jurisdiction.

[40] Article 60 of the Statute.

[41] Article 61 (1) of the Statute and Article 78 (1) of the Rules. As of July 31, 1968, no such application had been made to the Court. United Nations, I.C.J., *Yearbook: 1967–68* (No. 22), p. 32.

[42] Article 94 (1) of the Charter. Non–United Nations members must make a similar undertaking under the terms of Article 93.

Nicaragua	Switzerland
Nigeria	Turkey
Norway	Uganda
Pakistan	United Arab Republic
Panama	United Kingdom of Great
Philippines	Britain and Northern
Portugal	Ireland
Somalia	United States of America
Sudan	Uruguay[43]
Sweden	

One comment on this state of affairs notes sadly that "never in the joint history of the Permanent Court or the present Court has the percentage of members of the organized international community having accepted the compulsory jurisdiction been so low."[44] An important feature of the above list of states, however, is the fact that every Great Power except the Soviet Union has accepted compulsory jurisdiction. Even the cantankerous U.S. Senate rose to the occasion and approved acceptance by the United States.

Unfortunately, the acceptance by the 43 states in the above list of compulsory jurisdiction is illusory. Every state has set down reservations—some quite simple and some so complex, with so many qualifications, that it is not really clear exactly to what extent the Court's jurisdiction is valid. A survey of these reservations reveals five basic categories: (1) time restrictions; (2) reciprocity; (3) reservation if previous agreement provides for another tribunal; (4) pending ratification; (5) special categories (e.g., fishing rights, wartime suspension, etc.).[45]

The tenor of the reservations made by many nations is very restrictive. One of the leading examples has been Great Britain, which has consistently attached reservations to her declaration excluding questions concerning Commonwealth matters and imposing extensive *rationae temporis* reservations.[46] The effect, of course, is discouraging to attempts to build a supranational court.

---

[43] Includes all declarations made under Article 36 (2) of the Statute, which had not lapsed or been withdrawn by July 31, 1968, the beginning of the period covered by the present *Yearbook*. See United Nations, I.C.J., *Yearbook: 1967–68* (No. 22), pp. 41–69.

[44] Rosenne, *op. cit.*, p. 83.

[45] See United Nations, I.C.J., *Yearbook: 1967–68* (No. 22), pp. 41–69. Actually there had been similar reservations under the PCIJ, but not of the extent to which they appeared under the United Nations' Court. See Manley O. Hudson, *International Tribunals: Past and Future* (Washington, D.C.: Carnegie Endowment for International Peace and Brookings Institution, 1944), pp. 76–77.

[46] The most far-reaching reservation was made in the British declaration of April 18, 1957 (par. v), excluding *inter alia* "disputes . . . relating to any question which, in the opinion of the Government of the United Kingdom, affects the national security of the United Kingdom or any of its dependent

Perhaps a more serious sort of reservation, in contrast with the rather "standard" ones just listed, is a sixth type of reservation introduced by the United States. This is the so-called "self-judging" clause, frequently called the "Connally" or "Connally-type" Amendment.

THE CONNALLY AMENDMENT A statement attributed to Judge Manley O. Hudson seems to sum up the position of the United States vis-à-vis the International Court of Justice. The United States, he says, "seldom loses an opportunity to profess its loyalty to international arbitration in the abstract. . . . The expression of this sentiment has become so conventional that a popular impression prevails that it accords with the actual policy of the United States."[47]

The policy mentioned refers to the nature of U.S. acceptance of the compulsory jurisdiction of the International Court. The story, briefly retold, goes as follows.

The filing of a U.S. declaration of acceptance was delayed for over a year—pending Senate approval. During this time there was much debate, although there was none of the bitterness and stubbornness which had marked the Senate's performance 25 years earlier.

On July 28, 1945, the date the Charter was approved, Senator Wayne Morse (R, Ore.) introduced a resolution (S. Res. 160) "providing that the Senate recommend to the President that he accept, on behalf of the United States, the compulsory jurisdiction of the Court," which was not considered.[48] On November 28, 1945, Senator Morse, along with 15 other senators, introduced a second resolution (S. Res. 196) which would accept the compulsory jurisdiction of the International Court of Justice—with the following exceptions:

Provided, that such declaration should not apply to:
a. disputes the solution of which the parties shall entrust to other tribunals by virtue of agreements already in existence or which may be concluded in the future; or

---

territories" (see United Nations, I.C.J., *Yearbook, 1957–58* (No. 12), pp. 211–212). This reservation was subsequently revoked by a new declaration of November 26, 1958, although a new reservation was added (par. vi) excluding disputes which might have arisen while the prior reservation was in effect (see *ibid., 1960–61* (No. 15), pp. 216–217). For one of the most complete (although dated) discussions of British and other reservations, see C. H. M. Waldock, "Decline of the Optional Clause," *British Yearbook of International Law*, XXXII (1955–56), 244–287.

[47] Cited by Lawrence Preuss, "The International Court of Justice, the Senate, and Matters of Domestic Jurisdiction," *American Journal of International Law*, XL, 4 (October, 1946), 720.

[48] See description by Wilcox, *op. cit.*, p. 701.

b. disputes with regard to matters which are essentially within the domestic jurisdiction of the United States.[49]

The Senate Committee on Foreign Relations, chaired by Senator Tom Connally (D, Tex.), appointed a subcommittee to conduct hearings on S. Res. 196. Hearings were held on July 11, 12, and 15, 1946.[50] On July 25, 1946, the Committee on Foreign Relations unanimously reported S. Res. 196 (with the Morse reservations quoted above) for favorable action by the Senate. The Senate began to consider the resolution on July 31, 1946. It was during this debate that the famous "Connally Amendment" was added. The essence of this amendent was to append to the end of proviso b of the Morse resolution the phrase "as determined by the United States." The Connally Amendment was adopted by a vote of 51 to 12.[51] On August 2, 1946, the resolution (S. Res. 196) as amended was adopted by the overwhelming vote of 60 to 2.[52] Finally, on August 16, 1946, President Truman transmitted to the Secretary-General of the United Nations a declaration accepting the jurisdiction of the Court under the terms of Article 36, paragraph 2 of the Statute.[53]

This act ostensibly marked the end of an era. The United States had pulled itself out of isolation and distrust for the international community. The proof was there: the United States had led in the establishment of the United Nations, the Senate had overwhelmingly ratified the Charter and the Statute, and as final evidence that the last great bastion against any sort of "creeping supranationalism" was falling, the United States had submitted to the compulsory jurisdiction of the World Court. Unfortunately, this evidence was more apparent than real.

The most obvious implication of the Connally reservation is that it *retains for the United States* the decision as to whether a dispute falls within its domestic jurisdiction. This appears to be in direct conflict with Article 36 (6) of the Statute which *explicitly* provides for the transfer of this decision-making power to the Court.

Interesting in this respect is the report of the Senate Committee

---

[49] Quoted in "The United States and World Court Jurisdiction," *Congressional Digest*, XL, 1 (January, 1961), 9.

[50] U.S. Senate, Subcommittee of the Committee on Foreign Relations, *Hearings, on S. Res. 196, a Resolution Proposing Acceptance of Compulsory Jurisdiction of the International Court of Justice by the United States Government*, 79th Cong., 2nd Sess., 1946 (hereinafter cited as *Hearings*).

[51] See Wilcox, *op. cit.*, p. 714.

[52] Figures from Preuss, *op. cit.*, p. 721.

[53] For the text of the declaration see "Recognition of Compulsory Jurisdiction of the International Court of Justice," *Department of State Bulletin*, XV, 375 (September 8, 1946), 452.

on Foreign Relations itself,[54] which could not have made the matter clearer:

> The question of what is properly a matter of international law is, in case of dispute, appropriate for decision by the Court itself, since, if it were left to the decision of each individual state, it would be possible to withhold any case from adjudication on the plea that it is a matter of domestic jurisdiction.
>
> A reservation of the right of decision as to what are matters essentially within domestic jurisdiction *would tend to defeat the purposes which it is hoped to achieve by means of the proposed declaration as well as the purpose of Article 36, paragraphs 2 and 6, of the Statute of the Court* [italics mine].[55]

The Senate was clearly not swayed by the wisdom of this report. That the Administration favored the stand taken in the Committee report was revealed in testimony by Mr. Dean Acheson (then Undersecretary of State) before the Senate Subcommittee on the World Court. Mr. Acheson noted: "The rule of law becomes effective to the extent that states agree to submit themselves to the decision of the Court in all cases involving questions of law. It cannot become effective if states may reserve this decision to themselves, regardless of the degree of good faith by which they govern their actions."[56]

Judge Lauterpacht of the International Court of Justice was also not impressed by the Senate's amendment. In his well-known separate opinion in the *Norwegian Loans* Case (*France* v. *Norway*), he questioned the validity of the Connally-type reservation:

> I consider it legally impossible for the Court to act in disregard of its Statute which imposes upon it the duty and confers upon it the right to determine its jurisdiction. That right cannot be exercised by a party to the dispute. The Court cannot, in any circumstances, treat as admissible the claim that the parties have accepted its jurisdiction subject to the condition that they, and not the Court, will decide on its own jurisdiction. To do so is in my view contrary to Article 36 (6) of the Statute which, without any qualification, confers upon the Court the right and imposes upon it the duty to determine its jurisdiction.[57]

---

[54] In light of the apparent general support for acceptance of compulsory jurisdiction (especially on the Foreign Relations Committee but also in the whole Senate as well), most observers, like Prof. Herbert W. Briggs, were startled by the "sudden appearance of reservationist sentiment." See in this regard Herbert W. Briggs, "Reservations to the Acceptance of Compulsory Jurisdiction of the International Court of Justice," *Recueil des Cours*, XCIII (1958), 223–367.

[55] U.S. Senate, *A Report to Accompany S. Res. 196*, 79th Cong., 2nd Sess., 1946, Senate Report No. 1835, p. 5.

[56] *Hearings*, p. 129.

[57] United Nations, I.C.J., *Reports of Judgments, Advisory Opinions and Orders* (hereinafter cited as *Reports*), 1957, p. 43. In the *Interhandel* Case (*Switzerland*

Because of the Senate's attitude the United States has been forced, in large measure, to revert to the two-faced international role that characterized the League years. As one of the loudest proponents of an international rule of law, the United States has unfortunately been unprepared to take one of the first real steps toward implementing that rule of law.[58] Even more unfortunate is the fact that by far the majority of nations are equally unprepared.

EFFECT OF THE CONNALLY AMENDMENT   According to Ruth Lawson, there was no question that the Court would decide matters of jurisdiction until the problem was raised by the United States' declaration of August 14, 1946.[59] Furthermore, the U.S. declaration prompted a series of other countries to make similar reservations. Currently, only 5 of the 43 nations accepting compulsory jurisdiction have self-judging clauses (Liberia, Malawi, Mexico, Sudan, and U.S.A.).[60] At one time, however, France, Great Britain, India, Pakistan, and South Africa all had a "Connally Amendment."[61]

Although U.S. foreign policy is not the central object of study here, it is nevertheless worthwhile to examine briefly U.S. experience with the Connally Amendment. The implications of such a case study clearly have value in the larger context of international relations.

Secretary of State Christian Herter, speaking of the U.S. "fear" of the Court's jurisdiction providing an inroad for an international organization to intervene in affairs of domestic jurisdiction, has noted that "deletion of our self-judging reservation will not operate to give the International Court jurisdiction of domestic matters. There should be no misapprehension on this score."[62] He cited as evidence of protection the fact that the U.S. declaration accepting

---

v. *the United States of America*) two years later Judge Lauterpacht again questioned the "self-judging" clause: "My view as to the validity of the automatic reservation and that of the Declaration of Acceptance which incorporates it, is the same as that expressed in my Separate Opinion in the case of *Certain Norwegian Loans*." See United Nations, I.C.J., *Reports*, 1959, p. 100.

[58] In this connection see, for example, the position of the United States in the *Interhandel* Case. United Nations, I.C.J., *Reports*, 1959, p. 6.

[59] Lawson, *op. cit.*, p. 273.

[60] United Nations, I.C.J., *Yearbook: 1967–1968* (No. 22), pp. 41–69.

[61] *Ibid., 1947–68* (Nos. 1–22).

[62] "The Self-Judging Aspect of the U.S. Reservation on Jurisdiction of the International Court," *Department of State Bulletin*, XLII, 1077 (February 15, 1960), 230. This article is a reprint of a statement by Secretary Herter before the Senate Committee on Foreign Relations on January 27, 1960, during hearings on S. Res. 94.

the compulsory jurisdiction of the World Court is governed by: (a) proviso b of the U.S. declaration; (b) Article 36, paragraph 2 of the Statute; (c) Article 2, paragraph 7 of the Charter.[63]

Nations are understandably anxious to protect their national sovereignty, of which domestic jurisdiction is clearly an intrinsic element. If nations are unwilling to accept the above guarantees, however, then they should be unwilling to accept compulsory jurisdiction. Such a policy would at least be consistent. To accept compulsory jurisdiction and at the same time "not accept" it through a Connally reservation is farcical.

If it is the purpose of the Connally Amendment to protect U.S. interests, then one must look at self-judging clauses in practice. Only then can a proper perspective be obtained. Two main points need to be made. First, the self-judging clause has not served the United States well in practice. Second, the Connally Amendment is probably a greater potential threat to U.S. interests than a protection.

The United States has invoked the Connally reservation twice—in the first and second phases of the *Interhandel* Case (*Switzerland v. United States of America*).[64] The United States won the judgment, but it was *not* due to its peremptory claim of domestic jurisdiction. The Court decided *sub silentio* the jurisdictional issues anyway.

Probably of far more significance is the fact that the United States has a great deal to gain from an international rule of law.[65] The danger to the United States posed by the Connally Amendment was shown in the *Norwegian Loans* Case in 1957 (*France v. Norway*).[66] France, which had earlier filed a reservation very similar to the Connally Amendment, sued Norway in 1957 over the latter's refusal to pay off certain bonds in gold. Norway, which had also earlier accepted compulsory jurisdiction (but without a Connally-type reser-

---

[63] For the text of the U.S. declaration see *supra,* pp. 95–96.

[64] United Nations, I.C.J., *Reports,* 1959, p. 6.

[65] For example, the United States is the world's largest creditor nation. This position is obviously enhanced by the security afforded through law.

[66] United Nations, I.C.J., *Reports,* 1957, p. 7. This had also been shown when Bulgaria invoked the Connally Amendment against the United States in the case of the *Aerial Incident of 27 July 1955* (*United States of America v. Bulgaria*). The case was removed from the Court's list on May 30, 1960, when the United States accepted Bulgaria's preliminary objection based on the Connally Amendment. See United Nations, I.C.J., *Reports,* 1960, p. 146 (order of May 30, 1960). See also Leo Gross, "Bulgaria Invokes the Connally Amendment," *American Journal of International Law,* LVI, 2 (April, 1962), 357–382.

vation) invoked France's own reservation against her, claiming the matter was "domestic." Because of the principle of reciprocity, the Court held, any country can invoke peremptory domestic jurisdiction when hailed into Court by a country having a self-judging clause. What the United States has done then, in effect, is to arm every country in the world with the provisions of the Connally Amendment. This can only hurt the United States, as a country highly likely to go to court seeking redress of grievances. Such a situation undoubtedly explains why France, after losing the *Norwegian Loans* Case on these grounds, modified her domestic jurisdiction reservation in 1959.[67]

By way of summation of national practice, two points have become evident. First, if acceptance of compulsory jurisdiction represents a step toward handing over supranational decision-making powers to an international court, then the ICJ probably represents, if not a step backward, then at least no advance over the PCIJ. Second, the use of the Connally-type amendment (although slight) appears as a curious national political maneuver of dubious legality.[68] In terms of supranationalism, its effect in practice is unclear.

WORK OF THE COURT   Table 7 shows the amount of business that has occupied the Court. The national suspicions that seemed to prevail at San Francisco are apparently reflected in the general lack of interest in the Court. In comparison with the Permanent Court, the International Court of Justice has not been used as much, although it has dealt with several politically important cases.[69]

Table 8 outlines the nature of the cases that have come before the Court. The first column illustrates the questions raised regarding jurisdiction. In all, preliminary questions were raised against the Court's jurisdiction in 13 cases (Judgments 1, 8, 10, 13, 14, 16, 17, 20, 21, 24, 26, 27, and 28). To partially quell the doubts of those who fear the Court will construe its jurisdiction expansively, the evidence shows that the Court has upheld the objections in eight of these cases (Judgments 8, 10, 13, 14, 16, 17, 21, and 27). In all of the five remaining cases, in which the Court assumed jurisdiction over

---

[67] For discussion see testimony by Prof. Herbert W. Briggs, on January 27, 1960, before the Senate Committee on Foreign Relations during hearings on S. Res. 94. Reprinted in "The United States and World Court Jurisdiction," *op. cit.*, p. 29.

[68] Cf. Article 36 (6) of the Statute.

[69] Cf. the *Fisheries, Anglo-Iranian Oil Company,* and the *Right of Passage* cases.

Table 7 Work of the International Court of Justice[a]

Year	New Cases Registered			Nature of Solution		
	Total	Conten-tious Cases[b]	Req. for Adv. Opinions	Judg-ments Rend.	Advisory Opinions	Case Discon-tinued
1946	—	—	—	—	—	—
1947	3	2	1	—	—	—
1948	1	—	1	1	1	—
1949	6	3	3	2	1	—
1950	4	3	1	2	4	1
1951	4	4	—	2	1	—
1952	—	—	—	3	—	—
1953	3	2	1	3	—	—
1954	3	2	1	1	1	3
1955	8	6	2	1	1	—
1956	—	—	—	—	2	4
1957	6	6	—	2	—	—
1958	3	3	—	1	—	—
1959	4	3	1	3	—	2
1960	2	2	—	2	1	2
1961	2	1	1	1	—	1
1962	1	1	—	2	1	—
1963	—	—	—	1	—	—
1964	—	—	—	1	—	—
1965	—	—	—	—	—	—
1966	—	—	—	1	—	—
1967	2	2	—	—	—	—
1968	—	—	—	—	—	—
Total	52[c]	40	12	29	13	14

a Data derived from United Nations, I.C.J., *Yearbook: 1965–66* and *1967–68* (Nos. 20 and 22); and United Nations, Press Services, Office of Public Information, *Weekly News Summary* (Press Release WS/251, 22 July 1966), pp. 2–3.

b The *Corfu Channel* cases are numbered 1, 1a, and 2 by the I.C.J *Yearbook*. They are counted as two cases under the total of new cases registered, although all three judgments rendered are counted.

c To July 31, 1968, inclusive. The latest two cases registered concern the North Sea Continental Shelf: *Denmark* v. *Federal Republic of Germany* and *Federal Republic of Germany* v. *Netherlands*.

the protests of a nation, the preliminary decision was complied with.

The jurisprudence of the Permanent Court regarding jurisdiction has of course been assumed by the International Court of Justice. In addition to what has been said in the preceding chapter, the Court has further defined its jurisprudence in two areas: consent and *compétence de la compétence*.

Regarding consent, the Court has noted that the principle of consent to jurisdiction extends so far as to exclude the assumption of jurisdiction by the Court in a case brought by two parties to the proceedings when the interests of a third state, which has not consented and which is not a party, are vitally affected by the outcome.

Table 8 Nature and Solution of Contentious Cases Before the International Court of Justice[a]

Case/Jurisdiction[b]	Issue	Disposition	Judges' Vote[c]
1. *Corfu Channel* (jurisdiction) (*United Kingdom v. Albania*); contested by Albania/A; ICJ *Reports* 1947–48, p. 7; 25 March 1948	Albania protested Court's jurisdiction.	For United Kingdom.	15 to 1. The *ad hoc* judge sent by Albania was the lone dissenter.
2. *Corfu Channel* (merits) (*U.K. v. Albania*); accepted; ICJ *Reports* 1949, p. 4; 9 April 1949	a) Responsibility of Albania for mined channel.	a) For U.K.	a) 11 to 5. The U.K. judge voted for the U.K.; the Albanian *ad hoc* judge dissented.
	b) Court has jurisdiction to determine amount of compensation due U.K.	b) For U.K.	b) 10 to 6; the U.K. judge voted for the U.K.; the Albanian *ad hoc* judge dissented.
	c) U.K. violation of Albanian waters on 12–13 Nov. 1946.	c) For Albania.	c) Unanimous.
	d) U.K. violation of Albanian waters on 22 Oct. 1946.	d) For U.K.	d) Unanimous.
3. *Corfu Channel* (fixing amount of compensation) (*U.K. v. Albania*); accepted; ICJ *Reports* 1949, p. 171; 15 Dec. 1949	Amount of damages due U.K.	For U.K.	12 to 2. The U.K. judge voted with the majority; the Albanian *ad hoc* judge was one of the dissenters.

[a] Data derived from United Nations, I.C.J., *Reports of Judgments, Advisory Opinions and Orders*, 1947–64; United Nations, I.C.J., *Yearbook: 1965–66* and *1967–68* (Nos. 20 and 22); and United Nations, Press Services, Office of Public Information, *Weekly News Summary* (Press Release WS/251, 22 July 1966), pp. 2–3.

[b] Under this heading, the term "accepted" indicates the parties went before the Court on the basis of agreement stemming from declarations accepting jurisdiction, *ad hoc* agreements, or treaties conferring jurisdiction. "Contested" shows that a party objected to the Court's jurisdiction. A (affirmative) indicates that the objection was overruled and that the Court found it had jurisdiction. N (negative) means that the objection was upheld. This column includes only cases where preliminary objections related to jurisdiction were invoked. Jurisdictional questions of one kind or another, however, were raised in nearly all other cases. The case citation and date of decision are also indicated.

[c] It is not possible in some cases to see how a particular judge voted because all of the dissenters were not identified.

Case	Questions	Decision	Vote
4. *Asylum (Colombia v. Peru)*; accepted; ICJ *Reports* 1950, p. 125; 20 Nov. 1950	a) Colombia's right to bind Peru in its unilateral determination of Haya de la Torre's offense as political.	a) For Peru.	a) 14 to 2. The Peruvian *ad hoc* judge voted for Peru; the Colombian *ad hoc* judge dissented.
	b) Peru bound to grant safe-conduct.	b) For Peru.	b) 15 to 1. The Colombian *ad hoc* judge was the lone dissenter.
	c) Had Colombia violated Havana Convention?	c) For Peru.	c) 10 to 6. The Peruvian *ad hoc* judge voted with the majority; the Colombian *ad hoc* judge dissented.
5. *Request for Interpretation of the Judgment of 20 Nov. 1950, in the Asylum Case (Colombia v. Peru)*; accepted; ICJ *Reports* 1950, p. 395; 27 Nov. 1950	Colombia requested interpretation of preceding judgment.	For Peru.	12 to 1. The Peruvian *ad hoc* judge voted with the majority; the Colombian *ad hoc* judge was the lone dissenter.
6. *Haya de la Torre (Colombia v. Peru)*; accepted; ICJ *Reports* 1951, p. 4; 13 June 1951	a) Court is unable to indicate how previous judgment should be executed (questions not put in proper form).	a) Probably against Peru.	a) Unanimous.
	b) Colombia was not obliged to hand over Torre to Peru.	b) For Colombia.	b) 13 to 1. The Peruvian *ad hoc* judge was the lone dissenter.
	c) Asylum should have ceased after the first judgment.	c) For Colombia.	c) Unanimous.
7. *Fisheries (U.K. v. Norway)*; accepted; ICJ *Reports* 1951, p. 8; 18 Dec. 1951	U.K. claimed Norway's method of delimiting fisheries zone by base lines to be contrary to international law.	For Norway.	Voting on two aspects the Court ruled 10 to 2 and 8 to 4 in Norway's favor. The U.K. judge dissented on both votes. The Norwegian judge voted for Norway on the first question; his vote on the second is not known.

Table 8 *Continued*

Case/Jurisdiction	Issue	Disposition	Judges' Vote
8. *Ambatielos* (jurisdiction) (*Greece v. U.K.*); contested by U.K./N (in part—see issue); ICJ *Reports* 1952, p. 7; 1 July 1952	a) U.K. claimed Court had no jurisdiction on merits. b) Greece claimed Court had jurisdiction to decide arbitrability of dispute.	a) For U.K. b) For Greece (limited jurisdiction).	a) 13 to 2. The U.K. judge voted with the majority; the Greek *ad hoc* judge did not dissent. b) 10 to 5. The U.K. judge dissented; how the Greek *ad hoc* judge voted is unclear.
9. *Ambatielos* (merits) (*Greece v. U.K.*); accepted; ICJ *Reports* 1953, p. 10; 19 May 1953	Greek claim of U.K. obligation to arbitrate.	For Greece.	10 to 4. The Greek *ad hoc* judge voted for Greece; the U.K. judge dissented.
10. *Anglo-Iranian Oil Co.* (*U.K. v. Iran*); contested by Iran/N; ICJ *Reports* 1952, p. 13; 22 July 1952	Preliminary objection by Iran to Court's jurisdiction.	For Iran.	9 to 5. Both the U.K. and Iranian *ad hoc* judges voted with the majority.
11. *Rights of Nationals of the United States of America in Morocco* (*France v. U.S.A.*); accepted; ICJ *Reports* 1952, p. 22; 27 Aug. 1952	a) Validity of Moroccan decree against U.S. nationals. b) Several questions as to extent of U.S. consular jurisdiction. c) Necessity of U.S. approval of laws.	a) For U.S. b) Both (see votes). c) For France.	a) Unanimous. b and c) The French judge did not dissent from those questions decided unfavorably for France; the U.S. judge dissented in votes of 6 to 5 and 7 to 4 on issues unfavorable to the U.S., yet he appears to have agreed with the Court's vote on other questions unfavorable to the U.S.
12. *Minquiers and Ecrehos* (*France v. U.K.*); accepted; ICJ *Reports* 1953, p. 4; 17 Nov. 1953	Sovereignty over two groups of islets between the British Channel island of Jersey and the French coast.	For U.K.	Unanimous, with the French judge voting against France.

13. *Monetary Gold Removed from Rome in 1943* (preliminary question) (*Italy v. U.K., U.S.A., and France*); question raised by Italy/N;[d] ICJ *Reports* 1954, p. 10; 15 June 1954	Court's jurisdiction on two Italian submissions.	For Italy.	Unanimous on one question and 13 to 1 on the other. The Italian *ad hoc* judge voted for his government in both instances; the respondent judges did not dissent.
14. *Nottebohm* (preliminary objection) (*Liechtenstein v. Guatemala*); contested by Guatemala/A; ICJ *Reports* 1953, p. 7; 18 Nov. 1953	Guatemala claimed its acceptance of compulsory jurisdiction expired shortly after investigation of the case.	For Liechtenstein.	Unanimous.
15. *Nottebohm* (merits) (*Liechtenstein v. Guatemala*); accepted; ICJ *Reports* 1954, p. 4; 6 April 1955	Right of ex-German national to use his acquired Liechtenstein citizenship to transform enemy (German) property into neutral property.	For Guatemala.	11 to 3. The Guatemalan *ad hoc* judge voted for Guatemala; the Liechtenstein *ad hoc* judge dissented.
16. *Certain Norwegian Loans* (*France v. Norway*); contested by Norway; joined by agreement of the parties to merits; ICJ *Reports* 1957, p. 9; 6 July 1957	Norwegian claim to deny Court's jurisdiction on basis of reciprocity stemming from France's self-judging clause.	For Norway.	12 to 3. The Norwegian judge voted with the majority; the French judge dissented.
17. *Right of Passage over Indian Territory* (preliminary objection) (*Portugal v. India*); contested by India/unclear—probably N; ICJ *Reports* 1957, p. 123; 26 Nov. 1957	Six preliminary objections raised by India.	Probably for Portugal. Four of the six objections raised by India were rejected; the remaining two were joined to the merits.	On the fifth preliminary objection the vote was 15 to 2 for joining it to merits. The Portuguese *ad hoc* judge dissented; the Indian *ad hoc* judge apparently voted for India on all six objections.

---

[d] A prime consideration was whether Italy or Albania had a prior claim to the gold. If Italy had, then the case with the U.S., U.K., and France could be decided. But the Court refused jurisdiction to consider the original point without Albania's consent.

Table 8 *Continued*

Case/Jurisdiction	Issue	Disposition	Judges' Vote
18. *Right of Passage over Indian Territory* (merits) (*Portugal v. India*); accepted; ICJ *Reports* 1960, p. 6; 12 April 1960	a) Two preliminary objections. b) Portugal's right of passage in 1954 to exercise sovereignty. c) Portugal's right of passage for arms and armed forces. d) Did India act contrary to its international obligations?	a) For Portugal. b) For Portugal. c) For India. d) For India.	a) 13 to 2 and 11 to 4. b) 11 to 4. c) 8 to 7. d) 9 to 6. In all of these votes the Portuguese and Indian *ad hoc* judges voted for their countries.
19. *Application of the Convention of 1902 Governing the Guardianship of Infants* (*Netherlands v. Sweden*); accepted; ICJ *Reports* 1958, p. 55; 28 Nov. 1958	Guardianship of a Dutch child living in Sweden alone with the mother when the mother died. Both Dutch and Swedish courts appointed guardians.	For Sweden.	12 to 4. The Dutch *ad hoc* judge voted for the Netherlands; the Swedish *ad hoc* judge voted for Sweden.
20. *Interhandel* (*Switzerland v. U.S.A.*) (preliminary objection); contested by U.S.A./A; ICJ *Reports* 1959, p. 6; 21 March 1959	Four preliminary objections raised by the U.S.A.	a) For Switzerland; U.S. objection rejected. b) For Switzerland; U.S. objection rejected. c) (1) For Switzerland; U.S. objection rejected. c) (2) For U.S.; no need to adjudicate merits. d) For U.S.; case inadmissible: failure to exhaust local remedies.	a) 10 to 5. b) Unanimous. c) (1) 14 to 1. c) (2) 10 to 5. d) 9 to 6. The U.S. judge dissented on the first question, but otherwise voted with the majority, which means he voted against his country twice; the Swiss *ad hoc* judge dissented in those votes favorable to the U.S., and voted for Switzerland on questions favorable to it.

No.	Case	Issue	Decision	Result
21.	*Aerial Incident of 27 July 1955* (preliminary objection) (*Israel v. Bulgaria*); contested by Bulgaria/N; ICJ *Reports* 1959, p. 6; 26 May 1959	Court is without jurisdiction because Bulgaria's acceptance of compulsory jurisdiction under League had expired.	For Bulgaria.	12 to 4. The Bulgarian *ad hoc* judge voted for Bulgaria; the Israeli *ad hoc* judge voted for Israel.
22.	*Case Concerning Sovereignty over Certain Frontier Land (Belgium v. Netherlands)*; accepted; ICJ *Reports* 1959, p. 209; 20 June 1959	Sovereignty over 33 acres of border land.	For Belgium.	10 to 4. Neither side had a judge on the Court or sent an *ad hoc* judge.
23.	*Arbitral Award Made by the King of Spain on 23 Dec. 1906 (Honduras v. Nicaragua)*; accepted; ICJ *Reports* 1960, p. 192; 18 Nov. 1960	That the 1906 arbitral award should be carried out.	For Honduras.	14 to 1. The Nicaraguan *ad hoc* judge was the lone dissenter.[e]
24.	*Temple of Preah Vihear* (preliminary objection) (*Cambodia v. Thailand*); contested by Thailand/A; ICJ *Reports* 1961, p. 17; 26 May 1961	Thailand claimed her acceptance of compulsory jurisdiction was not valid.	For Cambodia.	Unanimous. Neither side had an *ad hoc* judge.
25.	*Temple of Preah Vihear* (merits) (*Cambodia v. Thailand*); accepted; ICJ *Reports* 1962, p. 6; 15 June 1962	Sovereignty over the temple, presence of Thai troops, and Thai return of articles removed from the temple.	For Cambodia.	Three votes of 9 to 3, 9 to 3, and 7 to 5. Neither party had an *ad hoc* judge.
26.	*South West Africa* (preliminary objection) (*Ethiopia and Liberia v. South Africa*);[f] contested by South Africa/A; ICJ *Reports* 1962, p. 319; 21 Dec. 1962	Whether Art. 7 of the mandate for South Africa is a treaty or convention still in force within the meaning of Art. 37 of the Statute of the Court.	For Ethiopia and Liberia.	8 to 7. The Ethiopian and Liberian *ad hoc* judges voted with the majority; the South African *ad hoc* judge dissented.

[e] An interesting note; neither *ad hoc* judge was a national of the parties to the dispute.
[f] Originally two cases (Nos. 46 and 47 in the General List) which were joined because of their similarity.

Table 8 *Continued*

Case/Jurisdiction	Issue	Disposition	Judges' Vote
27. *Northern Cameroons* (preliminary objection) (*Cameroons v. U.K.*); contested by U.K./N; ICJ *Reports* 1963, p. 14; 2 Dec. 1963	Cameroons asked declaratory judgment against U.K. for failing to respect the Trusteeship Agreement of 1946 for the Territory of the Cameroons under U.K. administration. The U.K. denied jurisdiction because the arrangement was no longer in force.	For U.K. The issue was already *res judicata*.	10 to 5. The U.K. judge voted with the majority; the Cameroons *ad hoc* judge dissented.
28. *Barcelona Traction, Light and Power Co., Ltd.* (preliminary objection) (*Belgium v. Spain*); contested by Spain/A (in part); ICJ *Reports* 1964, p. 6; 24 July 1964	Spain raised four objections to jurisdiction on the grounds that the Spanish government had never consented.	For Belgium. Two of Spain's preliminary objections were rejected and the other two were joined to the merits.	Four votes of 12 to 4, 10 to 6, 9 to 7, and 10 to 6. The Belgian *ad hoc* judge voted for his government on all counts; the Spanish *ad hoc* judge dissented on all counts.
29. *South West Africa* (merits) (*Ethiopia and Liberia v. South Africa*); accepted; ICJ *Reports* 1966, p. 260; 22 July 1966	Responsibility of South Africa for mandate of South West Africa.	For South Africa. Case dismissed because the applicant states could not be considered to have established any legal right or interest in the case.	8 to 7. The *ad hoc* judge for both parties voted for their side.

In the *Monetary Gold Removed from Rome* Case (*Italy v. the United Kingdom, the United States of America, and France*) the Court refused jurisdiction because Albania, who was vitally affected by the outcome, had not consented to it.[70] The Court established this rule: "Where, as in the present case, the vital issue to be settled concerns the international responsibility of a third State, the Court cannot without the consent of that third State, give a decision on that issue binding upon any State, either the third State, or any of the parties before it."[71]

While bolstering up the rule that its jurisdiction is clearly and completely grounded in national consent, the Court has also made it plain that it regards itself as the final interpreter of whether this consent has been given—that it is competent to determine its own jurisdiction (Statute, Article 36, paragraph 6).

The most extensive treatment of this principle occurred in the *Nottebohm* Case (preliminary objection). A unanimous Court stated in detail:

Paragraph 6 of Article 36 merely adopted, in respect of the Court, a rule consistently accepted by general international law in the matter of international arbitration. Since the *Alabama* case, it has been generally recognized following the earlier precedents, that, in the absence of any agreement to the contrary, an international tribunal has the right to decide as to its own jurisdiction and has the power to interpret for this purpose the instruments which govern that jurisdiction. This principle was expressly recognized in Article 48, 73 of the Hague Convention of July 29th, 1899, and October 18th, 1907, for the Pacific Settlement of International Disputes. . . .

This principle, which is accepted by general international law in the matter of arbitration, assumes particular force when the international tribunal is no longer an arbitral tribunal constituted by virtue of a special agreement between the parties for the purpose of adjudicating on a particular dispute, but is an institution which has been pre-established by an international instrument defining its jurisdiction and regulating its operation, and is, in the present case, the principal judicial organ of the United Nations.

And:

The Court "whose function is to decide in accordance with international law such disputes as are submitted to it" (Article 38, paragraph 1 of the Statute), should follow in this connection what is laid down by general international law. *The judicial character of the Court and the rule of general international law referred to above are sufficient to establish that the court is competent to adjudicate on its own jurisdiction in the present case* [italics mine].[72]

---

[70] United Nations, I.C.J., *Reports,* 1954, p. 19.
[71] *Ibid.*, p. 33.
[72] United Nations, I.C.J., *Reports,* 1953, pp. 111, 119, and 120 respectively.

The mere declaration of a "rule of international law," no matter how generally accepted, is of no particular significance for supranationalism, however, unless an international tribunal can *effectively* apply it. With realistic acknowledgment of the large dose of national consent that must be present before nations will even have anything to do with an international court, the fact is that the International Court of Justice has carefully preserved its power of determining its own jurisdiction. More important, its efforts in this direction have been complied with by parties before it.

It is true, however, that as in the *Interhandel* Case (*Switzerland v. the United States of America*) for example, the Court occasionally has had to base its judgment on a rather circuitous argument to avoid an outright confrontation with a nation-state. In this case, the Court overruled U.S. objections (based on the Connally Amendment) to its jurisdiction, although it decided the case in favor of the United States (see Table 8, Judgment 20). In doing this, though, the Court structured its decision in such a way that, while reasserting its right to determine its own jurisdiction, it really avoided the basic challenge of the Connally Amendment by ruling on this question last. After deciding that the case was inadmissible due to Switzerland's failure to exhaust local remedies, the Court was able to claim that there was no need to adjudicate on the final question of the Connally reservation.[73]

Judge Lauterpacht asserted in this case that *compétence de la compétence* justified the exercise by the Court of the power to discuss, even in the silence of the parties, the nature of the controversy and the validity of the jurisdictional instruments involved. This was inherent in the Court's function, Article 36 (6) of the Statute, being only "declaratory of one of the most firmly established principles of international arbitral and judicial practice."[74]

Judicial Impartiality

As was true in the Permanent Court of International Justice, there is a very strong suggestion that the judges of the United Nations Court vote along national lines. In the 29 judgments rendered by the Court, the correlation between a judge's nationality and his vote (determined by his vote when his country was a party before the Court) is strikingly high. In fact it is so high as to suggest that nationalism is rampant on the Court. In only 7 of the 29 judg-

---

[73] See United Nations, I.C.J., *Reports,* 1959, p. 6.

[74] *Ibid.,* p. 104 (dissenting opinion of Judge Lauterpacht). For a discussion of his views in this case on reservations see *supra,* footnote 57.

ments was there a clear lack of correlation.[75] On the other hand, in 17 cases there was a correlation.[76] The remaining five cases do not fit into either category, either because dissenters were not identified or because judges split several ways on a series of complicated questions.[77] Even in several of these cases there is enough evidence to suggest a possible link between nationality and vote.

Of the 17 cases reflecting a possible correlation, *ad hoc* judges were identified with the position of the country they represented in 14 of them.[78] In fact, *ad hoc* judges were often the lone dissenters when the Court majority voted against their country. Regular judges were identified with their country's position in seven cases.[79] Four of these seven involved dissents by a regular judge when the ruling went against his country,[80] but none were lone dissents. The obviously high proportion of dissents by *ad hoc* judges when the country they represented lost a decision has prompted one scholar to proclaim the following interesting view:

> Indeed, so prevalent is this that one may be tempted to speculate whether a judge *ad hoc* is not expected to act in this way, and whether it is not in the long-term interests of the Court as an institution that he should do so. The reason is that having regard to the fragile foundations of international adjudication, the presence of a judge *ad hoc* on the bench, and the inclusion of his dissenting opinion in the text of the judgment itself, lends reality to the dictum that justice must not only be done but that it must be seen to be done. It makes it easier for a government to decide to entrust its affairs to the International Court.[81]

On the other hand, such actions by judges raise the question of judicial impartiality. Perhaps the mere fact that the vote of an *ad hoc* judge is generally known is bad in itself. It seems a reasonable assumption that judges, especially *ad hoc* judges, will be more inclined to be "national representatives" if their votes are publicized. The Court of the European Communities, for example, publishes only a single opinion for the entire Court, with votes kept secret. Perhaps this is extreme for the International Court of Justice, but certainly some modification of this scheme is not beyond consideration. An example might be simply not to identify the authors of dissenting opinions. That such a step might be necessary, or at least desirable, reflects the highly sensitive role of nationality in an inter-

---

[75] Judgments 10, 12, 13, 14, 22, 24, and 25.
[76] Judgments 1, 3, 4, 5, 7, 8, 9, 15, 16, 18, 19, 21, 23, 26, 27, 28, and 29.
[77] Judgments 2, 6, 11, 17, and 20.
[78] Judgments 1, 3, 4, 5, 9, 15, 18, 19, 21, 23, 26, 27, 28, and 29.
[79] Judgments 1, 3, 7, 8, 9, 16, and 27.
[80] Judgments 7, 8, 9, and 16.
[81] Rosenne, *op. cit.*, pp. 64–65.

national court, not found of course in the average municipal tribunal.[82]

Enforcement

Writing about Article 94 (2) of the Charter (providing for recourse to the Security Council to give effect to a judgment) in 1946, two distinguished scholars of international organization made this prediction: "Judging from past experience, this paragraph is not likely to have any great importance in practice. It has happened very rarely that states have refused to carry out the decisions of international tribunals. The difficulty has always been in getting states to submit their disputes to a tribunal. Once they have done so, they have usually been willing to accept even an adverse judgment."[83]

Experience with the World Court has borne out this prediction. As seen in the previous chapter, in no case did the parties refuse to carry out the judgment of the Permanent Court of International Justice. Of the 29 judgments rendered by the International Court of Justice, non-compliance has occurred in two instances—a somewhat ironic twist because of the supposedly stronger enforcement mechanism available to the latter Court.

The only instance of complete failure to comply with a judgment of the Court is the Albanian refusal to pay the damages (£843,947) awarded to the United Kingdom in the *Corfu Channel* Case.[84] In this instance, the competence of the Security Council has not been invoked to secure compliance.[85] Presumably, unless the United Kingdom takes the initiative and brings the matter before the Security Council (highly unlikely at this point), the potentially supranational enforcement aspect of judicial decisions will not be tested.

The only other instance of non-compliance involved not a Court decision, but rather a Court order for interim measures of protection in the *Anglo-Iranian Oil Company* Case.[86] In this case, Great Britain did go to the Security Council seeking enforcement measures. Britain's experience in this effort is quite instructive. Not only

---

[82] This question is discussed further in Chapters 5 and 7.

[83] Leland M. Goodrich and Edvard Hambro, *Charter of the United Nations: Commentary and Documents* (Boston: World Peace Foundation, 1946), pp. 263–264. See also Edvard Hambro, *L'Exécution des Sentences Internationales* (Paris: Librairie de Recueil Sirey, 1936).

[84] See Judgments 2 and 3 in Table 8. See also Rosenne, *op. cit.*, p. 43.

[85] The *Monetary Gold Removed from Rome in 1943* Case represented a "self-help" measure to effect payment. Albanian funds in Italy were confiscated by the Allies (see Judgment 13 in Table 8).

[86] See Judgment 10 in Table 8.

does one get some sense of what is likely to happen when Security Council aid is called for, but also, this encounter with political reality clarifies the position that supranationalism really holds in the present United Nations community.

GREAT BRITAIN, IRAN, AND THE SECURITY COUNCIL By a letter dated September 29, 1951, the United Kingdom requested the inclusion of the following item on the provisional agenda of the Security Council: "Complaint of failure by the Iranian Government to comply with provisional measures indicated by the ICJ in the *Anglo-Iranian Oil Company* Case."[87] In this complaint the United Kingdom recalled that the International Court of Justice had notified the Council of the provisional measures indicated by the Court on July 5, 1951, under Article 41 (2) of the Statute.[88]

Further, the British complaint pointed out, the United Kingdom had accepted the findings of the Court. Iran, however, had rejected them and had ordered the expulsion from Iran of all the remaining staff of the Company—contrary to the interim measures ordered by the Court. Finally, the complaint continued, "His Majesty's Government in the United Kingdom are gravely concerned at the dangers inherent in this situation and at the threat to peace and security that may thereby be involved."[89] Appended to the British complaint was a draft resolution calling upon Iran to comply with the Court order.[90]

After the question had been placed on the Security Council agenda, the representative of the United Kingdom made the following statement at the 559th meeting on October 1, 1951:

The Council will, of course, bear in mind the position of the Court as the principal judicial organ of the United Nations; both Article 92 of the Charter and Article I of the Court's Statute establish this. Its position in this capacity has been affirmed by the Court itself. . . . To act in conformity with the decisions and findings of the Court must, therefore, necessarily be to act in conformity with the purposes and principles of the United Nations. This is a cardinal reason justifying both the present recourse to the Security Council on the part of the United Kingdom Government and its request for support. . . .[91]

---

[87] United Nations, Department of Political and Security Council Affairs, *Repertoire of the Practice of the Security Council: 1946–1951* (hereinafter cited as *Security Council Repertoire*) (New York: Department of Political and Security Council Affairs, 1954) , p. 360, from S/1745/Rev. 1, 501st meeting, p. 3.

[88] See S/2239, *S.C.O.R., 6th year, Suppl. for Oct., Nov., Dec. 1951*, p. 1, in *ibid.*

[89] *Security Council Repertoire*, p. 360.

[90] See S/2358, *S.C.O.R., 6th year, Suppl. for Oct., Nov., Dec. 1951*, pp. 2–3, in *ibid.*

[91] *Security Council Repertoire*, p. 360.

This question was considered by the Security Council at the 559th through the 563rd meetings (between October 1 and 17, 1951) and at the 565th meeting (October 19, 1951). The key aspects of the United Kingdom/Iran debate were outlined at the first meeting (559th) on October 1, 1951. The British argument was based on three main points:

1. Relying on Article 93 (1), which made all U.N. members *ipso facto* parties to the Statute and Article 94 (1), wherein United Nations members undertook to comply with Court decisions, the British government maintained that "the indication by the Court of provisional measures under *Article 41 of the Statute* of itself gave rise to obligations which it was the duty of the Security Council to uphold and which could not be regarded as being solely within the domestic jurisdiction of one of the parties."[92]

2. Noting that the Security Council had special functions in relation to decisions of the Court both under Article 94 (2) of the Charter (enforcement) and Article 41 (2) of the Statute (interim measures), the United Kingdom maintained that "Article 94 (2) applied not only to final judgments of the Court, but to decisions on interim measures as well, for there would be no point in making the final judgment binding if one of the parties could frustrate that judgment in advance by actions which would render it nugatory."[93]

3. Stressing that the formal basis of the reference to the Council was Article 35 of the Charter, the British government noted that "in these circumstances and quite apart from the decision of the Court, there was a dispute which should receive urgent consideration by the Council."[94]

The Iranian argument countered with four defensive points:

1. Iran claimed that the Security Council had no competence because of the traditional principle of international law guaranteeing sovereign rights in matters of domestic jurisdiction.

2. Iran further claimed that this principle of international law was also the law of the United Nations by virtue of Articles 1 (2) and 2 (7), which exempted members from any requirement to submit such matters to settlement under the Charter.

3. Also, the Security Council could not, as Great Britain claimed, enforce compliance under Article 94 with the provisional measures indicted by the Court under Article 41 of its Statute, because the

---

[92] *Ibid.,* p. 476.
[93] *Ibid.*
[94] *Ibid.*

Statute attributed binding force only to *final judgments* under Article 59.

4. Finally, Iran countered the suggestion that the Security Council ought to assume jurisdiction because of the existence of a threat (or potential threat) to the peace by claiming that "a nation as weak and small as Iran could not endanger world peace, that whatever danger there might be to peace lay in the actions of the Government of the United Kingdom, and that the only dispute between Iran and the United Kingdom related to the latter's attempts to interfere in the internal affairs of Iran."[95]

Security Council consideration of these questions was quite unhurried, characterized by an apparent desire to avoid doing anything. A draft resolution was submitted by Ecuador at the 562nd meeting on October 17, 1951, calling on "the parties concerned to reopen negotiations as soon as possible with a view to making a fresh attempt to settle their differences in accordance with the Purposes and Principles of the United Nations Charter."[96]

Beyond this point, Council debate closely followed the Cold War split. The Soviet Union took Iran's side.[97] The United States and China sided with the United Kingdom.[98] The leading neutrals of India and Yugoslavia proposed a wait-and-see-what-the-Court-does policy.[99] When France, at the 565th meeting (October 19, 1951), adopted this latter position by proposing that "the Council adjourn its debate on the question until the International Court of Justice had ruled on its own competence in the matter," the Council, for lack of ability to do anything else, adopted this stand.[100]

When the Secretary-General transmitted by a letter dated August 19, 1952, for the information of the members of the Security Council, a copy of the judgment of the International Court (given July 22, 1952) in which the Court found it had no jurisdiction in the case, the matter—if not settled—was at least forgotten.[101]

Writing about this incident, one scholar had this to say about Article 94 (2) : "the Security Council showed little enthusiasm for this procedure, which led to no concrete result. In fact, the efficacy of this provision depends upon the unanimity of the five Permanent Members. Their inability to reach agreement on major political is-

---

95 *Ibid.*
96 *Ibid.*, p. 360.
97 *Ibid.*, p. 476.
98 *Ibid.*, p. 477.
99 *Ibid.*, pp. 476–477.
100 *Ibid.*, p. 361.
101 *Ibid.*, p. 478 (S/2746) .

sues is the fundamental reason for the failure of the Security Council to face up to the challenge which was presented to it by the United Kingdom in 1951.[102]

Security Council inaction can in part be excused simply because the binding effect of Court orders of this type, as has been seen, is not beyond controversy—especially when they are given before the Court's jurisdiction is established. Although perhaps not excusable, the Iranian action is understandable. It can be argued that the circumstances in Iran at the time were of an exceptional nature and could hardly reflect the typical attitude of that government. Proof of this probably lies in the fact that the parties subsequently came to an agreement.[103] These circumstances notwithstanding, Security Council action was clearly circumscribed by basic factors in world politics, for example national sovereignty complicated by Cold War maneuvering.

In retrospect, one can see that these political factors, to a greater or lesser degree, have permeated the two international tribunals which have existed as part of a general international organization. The hopes and desires of some states to the contrary, neither the Permanent Court of International Justice nor the International Court of Justice were intended to be supranational in the sense outlined in Chapter 1. While these institutions possessed some supranational potential, it has not been realized—and there is no reason to expect that it will be until world politics changes.

The power of a United Nations organ is not likely to be much greater than the lowest common denominator of agreement that can be achieved among 124 nation-states (United Nations membership as of July, 1968). The difficulty of achieving agreement among 124 units of any kind suggests that the fewer the units the greater the chance of achieving a higher denominator of agreement—especially if these units have much in common like culture, legal system, and history. The Central American Court of Justice possessed these

---

[102] Rosenne, *op. cit.*, p. 44.

[103] Louis B. Sohn (ed.), *Cases on United Nations Law* (Brooklyn: The Foundation Press, Inc., 1956), p. 312, notes: "On 5 August 1954, an agreement was reached between Iran and the National Iranian Oil Company, on the one hand, and an international consortium of eight oil companies, on the other hand, on restoring the flow of Iranian oil to world markets and on compensation to be paid to the Anglo-Iranian Oil Company. Iran agreed to pay Anglo-Iranian $70,000,000 over a period of ten years beginning in 1957; in addition, the other companies agreed to pay to it approximately $510,000,000 in return for the shares they acquired in the Iranian oil production. The agreement was finally signed on 19 and 20 September and was ratified on 29 October 1954."

characteristics, but unfortunately the apparent agreement achieved was on a legal plane only and had no basis in political reality. The League and United Nations courts have been based upon political realities, but have been correspondingly weak.[104] The ideal of the well-grounded regional tribunal seems to have been realized in two European courts—the Court of the European Communities and, to a lesser degree, the European Court of Human Rights. Because of a strong base of political consensus among the six contracting parties, the Court of the European Communities has assumed a high degree of supranational power. Political consensus is not so strong for the European Court of Human Rights in the 18-member Council of Europe. Consequently, its supranational promise remains a potentiality.

---

[104] For an assessment of the success of these two courts see Rosenne, *op. cit.,* pp. 169–174. For a theoretical discussion of the limits of international adjudication see Kenneth S. Carlston, "Development and Limits of International Adjudication," *Proceedings of the American Society of International Law* (1965), pp. 182–189.

CHAPTER FIVE

COURT OF THE
EUROPEAN COMMUNITIES

A. EXPECTATIONS OF STATESMEN

Unfortunately, as one author writes regarding the drafting of the treaty establishing the European Coal and Steel Community (ECSC), "it is to be regretted that no record of the *travaux préparatoires* of the Treaty exists."[1] Also to be regretted is the fact that this same situation marks the creation of the two subsequent European communities—the European Economic Community (EEC) and the European Atomic Energy Community (Euratom).

In spite of this disadvantage, however, one can get at least some sense of statesmen's expectations concerning the Court of the European Communities from (1) the general tenor of the European integrative movement and (2) the ratification debates on the treaties following their signing.

European Integration

BEGINNINGS   Attempts at European integration, in some form or another, are probably as old as Europe itself—from pre–Holy Roman Empire to modern times. In the postwar era in Europe, the romantic attraction of integration has been as great as ever—bolstered by the note of urgency spawned in the aftermath of

---

[1] D. G. Valentine, *The Court of Justice of the European Communities*, I (London: Stevens & Sons Ltd., 1965), 2.

the cruel realities of World War II. The history of postwar integration—beginning with private federative groups and the U.S. Marshall Plan and resulting in a myriad of economic, political, and military regional organizations—does not need to be recounted here.[2]

The concrete beginnings of the modern European communities were in 1950, when on the afternoon of May 9, in the Salon d'Horloge at the Quai d'Orsay, French Foreign Minister Robert Schuman read to representatives of the world's press a proposal from his government. This revolutionary announcement (the so-called Schuman Plan), which signaled the beginning of the European Community, urged that:

a) the contribution which an organized, living Europe can make to civilization is indispensable to the maintenance of peace;

b) if the European nations are to draw together, the centuries-old struggle between France and Germany must be brought to an end; and

c) the pooling of French and German coal and steel production under a common authority, in an organization open to all the countries of Europe, would assure the immediate establishment of common bases of economic development—the first step in European federation.[3]

After ten months of negotiation, France, the German Federal Republic, Italy, and the three Benelux countries signed the treaty setting up the European Coal and Steel Community—the first "common market." Fourteen months later, the Treaty had been ratified by all six national parliaments. In signing the draft ECSC Treaty on April 18, 1951, the six governments declared themselves "resolved to substitute for historic rivalries a fusion of their essential interests; to establish, by creating an economic community, the foundation of a broad and independent community among peoples long divided by bloody conflicts; and to lay the bases of institutions capable of giving direction to their future common destiny."[4]

The ECSC was a unique step forward. The Treaty had set up the first European organization with a federal type of structure. This was the first time a "common European authority," independent of the various governments, was able to make its own decisions. Ex-

[2] A brief, readable account of this period is offered by Richard Mayne, *The Community of Europe: Past, Present and Future* (New York: W. W. Norton and Company, Inc., 1963).

[3] European Community Information Service, *The European Community* (London Office: Press and Information Office of the European Communities, 1961), p. 3.

[4] *Ibid.*, p. 4.

plaining his Plan before the Assembly of the Council of Europe (Fourth Sitting, August 10, 1950), Robert Schuman said: "The Authority would thus be the first example of a supra-national institution, in the interests of which the participating countries would have to agree to a partial abandonment of sovereignty."[5] Further, Schuman saw in this partial abandonment of sovereignty "not an end in itself but an absolute necessity if a solution were to be found for the present deadlocks."[6]

Under the bold leadership of Jean Monnet, the first European Community began when the ECSC Treaty went into force on July 15, 1952.[7] In 1953 the ECSC was opened, and coal, iron, and steel prices came under its control. With the year 1954, the first big stumbling block to further integration appeared. While the ECSC had made headway, the treaty for a second European community (European Defense Community—EDC), signed by the "Six" nine months after the ECSC in order to solve the problem of a German contribution to European defense, was rejected by the French Parliament.

At this point the project for setting up a political community of the Six was abandoned in favor of a return to the economic realm as the first prerequisite to integration. At a meeting at Messina, Sicily, on June 1, 1955, the six governments decided that the policy of integration inaugurated on May 9, 1950, must lead to the merger of the national economies as a whole.[8]

In 1956, the Six decided to open negotiations with a view to setting up the Common Market (EEC) and Euratom. A most important negotiation in this year was the agreement between German Chancellor Dr. Konrad Adenauer and Guy Mollet, the French Prime Minister, in Luxembourg on October 27, which returned the Saar both economically and politically to Germany, thus removing one of the last real obstacles to Franco-German reconciliation.

On March 25, 1957, the six foreign ministers, meeting in Rome, signed the treaties setting up the European Economic Community (EEC or the Common Market) and the European Atomic Energy Community (Euratom). Before the year's end the two treaties had

---

[5] "Summary of the Debates in the Consultative Assembly of the Council of Europe," *European Assembly*, I, 1 (August 7–11, 1950), 49. (Published by authority of the Council of Europe by the Hansard Society.)

[6] *Ibid.*

[7] Europäische Gemeinschaft, Presse- und Informationsdienst, "Zeittafel der europäischen Integration," *Die Europäische Gemeinschaft: EWG-Montanunion-Euratom* (Brüssel: Presse- und Informationsdienst der Europäischen Gemeinschaften, 1963), pp. 24–25.

[8] European Community Information Service, *op. cit.*, p. 3.

been ratified by the parliaments of all six member countries with even greater majorities than the treaty establishing the ECSC.[9] The EEC and Euratom treaties entered into force on January 1, 1958, with Brussels as the provisional headquarters, and in 1959 the EEC and Euratom actually started operation.

Figure 3 outlines the institutional framework of the communities as it existed prior to July 1, 1967, when the executive organs of the three communities were merged.[10] The former organizational structure is shown here for clarity as the bulk of this study concerns the communities prior to 1967. Further, only the institutions (and not the treaties themselves) were merged. Also, the merger treaty "does not alter the powers or the responsibilities of the institutions or their relations with one another."[11] The terminology of Figure 3 is employed throughout this study and is still referred to in the communities. The following paragraphs, briefly explaining the functions of the Community organs, clarify this.

1. The *Executives* originally comprised the Common Market Commission (nine members), the High Authority of the ECSC (nine members), and the Euratom Commission (five members). The three agencies have now been merged into one Commission of fourteen members, which will exercise their former powers and responsibilities.[12] One organ, then, will simply act in three different capacities. Highly independent of national governments, the task of the new Commission is roughly to supervise the implementation of the provisions of the respective treaties.

2. Also having an executive function were the *Councils of Ministers,* composed of one member from each national government (the only Community institution whose members are national represen-

---

[9] Europäische Gemeinschaft, Presse- und Informationsdienst, *op. cit.,* pp. 24–25.

[10] On this date the Brussels treaty of April 8, 1965, merging the executive branches of the EEC, Euratom, and ECSC, entered into force. No timetable was set for the merger of the communities themselves. See "Treaty Establishing a Single Council and a Single Commission of the European Communities," *Annuaire Européen,* XIII (1967), 461–503. For a discussion of the merger see Gordon Weil, "The Merger of the Institutions of the European Communities," *American Journal of International Law,* LXI, 1 (January, 1967), 57–65.

[11] See European Community Information Service, *European Community,* No. 104 (July-August, 1967), p. 4. One modification is that the single Commission will be responsible to the European Parliament for its actions. In this case, the merger treaty follows the same lines as the EEC and Euratom treaties, which allocated a more important role to the Parliament than did the ECSC Treaty.

[12] These fourteen members will serve maximum terms of three years, at which time the number will be reduced to nine members who will serve four-year terms. For biographical sketches on the new members of the Commission see *ibid.,* p. 6.

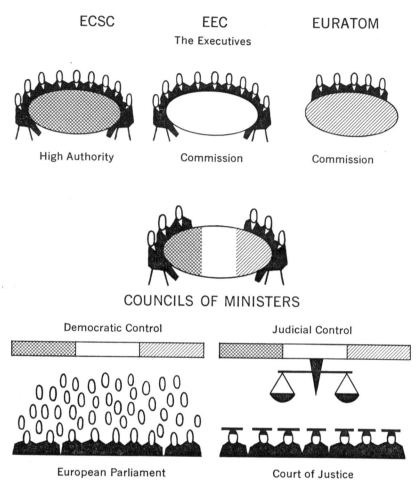

ECSC   EEC   EURATOM

The Executives

High Authority   Commission   Commission

COUNCILS OF MINISTERS

Democratic Control   Judicial Control

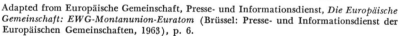

European Parliament   Court of Justice

Adapted from Europäische Gemeinschaft, Presse- und Informationsdienst, *Die Europäische Gemeinschaft: EWG-Montanunion-Euratom* (Brüssel: Presse- und Informationsdienst der Europäischen Gemeinschaften, 1963), p. 6.

FIG. 3 The Organs of the European Community Prior to July 1, 1967

tatives) and serving as an agent of intergovernmental control over the activities of the respective communities. As of July 1, 1967, the Councils were merged into a single Council sitting in three different capacities. On EEC and Euratom matters, the Council holds the final decision-making power (thereby preventing the communities from being fully supranational), but only on the basis of proposals by the Commission. It can only modify proposals by unanimous vote. For ECSC affairs, the Council has the last word on certain fundamental questions, but mainly its role is limited to giving an opinion before the Commission takes decisions. Its decisions are mainly taken by majority vote.

3. The *European Parliament* consists of 142 members, who are (for the time being) nominated by and from the six national parliaments, but who sit in European political parties irrespective of nationality.[13] Intended to serve in the future as the main element of democratic control over the Community's other institutions, the Parliament has the sole right to dismiss the commissions or the High Authority, and is consulted on all important issues. Both the Parliament and the Court of Justice have been common institutions for the three communities since their beginning.

4. Finally, the *Court of Justice,* consisting of seven independent judges, has the sole power to decide whether the acts of the Council of Ministers and the Executives should be upheld or not. Its judgments have the supreme force of law throughout the Community.[14] It is this Court which forms the subject of this chapter.

"EUROPEAN" VIEWS ON INTEGRATION   One may presume from the foregoing brief historical survey that European integration, and the institutional paraphernalia that accompanies it, have played a rather major role in postwar European politics. This development, which has been no overnight occurrence, has been marked by many years of tedious, calculating statesmanship. While the major part of this work is not a matter of public record, there are enough public pronouncements by statesmen involved in the integrative movement to suggest clearly that high—yet realistic—supranational hopes are the "tenor of the times" in Europe. This in turn of course reveals something about these statesmen's expectations for the Court.

Shortly after the proposal of the Schuman Plan, the German Bundestag adopted a rather startling stand against state sovereignty. With only four Communist votes dissenting, the Bundestag on July

---

[13] Christian Democrats, Socialists, and Liberals. For a discussion of the development of "supranational political parties" in the European Parliament see Ernst B. Haas, *The Uniting of Europe: Political, Social and Economic Forces, 1950–1957* (Stanford, Calif.: Stanford University Press, 1958) , Chap. 11.

[14] General treatments of the Community institutions can be found in Europäische Gemeinschaft, Presse- und Informationsdienst, *op. cit.,* pp. 6–8; European Community Information Service, *The European Community at a Glance* (London Office: Press and Information Office of the European Communities, 1964) , pp. 1–2, and *European Community: The Facts* (Washington Office: Press and Information Office of the European Communities, 1967) , pp. 4–8; and Michael Curtis, *Western European Integration* (New York: Harper and Row, 1965) , especially Chaps. 6, 7, and 8.

26, 1950, advocated the conclusion of a European federal pact in the following resolution: "Convinced that the present division of Europe into national sovereign states tends to lead the European nations into ever-increasing misery and to deprive them of their freedom, the Bundestag of the German Federal Republic, established by free elections, declares itself in favor of a European Federal Pact. . . ."[15]

Among the specific proposals embodied in this resolution was "the creation of a supranational Federal Authority . . . which has at its disposal legislative, executive and judicial competence."[16]

Chancellor Adenauer, speaking before the Bundestag on March 19, 1953, stated a similar position:

> We must free ourselves from thinking in terms of national statehood. The last war, and developments in the field of armament and modern technology, have created entirely different and new conditions in the world. . . . West European countries are no longer in a position to protect themselves individually; none of them is any longer in a position to salvage European culture. These objectives, which are common to all, can only be attained if the West European nations form a political, economic and cultural union, and, above all, if they render impossible any military conflicts among themselves.[17]

Later, summarizing the Common Market negotiations after his return from Paris in February, 1957, Chancellor Adenauer proclaimed that the delegates had "taken a long step forward on the road to a united Europe" and even labeled the negotiations "the most important postwar event."[18] These talks in the Hotel de Matignon in Paris were the crowning event of 18 months of thorough groundwork. According to the official *Bulletin* of the German government information service, the outcome of these talks was viewed in the German Federal Republic as "an integral part of the larger goal of European unity."[19] The same source noted that neither the Chancellor nor Foreign Minister von Brentano "have left any doubt that national economic interests should be subordinated to the idea of ultimate political unity."[20]

---

[15] "Deutscher Bundestag faßt Entschließung für einen Europäischen Bundespakt," in Heinrich Siegler, *Dokumentation der europäischen Integration* (Bonn: Siegler & Co. KG. Verlag für Zeitarchive, 1961), Doc. 44, p. 44 (my translation).

[16] *Ibid.*

[17] Cited by Hans Speier and W. Phillips Davison (eds.), *West German Leadership and Foreign Policy* (Evanston, Ill.: Row, Peterson and Company, 1957), p. 80.

[18] Germany, Federal Republic, Presse- und Informationsamt der Bundesregierung, *The Bulletin* (February 28, 1957), p. 1.

[19] *Ibid.*

[20] *Ibid.*

On February 28, 1957, Dr. Heinrich von Brentano commented specifically on these negotiations. One great advantage of the treaties on the European Common Market and Euratom, he felt, was that no attempt had been made to rush them to completion. Contrasting sharply with the supranational exuberance that characterized the hastily drawn-up Central American Court system, the European talks, von Brentano stressed, took careful account of economic and political realities.[21]

With the exception of France after De Gaulle's rise to power, all six of the European Community countries have generally supported a supranational position similar to that outlined above.[22] A distinguished Dutch diplomat active in European integration, writing in this context, notes that while there are both "internationalists" and "supranationalists" in European politics, Europe clearly has a supranational commitment.[23] His distinction between the two is interesting:

> "Supranationalists" and "internationalists" start from a different conception. The former intend to create an organization where the participating Governments transfer a portion of their powers of decision—I abstain on purpose from using the much abused and often misleading word "sovereignty"—to a body, to an independent authority, which recommends or decides, depending upon its powers in each case, in conformity with the interests of the Community which they serve as a whole, and not necessarily in accordance with the wishes of the individual member-states of that community.
>
> "Supranationalism", thus defined, constitutes a courageous attempt to break through the barrier of the veto, of the unanimity rule, which all too frequently means that the lowest common denominator constitutes the only basis upon which agreement can be reached. . . . Furthermore, it is only fair to admit that the supranationalists do not consider their kind of organization an end in itself. This is a point which is frequently missed and which has contributed considerably to mutual incomprehension and misunderstanding.[24]

An Italian federalist (Secretary-General of the European Federalist Movement) writes a further interesting note about three of these supranationalists who were destined to direct French, German, and

---

[21] *Ibid.*

[22] For a full documentation see "Von der Zürcher Rede Churchills (19. September 1946) bis zur Unterzeichnung der Römer Verträge (25. März 1957)" in Siegler, *op. cit.*, Kapitel I, Docs. 1–170.

[23] H. E. Jonkheer Van Vredenburch, "European Co-operation, as Seen from The Hague," *International Relations* (London), I, 11 (April, 1959), 521–528. At the time of writing the author was Netherlands Ambassador to Bonn. He had formerly been Director-General of European Co-operation at The Hague, Deputy-Secretary of NATO, and later Chief Representative of the ECSC in the United Kingdom.

[24] *Ibid.*, p. 523.

Italian foreign policy after the war—Schuman, Adenauer, and De Gasperi. All three "came from borderlands. Two of them in their time had belonged to two different states; the third, Adenauer, had been involved in the separatist movement in the Rhineland after World War I. All three were fundamentally conservative, but national sovereignty was not one of the values they were anxious to protect."[25]

Indicative of the deep commitment many European leaders have for supranational integration is the significant group of activists led by Jean Monnet (France). Monnet was the first President of the High Authority, but resigned because the organization, although generally acknowledged as the most powerful supranational organ yet created, was *not supranational enough!*[26] In his farewell address to the ECSC Common Assembly Monnet said:

The indispensable contribution which the Coal and Steel Community had made and will continue to make to European federation consists in its progress and success in the areas entrusted to it. However, the institutions of our community exercise only the powers delegated to them. It is not for them to extend them. The decision to transfer new powers to the European institutions belongs entirely to the [national] parliaments and governments. The impulse must, therefore, come from without.[27]

To supply this "impulse from without" Monnet founded his Action Committee in October, 1955. The purpose of the Action Committee was to "conduct a collective and concrete campaign directed at the governments and in the parliaments with a view towards the realization of a United States of Europe."[28]

The Committee consists of the leaders of all major political parties and trade unions in the Community except for the Communists, the Italian (Nenni) Socialist Party, and the Gaullist Union for the New Republic (UNR). The Committee's full impact on governmental policies is probably indeterminable, but it is clear that it has influence—important influence—on the governments of the Community. Walter Yondorf labels the Committee "one of the world's most prestigious organizations. Probably no other private association can boast such an array of ex–Prime Ministers, including

---

[25] Altiero Spinelli, "The Growth of the European Movement Since World War II," in C. Grove Haines (ed.), *European Integration* (Baltimore: The Johns Hopkins Press, 1957), p. 45.

[26] The immediate cause of his resignation was the French rejection of EDC.

[27] Jean Monnet, *Les États-Unis d'Europe Ont Commencé* (Paris: Robert Laffort, 1955), p. 102. Cited by Walter Yondorf, "Monnet and the Action Committee: The Formative Period of the European Communities," *International Organization*, XIX, 4 (Autumn, 1965), 889.

[28] Action Committee for the United States of Europe, "Note for Journalists" (Paris, May 4, 1957). Cited by Yondorf, *loc. cit.*

Prime Ministers with future prospects, among its members."[29] Among the more well-known names are: Guy Mollet, Erich Ollenhauer, Herbert Wehner, Guiseppe Saragat, Théo Lefèvre, Robert Lecourt, Heinrich Krone, Aldo Moro, Maurice Faure, Antoine Pinay, and René Pleven. The most recent rise to power by a member of the Committee occurred when the former President of Baden-Württemberg, Kurt Kiesinger, replaced Ludwig Erhard as West Germany's Chancellor.[30]

While there is clearly opposition within the Community to the pervading wave of supranationalism, most of it is directed not against the general theory but rather against specific repugnant manifestations (e.g., agriculture, transport, or anti-cartel policy). The only leading outspoken critic of supranationalism per se is General de Gaulle of France, whose formula is "l'Europe des États." Only the nation embodies legitimate political power, in this view, but nations may work closely together and may create *international bodies* that serve common purposes. According to Richard Mayne, General de Gaulle "sees the Community institutions as purely technical machinery with limited aims. The bulk of the Gaullist party, in fact, voted against ratification of the European Coal and Steel Treaty in December, 1951. But even General de Gaulle has since looked forward to 'an imposing confederation,' and under his leadership France has scrupulously respected the legal provisions of the Community Treaties."[31]

De Gaulle explained his position at a press conference in Paris on September 5, 1960:

> The creation of Europe, that is its unity, is indeed an important thing. It is banal to say this. Why should this great hearth of civilization, of strength, of reason and of progress be extinguished under its own ashes? Nevertheless one must not give himself over to dreams in this area, rather he must see things as they are. What are the realities of Europe and the cornerstones upon which one can build further? In reality it is the States. . . . It is a chimera to believe that one could create something operative or that the people would approve of something that would exist outside of, or above, the State. Certainly it is true that, before one has treated the European problem in its entirety, certain more or less supranational institutions could be created. These institutions have their technical worth, but they neither have nor can they possess authority and political effectiveness.[32]

---

[29] Yondorf, *op. cit.*, p. 912.

[30] For a full list of members of the Committee see *ibid.*, pp. 891–893.

[31] Mayne, *op. cit.*, p. 13.

[32] "De Gaulle gegen übernationale Einrichtungen, für regelmäßige Konsultationen der Regierungen und für europäische Volksabstimmung," in Siegler, *op. cit.*, Doc. 372, p. 378 (my translation).

Putting political considerations temporarily aside, it seems a fair summary of the preceding paragraphs to claim that the six members of the European communities have generally committed themselves to the idea of supranational integration. Various national constitutions and of course the treaties themselves are legal witness to this.

SUPRANATIONAL EXPECTATIONS IN NATIONAL CONSTITUTIONS   Three constitutions of the Six clearly foresaw the development of supranational institutions in their provisions for the "delegation of sovereignty" by treaty. The French Constitution of 1958—following that of 1946—consents "aux limitations de souveraineté nécessaires à l'organisation et à la défense de la paix (sous réserve de réciprocité) ."[33]

The new German Constitution (or Basic Law) has the following provisions:

1. The Federation may, by legislation, transfer sovereign powers to international institutions.
2. For the maintenance of peace, the Federation may join a system of mutual collective security; in doing so it will consent to those limitations of its sovereign powers which will bring about and secure a peaceful and lasting order in Europe and among the nations of the world.
3. For the settlement of disputes between nations, the Federation will accede to conventions concerning a general, comprehensive obligatory system of international arbitration.[34]

The Constitution of the Netherlands (since 1953) consents to the transfer of legislative, administrative, and judicial powers to international organizations.[35] In the case of the Netherlands, if the development of the international legal order so requires, treaty provisions (with approval of the States-General) can even depart from constitutional provisions.[36]

The Community treaties probably reveal the most in terms of what degree of supranationalism the Six would accept. The ratification debates following the submission of the ECSC Treaty to the national parliaments provide a fitting prelude to an examination of the constitutional basis of the Court. They emphasize the arguments and fears that apparently surrounded the creation of the Community institutions.

---

[33] France, *Constitution* (1958) , Preamble.
[34] Germany, Federal Republic, *Basic Law* (1949) , Article 24, pars. 1–3.
[35] Netherlands, *Constitution,* Article 67.
[36] *Ibid.,* Article 63.

Ratification Debates

The ECSC Treaty passed with respectable majorities in the national parliaments of all six countries with the most heated debates occurring in Belgium, Italy, and France.[37] Although all aspects of the Treaty were discussed, of interest here is a brief survey of some of the views expressed concerning supranationalism and the Court.

Professor Mason, in discussing the ratification debates, writes: "No attempt was made to hide the inroads on national sovereignty resulting from the Treaty; instead, these were called its greatest merit. While it is possible that such a display of 'supranationalism' was at times but a cloak for a variety of economic, political, and perhaps even nationalist considerations, it is remarkable that supranationalism evidently was considered a primary asset to assure ratification."[38]

The German position, which has already been outlined above, was further bolstered by Chancellor Adenauer's remark to the Bundestag that for the first time in history nations were voluntarily "giving up a portion of their sovereignty" to a supranational institution—"an event which signifies the end of nationalism . . . which has been the cancer of Europe. . . ."[39]

A. Coste-Floret, the *Rapporteur* of the French Assembly's Foreign Relations Committee, called the ECSC "a veritable revolution" destroying the "quasi-divine" principle of national sovereignty.[40] The Italian Undersecretary of State labeled the Community "a new experiment in history . . . the first tentative, revolutionary attempt to pass from the international to the supranational. . . . For the first time, six nations find themselves united in a community which overcomes national sovereignty. . . ."[41]

---

[37] The vote in the Netherlands' Second Chamber was 62 to 6 and in the First Chamber, 36 to 2. In the Luxembourg unicameral Chamber of Deputies it was 47 to 4. In the Italian Chamber the Treaty was approved 265 to 98 and in the Senate, 148 to 97. The vote in the German Bundestag was 232 to 143. In the Belgian Senate the vote was 102 to 4 compared to 165 to 13 in the Belgian Chamber. In France, the votes were 377 to 235 in the Assembly, 177 to 31 in the Council of the Republic, and 110 to 15 in the Economic Council. Figures cited by Henry L. Mason, *The European Coal and Steel Community: Experiment in Supranationalism* (The Hague: Martinus Nijhoff, 1955), pp. 10–11.

[38] *Ibid.*, pp. 12–13.

[39] Germany, Federal Republic, Bundestag, *Sitzungsbericht* (July 12, 1951), p. 6501.

[40] France, Assemblée Nationale, *Journal Officiel* (December 7, 1951), p. 8857.

[41] P. E. Taviani, *Il Plano Schuman* (Rome, 1953), p. 61. Cited by Mason, *op. cit.*, p. 13.

Of course, the Europeans also had their Senators Borah and Johnson. An outstanding example was M. Van Cauwelaert, a leading Social Christian in Belgium, who voiced the only real objection to that country's general acquiescence in the surrender of sovereignty. He protested: "If outside of war circumstances we would have demanded for our own Belgian government the powers which according to the Schuman Plan we would have to give to eight foreigners, they would have hissed and booed us. . . . We don't have the right to sell our national sovereignty just like that."[42]

A similar example was provided by French General A. Aumeran, an Independent Republican. He was certain that the Community would mean the ruin of France as a Great Power as well as the demise of the French empire. Quoting Jean Jaurès, a Socialist of the pre–World War I era, he concluded: "to destroy nations is to destroy all sources of light and liberty, leaving nothing but universal despotism."[43]

Critique of the Court itself was much more substantive. Prof. Schmid in the German Bundestag raised the question as to whether judges would be able to "jump over their national shadows." He cited the sad experiences of previous international courts and felt certain that judges would be bound to consider themselves national representatives. As evidence, he cited the experience of the "Hague Court" wherein the judges only voted against their nation's official position in two cases: a French judge in the *Lotus* Case and a Belgian judge in the *Austro-German Customs Union* Case.[44] Although his figures were incorrect, his stand bears out the warning of previous chapters that perhaps more important than the actual fact of judicial lack or presence of impartiality is whether or not observers *think* the Court is impartial.

A similar stand was taken by the French Economic Council, which felt that judicial impartiality was endangered because the judges would be directly appointed by the member governments (as was true with the Central American Court) for six-year terms with the possibility of reappointment.[45]

Perhaps a more serious criticism of the Court concerned its review

---

[42] Cited in Netherlands, *Handelingen Tweede Kamer* (October 30, 1951), p. 181. Quoted by Mason, *op. cit.*, p. 15.

[43] France, Assemblée Nationale, *Journal Officiel* (December 6, 1951), pp. 8878–79.

[44] Germany, Federal Republic, Bundestag, *Sitzungsbericht* (January 10, 1952), p. 7729, and (July 12, 1951), p. 6514.

[45] France, Conseil Economique, *Journal Officiel* (November 30, 1951), p. 243. Cited by Mason, *op. cit.*, p. 17.

powers over decisions of the High Authority. Since the High Authority was charged with handling highly technical iron and steel matters, one could legitimately wonder if these were properly a subject for judicial consideration. Dr. Veit, a German Socialist, noted: "It is the function of courts to consider facts in relation to the law. However, if a court is supposed to make difficult economic decisions, not only in relation to formal requirements on jurisdictional issues, but also concerning possible misuse of discretionary powers [*Ermessensmißbrauch*] . . . where will such a court get its norms?[46]

A similar argument appeared in the Parliament of the Netherlands.[47] The only defense seems to have been that the text of the Treaty was considered so detailed and precise that the judges would have no problems applying its provisions.[48]

Beyond all of the preceding general discussions, however, there is simply no public record of the drafting of the treaties establishing the Court, although one can undoubtedly extrapolate a great deal from the mood of these discussions. Professor D. G. Valentine insists that only "two glimpses" can be obtained of the Court in the *travaux préparatoires* that preceded the ratification debates. The first is provided in a report of the French delegation, which declared: "It was quite clear that the actions of the High Authority must be exercised with a respect for law, and especially for the rules set out in the Treaty. That is why the necessity of subjecting the High Authority to a judicial control was at once recognized."[49]

The other glimpse of which Valentine writes was provided by the *Exposé des Motifs* of the Luxembourg government, which stated that it was only "despite certain hesitations" that it was decided to establish a Court rather than an arbitral tribunal.[50]

With these high supranational expectations as a backdrop, the Court opened its first session on December 10, 1952, as the judicial arm of the Coal and Steel Community. Six years later, on October 7, 1958, the Court was seated the first time as the common Court of the European Communities, including the new EEC and Euratom

---

[46] Germany, Federal Republic, Bundestag, *Sitzungsbericht* (January 10, 1952), pp. 7729–30.

[47] See M. Klompé's remarks in Netherlands, *Handelingen Tweede Kamer* (October 30, 1951), p. 170. Quoted by Mason, *op. cit.,* pp. 25–26.

[48] See Netherlands, *Handelingen Tweede Kamer* (October 30, 1951), p. 170. Cited in Mason, *op. cit.,* p. 17. See also Germany, Federal Republic, Bundestag, *Sitzungsbericht* (January 10, 1952), p. 7732.

[49] France, Ministry of Foreign Affairs, *Rapport de la Délégation Française sur le Traité Instituant la CECA* (October, 1951). Cited by Valentine, *op. cit.,* p. 2.

[50] Luxembourg, *Compte Rendu, Session Ordinaire* (1951–52), p. 127. Cited by Valentine, *op. cit.,* p. 2.

in its jurisdiction.[51] Among the speeches given at the opening session of the first Court was this short statement by Jean Monnet: "The formation of the Court marks the supreme authority of law in the Community. . . . For the first time there has been created a sovereign European Court. I foresee in it also the prospect of a supreme federal European Court."[52] The following sections attempt to show the extent to which Monnet's foresight has materialized.

B. CONSTITUTIONAL BASIS

One description of the legal basis of the European communities labels it a "quadrilingual labyrinth."[53] Although perhaps a trifle overstated, this assessment does nevertheless highlight the complexity of the legal documents creating the communities. Three separate treaties form the basis of the communities, each one a formidable document—or rather collection of documents. The treaty establishing the Coal and Steel Community is relatively succinct, consisting of only 100 articles, 3 annexes, 4 protocols, and 1 convention.[54] The only official language is French.

The treaty establishing the European Economic Community consists of 248 articles, 4 annexes, 13 protocols, and 1 convention. The Euratom Treaty, drafted at the same time, has 225 articles, 5 annexes, and 2 protocols.[55] Added to all three of these treaties was an

---

[51] Europäische Gemeinschaft, Presse- und Informationsdienst, *Gerichtshof der Europäischen Gemeinschaften: Seine Aufgaben, seine Verfassung, sein Verfahren* (Bonn: Presse- und Informationsdienst der Europäischen Gemeinschaften, 1966), p. 4.

[52] *Chronique du Politique Étrangère* (January, 1953). Quoted in Valentine, *op. cit.*, p. 4.

[53] Eric Stein and Thomas L. Nicholson (eds.), *American Enterprise in the European Common Market: A Legal Profile* (Ann Arbor: University of Michigan Law School, 1960), p. 15.

[54] "Treaty Between the Federal Republic of Germany, the Kingdom of Belgium, the French Republic, the Italian Republic, the Grand Duchy of Luxembourg and the Kingdom of the Netherlands Instituting the European Coal and Steel Community," Signed at Paris on 18 April 1951, *United Nations Treaty Series*, CCLXI, 3229 (1957), 140–319 (hereinafter cited as *ECSC Treaty*).

[55] "Treaty Establishing the European Economic Community (with Annexes and Protocols)," Done at Rome on 25 March 1957, *United Nations Treaty Series*, CCXCVIII, 4300 (1958), 1–165, and "Treaty (with Annexes and Protocol) Establishing the European Atomic Energy Community (EURATOM)," Done at Rome on 25 March 1957, *United Nations Treaty Series*, CCXCVIII, 4301 (1958), 167–266 (hereinafter cited as *EEC Treaty* and *Euratom Treaty*). The English texts are not official and there seems to be great variance between the English text filed with the U.N. (by the Italian government) and certain translations used, for example, by the British. Some variance may occur within this chapter where quotes from English authors appear; however, the U.N. versions are used whenever possible. The official French, German, Italian, and Dutch texts appear respectively in *United Nations Treaty Series*, Vols. CCXCIV, CCXCV, CCXCVI, and CCXCVII.

additional convention merging the institutions of the communities.[56] For the latter two treaties and the final convention, all four Community languages (German, French, Dutch, and Italian) are official and legally equal.

There are varying views of this multilingual complex of overlapping treaties. Professor Daniel Villey of the Paris Law Faculty says, with particular reference to the EEC Treaty, that it is "interminable, complex, impossible to disentangle."[57] On the other hand, Professor Paul Reuter of the same Faculty, while admitting that the treaties are complex and have their faults, finds that they are basically "terse and clear."[58] While neither view seems completely validated, the treaties do clearly represent a major engineering effort designed to establish the constitutional foundations for three highly specialized international communities. Fortunately, the task at hand does not require a study of the more technical parts of the treaties. Rather, the concern is with those sections establishing the substance and procedures of the Court.[59] (Articles of the treaties cited in this chapter are reprinted in Appendix F.)

Composition of the Court

The Court of Justice is composed of seven judges.[60] There are no nationality requirements. Judges are simply "appointed for a term of six years by the Governments of Member States acting in common agreement."[61] The only qualification is that judges "be chosen from among persons of indisputable independence who fulfil the conditions required for the holding of the highest judicial office in their respective countries or who are jurists of a recognised competence."[62] The treaties further specify that the

---

[56] "Convention Relating to Certain Institutions Common to the European Communities," Done at Rome on 25 March 1957, *United Nations Treaty Series,* CCXCVIII, 4302 (1958), 267–274 (hereinafter cited as *Community Convention*).

[57] Daniel Villey, "Les Communautés Européennes et Leur Incidence sur la Profession d'Avocat," *Le Droit Européen,* XLIX, 2 (August–September, 1958), 52. Translated by Eric Stein and quoted in Stein and Nicholson, *op. cit.,* pp. 15–16.

[58] Paul Reuter, "Aspects de la Communauté Economique Européenne," *Revue du Marché Commun,* VI, 1 (March, 1958), 8.

[59] *ECSC Treaty,* Articles 31–45, with attached Protocol on the Code of the Court; *EEC Treaty,* Articles 164–188; *Euratom Treaty,* Articles 136–160; *Community Convention,* Articles 3–4. For further discussion of the constitutional bases of the communities see Peter Hay, *Federalism and Supranational Organizations: Patterns for New Legal Structures* (Urbana: University of Illinois Press, 1966).

[60] *ECSC Treaty,* Article 32; *EEC Treaty,* Article 164; and *Euratom Treaty,* Article 137.

[61] *ECSC Treaty,* Article 32; *EEC Treaty,* Article 167; and *Euratom Treaty,* Article 139.

[62] *Ibid.*

Court will be assisted by two advocates-general, who must fulfill the same qualifications as judges.[63] According to the treaties, "the duty of the advocate-general shall be to present publicly, with complete impartiality and independence, reasoned conclusions on cases submitted to the Court of Justice, with a view to assisting the latter in the performance of its duties. . . ."[64]

The selection system for judges is similar to the method used by the Central American Court of Justice, whereby judges were directly selected by the member states. Judges serve for a relatively short (although renewable) term of six years—a potential threat to judicial independence.[65]

There are two safeguards however. First, the Court's deliberations are secret, with only one opinion being rendered.[66] This at least gives the judges protection in anonymity. Second, the treaties provide the usual safeguards regarding conflict of interest (judges may not hold other offices, etc.). In addition to these, two other elements of judicial independence and impartiality appear. The treaties provide that "before entering upon his duties each judge shall in open court take an oath to perform his duties impartially and conscientiously and to preserve the secrecy of the Court's deliberations."[67] A unique provision, and a decided supranational advance over previous tribunals, is that "a party may not invoke the nationality of a judge, or the absence from the bench . . . of a judge of its own nationality, in order to ask for a change in the composition of the Court."[68] Unfortunately, the admirable daring of this latter provision is somewhat weakened by the fact that all six members are represented on the Court in any event.

Access to the Court and Jurisdiction

The Court of the European Communities may be invoked by a very wide variety of entities. Not only is it possible to cir-

---

[63] *Ibid.*

[64] *ECSC Treaty*, Article 32 (a) (as amended by *Community Convention*); *EEC Treaty*, Article 166; and *Euratom Treaty*, Article 138.

[65] *ECSC Treaty*, Article 32; *EEC Treaty*, Article 167; and *Euratom Treaty*, Article 139.

[66] See "Protocol on the Code of the Court of Justice," Signed at Paris on 18 April 1951, *United Nations Treaty Series*, CCLXI, 3729 (1957), 247–267, Articles 29 and 30; "Protocol and the Statute of Justice of the European Economic Community," Done at Brussels on 17 April 1957, *United Nations Treaty Series*, CCXCVIII, 4300 (1958), 147–156, Articles 32, 33, and 34; and "Protocol on the Statute of the Court of Justice of the European Atomic Energy Community," Done at Brussels on 17 April 1957, *United Nations Treaty Series*, CCXCVIII, 4301 (1958), 256–266, Articles 33, 34, and 35.

[67] See *ibid.*, respectively Articles 2, 2, and 2.

[68] *Ibid.*, respectively Articles 19, 16, and 16.

cumvent the nation-state in international legal proceedings, but various other entities have been given unprecedented legal standing vis-à-vis the nation-states before the Court. In one form or another, the following entities have access to this international court:

1. States: the six members of the Community
2. International organs:
   > the High Authority (ECSC)
   > the commissions (EEC and Euratom)
   > the Councils of Ministers
   > the Assembly
3. Private enterprises and associations
4. Individuals

The means through which these entities have access depends entirely upon the various forms of the Court's jurisdiction, which is as complex as the treaties themselves. The provisions granting jurisdiction to the Court are scattered throughout the myriad of documents that form the legal foundation of the communities. Although scholars disagree as to the nature and types of the Court's jurisdiction, Professor Valentine (whose effort seems the most comprehensive and analytical) finds six distinctive types:[69]

1. *International jurisdiction.* Under this category member states may appear as parties against each other. By the terms of Article 89 (1) of the ECSC Treaty: "Any dispute among member States concerning the application of the present Treaty, which cannot be settled by another procedure provided for in the present Treaty, may be submitted to the Court *at the request of one of the States parties to the dispute*" (italics mine).[70] It should be noted that the closing phrase, with simple dispatch, disposes with "compulsory jurisdiction," "acceptance declarations," and "Connally Amendments." Article 89 (2) of the ECSC Treaty also gives the Court "jurisdiction to settle any dispute among member states related to the purpose of the present Treaty, if such dispute is submitted to it by virtue of an agreement to arbitrate."[71]

---

[69] See Valentine, *op. cit.*, pp. 9–15. Cf. Werner Feld, *The Court of the European Communities: New Dimension in International Adjudication* (The Hague: Martinus Nijhoff, 1964), Chap. 3. He sees the Court as an international, constitutional, administrative, civil, and miscellaneous tribunal. Gerhard Bebr, *Judicial Control of the European Communities* (New York: Frederick A. Praeger, 1962), pp. 21–23, makes a similar distinction, but adds disciplinary jurisdiction. Uwe W. Kitzinger, *The Challenge of the Common Market* (Oxford: Basil Blackwell, 1962), p. 69, makes only a threefold distinction among international, constitutional, and administrative.

[70] Similar provisions in the other treaties are *EEC Treaty*, Article 170 (1), and *Euratom Treaty*, Article 142 (1).

[71] See also *EEC Treaty*, Article 182, and *Euratom Treaty*, Article 154 (a).

2. Jurisdiction over the legal validity of Community executive action.[72] Actions may be brought by a) organs of the communities, b) member states, and c) enterprises, associations of enterprises, other legal persons, and individuals.

As an example of the first category, the Council of Ministers could seek "annulment of decisions and recommendations of the High Authority on the grounds of lack of legal competence, substantial procedural violations, violation of the Treaty or of any rule of law relating to its application, or abuse of power" (*détournement de pouvoir*).[73]

Member states may appeal not only against administrative acts of the High Authority (or the two commissions) as outlined in the preceding paragraph, but "on the petition of a member State or of the High Authority, the Court may annul the acts of the Assembly or of the Council."[74]

Finally, enterprises and associations "have the right of appeal on the same grounds against individual decisions and recommendations concerning them, or against general decisions and recommendations which they deem to involve an abuse of power affecting them."[75] Also, "any natural or legal person may, under the same conditions, appeal against a decision addressed to him or against a decision which, although in the form of a regulation or a decision addressed to another person, is of direct and specific concern to him."[76]

3. Jurisdiction arising from enforcement of the treaties. The High Authority and the two commissions are the primary enforcement instruments under the treaties. Any of the legal persons listed above can appeal enforcement decisions (within a time limit) of these agencies.[77]

---

[72] The executive organs include the High Authority, the two commissions, the three (overlapping) Councils of Ministers, the European Investment Bank, and, to a limited extent, the Common Assembly. (The July 1, 1967, treaty merged the first three organs into the single 14-member Commission and created a single Council of Ministers.) The legal validity (but not economic or political desirability) of their executive acts (including regulations, directives, decisions, and recommendations) may be challenged.

[73] *ECSC Treaty*, Articles 33 (1), 35 (1), and 38 (1); *EEC Treaty*, Articles 173 (1), 175 (1), and 180 (b) and (c); *Euratom Treaty*, Articles 146 and 148.

[74] *ECSC Treaty*, Articles 38 (1) and 35 (1); *EEC Treaty*, Article 173 (1); *Euratom Treaty*, Article 146 (1).

[75] *ECSC Treaty*, Articles 33 (2), 35 (1), and 48 (3); *EEC Treaty*, Article 173 (2); *Euratom Treaty*, Article 146 (2).

[76] *Ibid.*

[77] See *ECSC Treaty*, Articles 36 (2) and 88 (1–4); *EEC Treaty*, Articles 93 (2), 169 (2), and 173 (2); and *Euratom Treaty*, Articles 21 (3), 38 (3), 82 (4), 141 (2), 145 (2), and 146 (2).

4. Sole jurisdiction over Community matters before certain municipal courts. Article 41 of the ECSC Treaty, for example, provides: "When the validity of acts of the High Authority or the Council is contested in litigation before a national tribunal, such issue shall be certified to the Court, which shall have exclusive jurisdiction to rule thereon."[78]

In addition to the foregoing categories of jurisdiction, the Court is able to (5) render advisory opinions in connection with the treaties,[79] and possesses (6) limited appellate jurisdiction (only under the Euratom Arbitration Committee).[80]

Overshadowing these six types of jurisdiction, of course, is the general limitation of the Court's (and Community's) jurisdiction to the technical and legal aspects of three highly detailed treaties, which, although clearly possessing political overtones, are themselves limited to carefully delimited economic spheres of activity.

Because of the uniqueness of the European Community experiment and the highly technical nature of its basis, it is somewhat difficult to draw strict parallels between the Court of the European Communities and earlier international courts. The Court is practically *sui generis*. Professor Bebr writes in this context: "Since the Communities are not traditional international organizations, the Court may not be compared with an international tribunal. It is a unique court which has very little in common with the International Court of Justice, if anything at all."[81]

The communities, of course, were not designed to be traditional. They were designed to fulfill the supranational expectations of their founders—expectations which never materialized with the universal international organizations. The European communities fulfill all the requirements of the "traditional international organizations" and add some contributions of their own. The communities are the result of multilateral international treaties drawn up by sovereign nation-states. The treaties form the constitutional basis of the Court and define its jurisdiction.

Comparison with other "international" tribunals is difficult because much of the Court's activities deal with administrative and constitutional matters—but comparison is not impossible. The Court is clearly an "international" tribunal—both in basis and in

---

[78] Similar provisions in the other treaties are *EEC Treaty*, Article 177 (1/b), and *Euratom Treaty*, Article 150 (1/b).

[79] *ECSC Treaty*, Articles 2, 3, 4, and 95 (4) ; *EEC Treaty*, Article 228 (1 and 2) ; *Euratom Treaty*, Article 103 (3).

[80] *Euratom Treaty*, Article 18 (2).

[81] Bebr, *op. cit.*, pp. 21–22.

subject matter. It is simply a "traditional international" court presenting a "new dimension in international adjudication."[82] Even administrative acts and constitutional interpretation are done across international boundaries. A look at Court practice should clarify the nature of this "new dimension."

Judgments

Judgments and orders of the Court are final and have the force of law throughout the Community. There are, however, two aspects of enforcing these judgments: (1) against member states and (2) against other legal entities.

There is no enforcement machinery against the states themselves. The members of the Six simply bind themselves to

take all general or particular measures which are appropriate for ensuring the carrying out of the obligations arising out of this Treaty or resulting from the acts of the institutions of the Community. They shall facilitate the achievement of the Community's aims.

They shall abstain from any measures likely to jeopardise the attainment of the objectives of this Treaty.[83]

In a proper legal system the member states could not be the final judge of their own obligations under the law of the Community, and such is indeed the case. The Court of the European Communities is exclusively competent to pass judgment on alleged violations of obligations by member states. In the case of the ECSC, the High Authority simply demands compliance,[84] and the member states may appeal this demand to the Court.[85] In EEC and Euratom disputes must first go to the commissions, who send "reasoned opinions" to the states.[86] If the states fail to comply within three months, the commission refers the matter to the Court.[87] Article 171 of the EEC Treaty, for example, provides: "If the Court of Justice finds that a Member State has failed to fulfil any of its obligations under this Treaty, such State shall take the measures required for the implementation of the judgment of the Court."[88] Article 172 of the same Treaty further provides: "The regulations laid down by the Council pursuant to the provisions of this Treaty may confer on the

---

[82] From the title of the work by Feld, *op. cit.*

[83] *EEC Treaty*, Article 5. Similar provisions in the other treaties are *ECSC Treaty*, Article 5, and *Euratom Treaty*, Articles 2 and 3.

[84] *ECSC Treaty*, Article 14.

[85] *Ibid.*, Article 33 (1).

[86] *EEC Treaty*, Article 170 (1), (2), and (3); *Euratom Treaty*, Article 142 (1), (2), and (3).

[87] *Ibid.*, Articles 170 (4) and 142 (4) respectively.

[88] Cf. *Euratom Treaty*, Article 143.

Court of Justice full jurisdiction in respect of penalties provided for in such regulations."[89]

If the Court finds that a member state has failed to carry out its obligation, enforcement rests ultimately upon that state. Michel Gaudet, Director-General of the Legal Service of the European Executives, finds this a weighty responsibility:

> In reality, failing to comply with a decision of the Court stating its obligations under the Treaty is highly improbable on the part of a Member State. A failure would mean that the Member State is questioning the *affectio societatis* without which the Community cannot live, and would therefore raise a basic political problem. When drafting the Rome Treaties, the Member States have considered that such a situation should be handled between them on a political and not on a legal basis.[90]

The second aspect of the enforcement of Court decisions, namely against other legal entities (enterprises and individuals), does not raise the same problems. The decisions of the executive organs are *directly* binding on enterprises and individuals. Failure to comply can result in the issue being taken before the Court, which can order compliance and impose penalties directly on such entities. The Court's decisions are "enforced on the territory of member States through the legal procedures in effect in each of these States," and this will be accomplished "with no other formality than the certification of the authenticity of such decisions."[91]

Both on the basis of the expectations of the drafters and the actual provisions of the three treaties, the Court of the European Communities represents a strong supranational advance over the so-called "traditional" international courts.[92] The practice of the Court shows the extent to which this is true.

C. PRACTICE OF THE COURT
Jurisdiction

WORK OF THE COURT   The most striking feature about the work of the Court of the European Communities is that it has been a very busy court. The tradition in international tribunals has

---

[89] *Ibid.*

[90] Michel Gaudet, "The Legal Framework of the Community," *International and Comparative Law Quarterly*, Supplementary Publication No. 1 (1961), p. 17.

[91] *ECSC Treaty*, Articles 44 and 92; *EEC Treaty*, Articles 187 and 192; *Euratom Treaty*, Articles 159 and 164.

[92] The most strongly supranational of the Community institutions is, however, the High Authority (see *ECSC Treaty*, Chap. I), and to a lesser extent the commissions as well (*EEC Treaty*, Articles 155–163, and *Euratom Treaty*, Articles 124–135). All have rather broad discretionary decision-making powers, many with important political overtones.

been for nations to avoid not only acceding to compulsory jurisdiction, but to avoid using the court under most circumstances. Table 9, although it does not include the many advisory opinions, orders, and requests for interpretation, does nevertheless convey some idea of the volume of business.[93]

In roughly a 15-year period, the European Court has already handled seven times the volume of contentious cases the International Court of Justice had in nearly a 25-year period. Also, the average number of decisions per year has been roughly 15, compared with 1.4 for the ICJ. Also encouraging is the fact that the number of

Table 9 Work of the Court of the European Communities[a]

Year	Judgments Rendered in Contentious Cases
1954	2
1955	5
1956	7
1957	3
1958	10
1959	13
1960	19
1961	11
1962	19
1963	15
1964	24
1965	46
1966	21
1967 (to November 30)	10
Total	205

[a] Data derived from Appendix G.

cases has generally increased since the establishment of the Court.[94]

NATURE OF COMMUNITY LAW   Closely related to the question of jurisdiction is the nature or type of law the Court may or may not apply (and has or has not applied). The Court is given the power under all three treaties to "ensure the rule of law in the interpretation and application of the present Treaty and of its implementing regulations."[95] Two questions are immediately raised by

[93] For a more complete description of the nature of the cases see Appendix G.
[94] Particularly since 1958, when the court for the Coal and Steel Community became the court for all three European communities.
[95] *ECSC Treaty*, Article 31; *EEC Treaty*, Article 164; *Euratom Treaty*, Article 134.

this phrase: (1) what is meant by "ensure the rule of law?" and (2) what law?

In the context of the first question, J. F. McMahon of Oxford notes that "judicial interpretation of the charter of an international organization is the exception rather than the rule."[96] Neither the Covenant of the League nor the Charter of the United Nations contains any provisions for the authoritative interpretation of the document itself.[97] In fact, the implication with the Charter seems to be that each organ will work out informally its own interpretation. The Committee report (IV/2) at San Francisco read:

> In the course of the operations from day to day of the various organs of the Organization, it is inevitable that each organ will interpret such parts of the Charter as are applicable to its particular functions. This process is inherent in the functioning of any body which operates under an instrument defining its functions and powers. . . . Accordingly, it is not necessary to include in the Charter a provision either authorizing or approving the normal operation of this principle.[98]

The Community treaties say nothing beyond the fact that the Court "shall ensure the rule of law." Professor Valentine, after studying the treaties, admits that the Court's function as set forth in this phrase is simply "not clear." There is no indication whether the phrase means

> that the Court is to be guided by the general principles of international law, and is to subordinate the interpretation and application of the Treaty to these principles; or whether the phrase has a more restricted sense and merely implies that in the interpretation of the Treaty, the Court is to be bound by recognized rules of interpretation and that the application of the Treaty shall be subordinate to the law as set out in the Treaty thus interpreted.[99]

The preceding remarks also touch upon the second question of what law the Court may apply. In this case, the International Court of Justice (and formerly the Permanent Court of International Justice) is able to rely on the comparatively precise text of Article

---

[96] J. F. McMahon, "The Court of the European Communities: Judicial Interpretation and International Organization," *British Yearbook of International Law*, XXXVII (1961), 320.

[97] Although under Article 96 (1) of the Charter either the General Assembly or the Security Council may request the International Court of Justice to render an advisory opinion "on any legal question." The Court has built up considerable jurisprudence in this area. See, for example, footnote 21 in Chapter 1 of this study.

[98] "Report of Rapporteur of Committee IV/2," *U.N.C.I.O.*, Vol. XIII, Doc. 933, IV/2/42 (2), pp. 7–8.

[99] D. G. Valentine, *The Court of Justice of the European Coal and Steel Community* (The Hague: Martinus Nijhoff, 1955), p. 56.

38 of the Statute. There is nothing, however, which indicates the sources of law the European Court is supposed to apply when interpreting the treaties. Professor Reuter suggests that it was intended to allow the Court room for experimentation. Rather than attempting to define carefully the sources of Community law, he feels the drafters of the treaties wished to "allow the law of the Community to draw freely from whatever sources it needed."[100]

It is possible to isolate at least eight different sources of Community law in practice.[101]

1. The three treaties (and related protocols, conventions, etc.), of course, form the constitutional basis of the communities.

2. The executive decisions issued by the Councils of Ministers, the two commissions, and the High Authority.

3. The Court's own jurisprudence.

4. Municipal laws and municipal decisions.[102] The relation of Community law to municipal law has received a great deal of attention within the communities. The European Parliament, for example, has debated the question at length. The most extensive consideration came on June 16, 17, and 18, 1965, when the European Parliament debated the Legal Committee's report drafted by Mr. Dehousse on the supremacy of Community law over the national law of the member states.[103]

The Dehousse report endeavored

to demonstrate that the provisions of the Treaties and, hence, their direct application to various subdivisions of law, are a direct adjunct of domestic law. This means that existing provisions become void where they clash with the provisions of the Treaty and that Member States are bound to take the necessary steps to implement the Treaties without there being any need for the national Parliaments to intervene.

---

[100] Paul Reuter, *La Communauté Européenne du Charbon et de l'Acier* (Paris: Librairie Générale de Droit et de Jurisprudence, 1953), p. 89 (my translation).

[101] Adapted from sources suggested by McMahon, *op. cit.*, pp. 327–328.

[102] Especially of the French Conseil d'État, the administrative tribunal which apparently served as the model for the drafters of the Community Court. The Conseil d'État is rather highly regarded and is frequently referred to, both by politicians and academicians. An interesting discussion of "dualism" and "monism" as viewed by the Six is provided by the Vice-President of the District Court of Rotterdam and Editor-in-Chief of the *Netherlands International Law Review,* L. Erades, in "International Law, European Community Law and Municipal Law of Member States," *International and Comparative Law Quarterly,* XV, Part 1, 4th Series (January, 1966), 117–132.

[103] European Parliament, General Directorate of Parliamentary Documentation and Information, *Monthly Bulletin of European Documentation,* VII, 7 (July, 1965), 69–82.

Endowing the Communities with legislative powers implies a transfer of powers from national constitutional bodies to the Community institutions and consequently subordinating national legal systems.

This is why the terms of the Treaties[104] . . . as well as the implementing regulations cannot be repealed by subsequent national laws. In the event of any clash between national and Community regulations, the national judge is explicitly empowered to sanction the supremacy of Community law in that he can always refer the matter to the Court of Justice of the European Communities for a preliminary ruling.[105]

On October 22, 1965, the *Rapporteur,* summing up the report and the debate, indicated "the paramountcy of Community law was a legal principle" that had to be recognized. "This was," he said, "the political aim of the European Parliament for it was the only way in which the Community could be given any substance."[106] A resolution giving effect to the report was passed overwhelmingly by a show of hands.[107]

This resolution could not be regarded as other than a supranational challenge leveled at the six nation-states by their own legal creation. On the other hand, experience teaches that "resolutions" by international organs frequently carry little or no weight. Yet the practice of the Court itself indicates that there may be "real teeth" in the high principles of the supremacy of Community law.

The Court of the European Communities, in a rather significant supranational action, recently upheld a Community norm even though the highest constitutional court of a member state specifically favored the primacy of a national law. This occurred in a preliminary decision delivered in 1964 in the case of *M. Flaminio Costa*

---

[104] See *ECSC Treaty,* Article 86; *EEC Treaty,* Article 5; *Euratom Treaty,* Article 192.

[105] European Parliament, General Directorate of Parliamentary Documentation and Information, *op. cit.,* p. 70. For preliminary rulings see *ECSC Treaty,* Article 41; *EEC Treaty,* Article 177; and *Euratom Treaty,* Article 150, which provide: "The Court of Justice shall be competent to make a preliminary decision concerning: a) the interpretation of this Treaty; b) the validity and interpretation of acts of the institutions of the Community; and c) the interpretation of the statutes of any bodies set up by an act of the Council, where such statutes so provide."

[106] European Parliament, General Directorate of Parliamentary Documentation and Information, *Monthly Bulletin of European Documentation,* VII, 11 (November, 1965), p. 59. The Legal Committee had previously indicated it "was not seeking to bring pressure to bear on national courts but to draw attention to the existence of Community law, which all the States undertook to respect, and to provide national authorities with the information that would ensure the balanced development of the Communities." *Ibid.,* p. 69.

[107] *Ibid.,* p. 60.

v. *E.N.E.L.*[108] Briefly, this case involved a showdown between the Court and the Italian Constitutional Court. A resident of Milan had refused to pay his electric bill of slightly more than three dollars, claiming that the nationalization of the electric utilities by the Italian government contravened certain articles of the EEC Treaty.[109] The matter was referred by the Italian trial court to *both* the Community Court and the Italian Constitutional Court.

The Italian court upheld the validity of the nationalization, but it based its decision only upon the constitutional question of whether a subsequent Italian law could modify a prior international treaty imposing certain limitations on Italy's sovereignty. The Constitutional Court completely ignored the alleged Treaty violations or the legal nature of the Treaty in upholding the Italian law, although it did acknowledge that the Italian Constitution provided for such limitations of sovereignty.[110]

The landmark decision of the Court of the European Communities vigorously upheld the primacy of Community law. It stated:

> Contrary to other international treaties, the Treaty instituting the EEC has created its own legal order which was integrated with the national order of the member states the moment the Treaty came into force and which the domestic courts have to take into account; as such it is binding upon them. In fact, by creating a Community of unlimited duration, having its own institutions, its own personality and its own capacity in law, the right of international representation, and more particularly, real powers resulting from a limitation of competence or a transfer of duties from the States to the Community, the member states, albeit within limited spheres, have restricted their sovereign rights and created a body of law applicable both to their nationals and to themselves.
>
> The integration, with the laws of each member state, of provisions

---

[108] Cases are cited in two ways: X *Rec* 1141 [*Recueil de la Jurisprudence de la Cour*] or by their folio number (e.g., 6–64), which gives the case's number in the General List and the year of registration. The former method is used here (Appendix G shows both references). The Court reports are available only in the official languages of the Community. The French version is used here throughout, although occasional variations may occur when authors cited in the text have relied on other versions. However, the case citation, which will always be given, can be compared with Appendix G for the French version, should confusion about the case arise. Two similar cases are the *Bosch* decision, VIII *Rec* 89 (April 6, 1962), and the *Van Gend & Loos* decision, IX *Rec* 1 (February 5, 1963).

[109] Articles 37, 53, 93, and 102 were allegedly violated. These articles deal with the obligations of member states in connection with enactments of laws likely to distort the Common Market, state aids, restrictions on the right of establishment, and state monopolies.

[110] See Republic of Italy, *Constitution*, Article XI. For a partial text of the judgment see *Common Market Law Review*, II, 2 (September, 1964), 224–225. An analysis of this decision is offered by Nicola Catalano, former Justice of the Court of the European Communities, in *ibid.*, pp. 225–235.

having a Community source . . . have as their corollary the impossibility for the member states to give precedence to a unilateral and subsequent measure which is inconsistent with . . . a legal order accepted by them upon a basis of reciprocity. . . . The rights created by the Treaty by virtue of their specific original nature, cannot be judicially contradicted by an internal law . . . without undermining the legal basis of the Community. . . . A subsequent unilateral law, incompatible with the concept of the Community, cannot prevail.[111]

5. Textbook writers. The writings of various scholars seem to be frequently relied upon, especially by the advocates-general. One of the more frequently cited "authorities" has been Paul Reuter. In *Friedrich Stork et Cie., Kohlengroßhandlung* v. *Haute Autorité,* for example, Maurice Lagrange concluded in the advocate-general's presentation that the High Authority could not exercise its power in the subject matter of the case. "Such is the thesis at least upon the first point," he said, "of Paul Reuter on page 285 of his work. . . ."[112]

6. International law. The general body of traditional international law is rarely cited in the jurisprudence of the Court. The conclusions of Maurice Lagrange are illustrative in this respect:

One is able to recall without doubt that our Court does not have an international jurisdiction, but rather the jurisdiction of a Community created by six States along lines which resemble more a federal organization than an international organization, and that the Treaty, of which the Court has the mission of insuring its application, even if it has been concluded in the form of international treaties, and even if it is incontestably an international treaty, it constitutes none the less, from a material point of view, the Charter of the Community, of which the derived rules of law constitute the *internal law of this Community*. As for the *sources* of this law, clearly nothing prevents one, depending upon the case, from searching for them in international law, but normally and more often one will find them sooner in the internal law of the several Member States [italics in original].[113]

7. Laws of other municipal systems. Laws of countries outside the Six are seldom, if ever, cited. McMahon finds only two instances in nearly ten years of the Court's jurisprudence. English law was cited once in *Hamborner Bergbau AG et Friedrich Thyssen Bergbau AG* v. *Haute Autorité,*[114] and American law once in *Barbara Erzbergbau AG et Autres* v. *Haute Autorité.*[115]

---

[111] *M. Flaminio Costa* v. *E.N.E.L.*, X *Rec* 1143, 1158–60 (July 15, 1964) .

[112] *Friedrich Stork et Cie., Kohlengroßhandlung* v. *Haute Autorité,* V *Rec* 83 (February 4, 1959) (my translation) .

[113] *Fédération Charbonnière de Belgique* v. *Haute Autorité.* Conclusions de M. Lagrange. II *Rec* 263 (July 16, 1956) (my translation) .

[114] VI *Rec* 1049 (December 16, 1960) .

[115] VI *Rec* 386 (May 10, 1960) . See also McMahon, *op. cit.,* p. 328.

8. *Travaux préparatoires* and ratification debates. The Court has had to face the problem recognized earlier in this chapter, namely, the unavailability of the *travaux préparatoires*. Maurice Lagrange has noted in this connection, "en ce qui concerne le Traité du 18 avril 1951, les travaux préparatoires du Traité lui-même sont pratiquement inexistants . . . ou secrets (ce qui revient au même)."[116] But, Lagrange continues, *travaux préparatoires* do play a limited role interpreting the proper function of the Court, in the guise of the ratification debates.[117]

SOVEREIGNTY AND SUPRANATIONALISM   From the foregoing remarks it is clear that Community jurisprudence is quite "inner-directed" in the sense that it relies little on legal sources outside the Community (i.e., international law or laws of other municipal systems). That the Court has been expansive within the Community itself, however, will become clear during the course of this chapter. Yet on the other hand, there does not seem to be any "John Marshall" on the Court, and the Court's attitude toward adopting such a role appears to be quite ambivalent. For example, Maurice Lagrange believes that state sovereignty is something the Court had best leave untouched except where the treaties expressly provide for Court action. He expresses this passive view in the following words:

The Treaty rests upon a delegation of sovereignty to supranational institutions, consented to by Member States *for a very specific end,* to realize the functioning of a common market of coal and steel. The juridical principle which is at the base of the Treaty is a principle of *limited competence.* The Community is a moral person of public law, and under this heading it enjoys the juridical capacity *necessary for carrying out its functions and attaining its goals* (Article 6), *but for that purpose and only that purpose* [italics in original].[118]

Yet in another case, the other advocate-general, Karl Roemer, has taken the opposite position in arguing for a more active role for the Court. He says: "The Treaty has gone particularly far in the juridical codification of economic facts. . . . The result is that, in the application and interpretation of the Treaty, it would be dangerous to follow only the letter of its text. In order to discover the economic objectives assigned to this or that particular arrangement, it is necessary to go back to the objectives and fundamental principles of the Treaty."[119]

---

[116] *Fédération Charbonnière de Belgique* v. *Haute Autorité.*
[117] *Ibid.*
[118] *Algera et Autres* v. *Assemblée Commune.* Conclusions de M. Lagrange. III *Rec* 159 (July 12, 1957) (my translation).
[119] *Gouvernement du Royaume des Pays-Bas* v. *Haute Autorité.* Conclusions de

A further look at the practice of the Court may help bring into better focus the actual role the Court seems to have assumed.

Parties and Disposition

The Court of the European Communities has not only equaled the Central American Court of Justice in terms of the variety of parties other than nation-states that could appear before it, but has surpassed it. This is most noticeable of course in the practice of the Court, which proves the effectiveness of those articles guaranteeing access to such other legal persons as individuals and enterprises. Table 10 provides some idea of the extent to which nation-states have shared this international tribunal with "lesser" entities (Appendix G provides the same information in greater detail).

The data in Table 10 shows first that the Court has heard a broad sampling of those parties eligible to appear before it. Second, the majority of cases have involved private enterprises appealing decisions of the Community organs (mostly against the High Authority) and private individuals (all civil servants of the communities) appealing against Community personnel practices. It is for this reason that some scholars claim the Court is more of a *conseil d'état* rather than an international tribunal.[120] Table 10 clearly shows, however, that the Court deals with international disputes (many of them quite unique for an international court), and the fact that many of these disputes are of an administrative nature does not change the basic nature of the Court. Finally, Table 10 makes clear that the nation-states have successfully been challenged. They have been "hauled into court" by international organs and have even lost a substantial number of such cases.

One of the most significant cases in this area, however, is the unprecedented case of an individual taking his own country to court and winning[121] (Table 10, Category IV). The fact that an individual has legal appeal beyond his state, and the fact that he can actually win, demonstrates that the Court is supranational in fact as well as theory.

This particular case involved a Belgian national, Jean-E. Humblet (who was also an ECSC official), and an income tax dispute with his government. Community rules provide that Community civil servants are exempted from national taxes on salaries paid to

---

M. Roemer. I *Rec* 233 (March 21, 1955) (my translation). It is an interesting coincidence that the views of Lagrange and Roemer correspond to the positions of their respective countries of France and Germany vis-à-vis supranationalism.

[120] *Supra,* footnote 81.

[121] *Jean-E. Humblet* v. *État Belge,* VI *Rec* 1125 (December 16, 1960).

them by the three communities.[122] In this case the wife of Jean-E. Humblet had a separate, taxable income in Belgium. Belgian internal revenue authorities demanded Humblet declare his income from the Community so they could determine the combined income of husband and wife for the purpose of assessing the wife's tax. Although faced with the unusual case of an individual suing his own government, the Court declared itself competent to hear the case:

it is perfectly acceptable for an individual of the Community to present himself before the Court as a plaintiff against the Government of his native country just as enterprises have already challenged before the Court arguments presented by the Government of their country when intervening on the side of the High Authority.

Furthermore, as has already been stated above, the privileges granted by the Protocol confer rights upon the person concerned. . . . It is natural to suppose that an actual right has as corollary the ability of the beneficiary

Table 10   Parties Before the Court of the European Communities[a]

Parties	Winner		
I. *Enterprise* v. *Intl. Organ* 104[b]	*Enterprise* 16	*Intl. Org.* 79[b]	*Unclear* 9
II. *State* v. *Internatl. Organ* 21[c]	*State* 5	*Intl. Org.* 16[c]	
III. *Individual* v. *Intl. Organ* 78[d]	*Individual* 24	*Intl. Org.* 51	*Unclear* 3
IV. *Individual* v. *State* 1	*Individual* 1	*State* 0	
V. *Enterprise* v. *State* 1[c]	*Enterprise* 1	*State* 0	
VI. *Enterprise* v. *Enterprise* 2[b]			
VII. *Intl. Org.* v. *Intl. Org.* 1[d]			

a Data taken from Appendix G, which includes only parties to contentious cases wherein a decision was rendered. Intergovernmental disputes (i.e., *State* v. *State*) do not appear in this table because they have gone before the Court as requests for advisory opinions or interpretation, or have fallen under the category *State* v. *International Organ*. This latter situation results from an interstate dispute over a decision by an international organ.

b Indicates an instance where a case has been cited twice, once in each of two categories. This occurs when there are three parties to a dispute. See Appendix G, Case 42/49–59.

c *Ibid.*, Case 9/12–60.

d *Ibid.*, Case 70–63.

122 See *Euratom Treaty,* Article 192, and "Protocol on the Privileges and Immunities of the EEC," Article 12, reprinted in Alan Campbell and Dennis Thompson, *Common Market Law: Text and Commentaries* (London: Stevens & Sons Ltd., 1962) , pp. 357–372.

himself to avail himself of it by a law-suit rather than by the use of a third person as intermediary.[123]

Although the Court could not invalidate an administrative act of a member state, the Court found the Belgian government obligated under the ECSC Treaty to abide by Court decisions.[124] The Court noted:

> Community law does not confer on institutions of the Community the right to annul the legislative or administrative acts of a Member State.
>
> Thus, if the High Authority considers that a State has failed in one of the obligations incumbent upon it by virtue of the Treaty, by enacting or upholding provisions contrary to that Treaty, it may not itself annul or repeal those provisions, but may merely set out such failure, in accordance with Article 88 of the Treaty, and then adopt the procedure which is laid down therein to lead the State in question itself to withdraw the measure it has taken.
>
> The same applies to the Court of Justice. . . . The Court may not of its own authority, annul or repeal the municipal laws of a Member State in the administrative acts of its authorities.[125]

The Court then went on to point out that this position under the ECSC Treaty was identical with that under the two later treaties,[126] "which confer only a declaratory effect upon the decisions of the Court in the case of a failure [of a member state] to carry out the provisions of the Treaties, while obliging the States to take the measures required to carry out the judgment."[127]

The Belgian government apparently felt itself so obliged, because it complied immediately with the Court's decision.[128]

Judicial Impartiality and Enforcement

There is no evidence that the impartiality of judges is impaired by the selection process, although some authors have evidenced this fear. Werner Feld, for example, writes: "Since for re-appointment the judges of the Court are exclusively dependent upon their own governments, which are often parties to disputes before

---

[123] *Jean-E. Humblet* v. *État Belge* (translated by Valentine, *Court of Justice of the European Communities*, pp. 266–267) .

[124] See *ECSC Treaty*, Article 86; cf. *EEC Treaty*, Article 192; *Euratom Treaty*, Article 192.

[125] *Jean-E. Humblet* v. *État Belge* (translated by Valentine, *Court of Justice of the European Communities*, p. 391) .

[126] Cf. *EEC Treaty*, Article 171, and *Euratom Treaty*, Article 143.

[127] *Jean-E. Humblet* v. *État Belge* (translated by Valentine, *Court of Justice of the European Communities*, p. 392) .

[128] See Werner Feld, "The European Community Court: Its Role in the Federalizing Process," *Minnesota Law Review*, L, 3 (January, 1966) , 423–442.

the Court, it is certainly within the realm of possibility that they may be tempted on occasion to let thoughts of the future color their thoughts of the present."[129] In this context, the fact that three judges were simply dropped from the Court in the changeover from the ECSC Court to the Court of the European Communities is surely not lost on the current judges, with their short terms of office.[130]

In what seems to be the only real effort at studying judicial impartiality (and really a rather modest effort), the conclusion was that there was no noticeable attempt on the part of the member states to influence the deliberations of the Court.[131] The only conclusion was that there seems to be an informal political understanding among the member states that the positions on the Court (president, judges, advocates-general, and clerk) will be assigned according to an agreed-upon formula—although there is no Treaty requirement for this.[132] Such a provision, however, is neither unusual, contemptible, nor dangerous.

A basic guarantor of the independence of the judges is the fact that the secretness of their deliberations is protected through the single opinion rendered by the Court. This system was advanced in the previous chapter as a solution to the problem of an apparent lack of impartiality on the part of judges—especially *ad hoc* judges. Given the fact of the direct political appointment and short tenure of Community judges, this secretness has undoubtedly been a major factor in preserving judicial impartiality. The apparent success this secretness has had within the Community justifies at least its consideration as a possible reform of the International Court of Justice (where separate opinions can reveal how individual judges voted in a given case).

One disadvantage of the Community system is that decisions might lack vitality because of the lack of dissenting opinions. However, the publication of the conclusions of the advocate-general with each decision serves to fill this void. The former President of the Court of the European Communities, A. M. Donner, vigorously defended the "secret" system in the following words:

the deliberations of the Court are and must remain secret. If differences of opinion occur, they cannot be made public. So the ruling has to be given

---

[129] Feld, *The Court of the European Communities*, pp. 19–20.
[130] The reasons for the judges being dropped is not known.
[131] Stuart A. Scheingold, *The Rule of Law in European Integration: The Path of the Schuman Plan* (New Haven: Yale University Press, 1965), pp. 34–35.
[132] *Ibid.*, pp. 25–35.

in one judgment. This difference from the practice of most international adjudications has been deplored by some people. I myself do not share this regret. The exclusion of the possibility of giving separate or dissenting opinions protects the independence of the judges . . . it forces us to work out an agreement, which is perhaps not approved by all, but which is considered clear and adequate by lawyers from all six of the Member States. It demands much longer discussion *in camera* and a very careful wording of decisions, but it ensures rulings that are understandable throughout the Communities and contributes to the establishment of a common fund of legal notions and principles.[133]

Regarding the enforcement of the decisions handed down by the Court, only a brief comment needs to be made about practice. Judgments, as indicated earlier in this chapter, have executive force throughout the Community. Judge Donner notes that "a party who wants the Court's ruling executed can address himself immediately to the national judicial authority which verifies the ruling before it. The judgment is then executed in the same way as national judgments."[134] In practice, the Court's decisions have always been honored. Uwe Kitzinger has observed very succinctly that "the Court has in fact acquired considerable prestige and no one has yet dared to challenge or obstruct its rulings."[135]

In retrospect, one can see that the drafters intended the communities to be supranational and the treaties clearly reflect this. That the Court is supranational is clear both from the treaties and the Court's practice itself. The power wielded by the Community Court represents a significant advance beyond previous international tribunals. So that this advance can be properly evaluated in light of the perspective provided by a look at the experience of all the international adjudicative tribunals, it seems convenient to postpone this evaluation until one other tribunal can be examined—the European Court of Human Rights.

---

[133] A. M. Donner, "The Court of Justice of the European Communities," *International and Comparative Law Quarterly,* Supplementary Publication No. 1 (1961), pp. 67–68. See also Judge Donner's article, "The Single Voice of the Court," *European Community,* No. 107 (November, 1967), pp. 14–15.

[134] *Ibid.,* p. 72.

[135] Kitzinger, *op. cit.,* p. 70.

CHAPTER SIX

EUROPEAN COURT
OF HUMAN RIGHTS

A. EXPECTATIONS OF STATESMEN

A former President of the European Commission of Human Rights, C. H. M. Waldock, in a speech delivered at Brussels on Council of Europe Day[1] at the Brussels Exhibition, compared the Council of Europe to the European communities. He noted that "the Statute of the Council of Europe set up no supranational organ and left a closer European unity to be won by further agreements between Member States."[2] On the other hand, "the Rome Convention was hailed as a great achievement precisely because it did set up special European organs of a supranational kind."[3]

The Council of Europe, then, is not supranational. The "closer European unity" to be worked toward has found its most notable manifestation in the creation, under the auspices of the Council of Europe, of international machinery for the protection of human rights. This machinery consists of the European Commission of Human Rights and the European Court of Human Rights, the latter of which forms the subject of this chapter. These organs, like the Council of Europe itself, are intergovernmental.

The European Court of Human Rights deserves a brief examina-

---

[1] September 3, 1958.
[2] Speech reprinted in C. H. M. Waldock, "The European Convention for the Protection of Human Rights and Fundamental Freedoms," *British Yearbook of International Law,* XXXIV (1958), 356.
[3] *Ibid.*

tion in this study for a series of reasons. First, the statesmen who created the Court clearly had supranational hopes for it. Although these hopes were not fulfilled, it is of interest to review the powers and structure of the resultant Court in light of the drafters' intent. Second, the European Court of Human Rights does have some supranational potential, for example in its provisions for compulsory jurisdiction. Third, and related to this second point, is the fact that the Council of Europe has created a new and special type of legal situation by trying to define and protect human rights. Individuals arc in a position to carry grievances against nation-states (although under special and highly restrictive conditions) to international organs. While these organs are not supranational, conceivably this growing emphasis on the international protection of human rights might in the long run represent the most significant penetration of national sovereignty.

This study of the European Court of Human Rights must necessarily be brief. As was the case with the Court of the European Communities, the *travaux préparatoires* are simply not a matter of public record. Plans and expectations concerning the Court have to be deduced from more general materials. Further, the Commission is actually the basic organ of the Human Rights machinery. The Court itself is somewhat of a little-used adjunct. The goal of this chapter then is to measure the European Court of Human Rights against the supranational intent of its drafters and highlight potentially supranational aspects.

Beginnings

The "beginnings" of the Council of Europe—and the resultant Court of Human Rights—can be linked with the general postwar "movement" in Europe toward unification. Within this movement one finds the periodic surfacing of demands for a tribunal to guarantee human rights.

One of the earliest efforts in this direction began on December 14, 1947, when the four main organizations working for European union united to form the International Committee of the Movements for European Unity, which set about organizing a massive European conference.[4] The resultant conference, the Congress of

---

[4] "Internationales Komitee der Bewegung für die Einheit Europas Gebildet," in Heinrich Siegler, *Dokumentation der europäischen Integration* (Bonn: Siegler & Co. KG. Verlag für Zeitarchive, 1961), Doc. 11, p. 9. The organizations were: Conseil Français pour l'Europe Unie (President Edouard Herriot), Ligue Independante de Coöpération Européenne (Paul van Zeeland), Union Européenne des Fédéralistes (Henri Brughams), and the United Europe Movement (Winston Churchill). Churchill's son-in-law, Duncan Sandys, was named President of the International Committee.

Europe, met from May 7 to 10, 1948, in The Hague with Winston Churchill as Honorary President.[5] Some 700 to 750 delegates attended the Congress representing 16 countries.[6] Observers (most of whom were refugees) came from 10 other countries.[7] The purposes of the Congress were "to demonstrate the wide support for the cause of European unity, to provide fresh impetus to the movement and to make practical recommendations for its accomplishment."[8]

In the "Message to Europeans" adopted by the delegates at the final plenary session, it was proclaimed *inter alia:*

We desire a Charter of Human Rights guaranteeing liberty of thought, assembly and expression as well as the right to form a political opposition;

We desire a Court of Justice with adequate sanctions for the implementation of this Charter. . . .[9]

Most important were the 11 political resolutions agreed upon at The Hague. Those resolutions concerning sovereignty, supranationalism, and the Court can be summarized as follows:

The Congress:

1. recognizes that no attempt to rebuild Europe upon the basis of rigidly divided national sovereignty can prove successful.

2. declares that for the people of Europe the hour has come to hand over and merge a part of their sovereign rights in order to secure common political and economic measures for integration and for the appropriate development of their common resources.

3. demands the creation of a European Parliament.

4. proclaims that this Parliament must recommend the establishment of a Court, for the protection of the rights of the individual person and the fundamentals of freedom, which has adequate sanctions to implement a Charter of Human Rights; that to this end it must be possible for each citizen of the acceding nations, at any time and within the shortest waiting period, to lodge an appeal with the Court concerning the violation of his rights as defined in the Charter.

5. proclaims that the creation of a United Europe represents an essential factor in the creation of a United World.[10]

---

[5] "Europa-Kongreß im Haag; Resolutionen," in *ibid.*, Doc. 16, p. 17.

[6] Austria, Belgium, Britain, Denmark, Ireland, France, Germany, Greece, Italy, Liechtenstein, Luxembourg, Netherlands, Norway, Saar, Sweden, and Switzerland.

[7] Bulgaria, Canada, Czechoslovakia, Finland, Hungary, Poland, Rumania, Spain, U.S.A., and Yugoslavia.

[8] From European Movement, *The European Movement and the Council of Europe* (London, 1950), pp. 47–48. Cited by A. H. Robertson, *European Institutions: Co-operation, Integration, Unification* (New York: Frederick A. Praeger, 1959), pp. 10–11.

[9] *Ibid.*, p. 11.

[10] "Europa-Kongreß im Haag; Resolutionen," in Siegler, *op. cit.*, pp. 17–18 (summary of my translation).

Debates

This plea for a European parliament was of course realized in the Council of Europe. Article I of the Statute of the Council of Europe, which was signed in London on May 5, 1949, embodied most of the foregoing resolutions.

The aim of the Council of Europe is to achieve a greater unity between its members for the purpose of safeguarding and realizing the ideals and principles which are their common heritage and to facilitate their economic and social progress. This aim shall be pursued through the organs of the Council by discussion of questions of common concern and by agreements and common action in economic, social, cultural, scientific, legal and administrative matters, *and in the maintenance and further realization of human rights and fundamental freedoms* . . . [italics mine].

Following up Article I, the Consultative Assembly of the Council of Europe immediately began debates on a draft European Convention on Human Rights. In the absence of *travaux préparatoires,* the debates at least serve to give one a spattering of expectations concerning the Court. One of the most supranational views was expressed by Jean Silvandre (France), who thought: "The Court ought to have the power to annul any law or any decree which violated the Convention defining Human Rights and Fundamental Freedoms. It was only in this way that it would be fulfilling its proper role."[11]

A Netherlands delegate, L. J. C. Beaufort, who stated a similar position, felt "that the establishment of a supranational Court of Justice with powers of enquiry and decision would effectively safeguard the rights of Europeans and would constitute a first step towards the unification of Europe, which must be pressed forward with all speed."[12]

The main opposition to a supranational court—or even to a court at all—came from M. Rolin of the Belgian delegation and Mr. Ungoed-Thomas of the English delegation.[13] M. Rolin, whose views were typical, questioned the very necessity for a special court. Lauterpacht's summary of his speech at the eighteenth meeting of the Assembly (September 8, 1949) notes:

He said . . . "we have to admit that the good will of our Governments to conform to the Convention will be certain, and that if there is a mistake

---

[11] "Summary of the Debates in the Consultative Assembly of the Council of Europe," *European Assembly,* I, 2, 3, and 4 (August 14–28, 1950), 106. (Published by authority of the Council of Europe by the Hansard Society.)

[12] *Ibid.,* p. 109.

[13] See discussion by Hersh Lauterpacht, *International Law and Human Rights* (New York: Frederick A. Praeger, 1950), pp. 449–451.

and a report from the Commission of enquiry redress will be given." He doubted whether more than one case a year would come before the Court [a prediction that has been well vindicated]; the judges would thus hold a sinecure which would be unnecessarily expensive and hardly conducive to the dignity of the Court. He urged that the proposal was useless and illogical, and that if accepted it would be detrimental to the authority of the International Court of Justice inasmuch as it would remove a substantial source of litigation from its jurisdiction.[14]

This position notwithstanding, however, John Foster (United Kingdom) noted that the majority of the delegates favored not only a court, but a relatively strong one.[15] A motion to this effect was adopted by an overwhelming vote of 76 to 0.[16]

Other Views

Beyond the very sketchy information provided in Assembly debate, one can glean some sense of expectations from later statements by Council of Europe officials. The Head of the Human Rights Department of the Council of Europe, M. Polys Modinos, says, "the *aim* of the authors of the Convention [*"le souci dominant* des promoteurs de la Convention"] was to guarantee the maintenance and the working of democratic régimes by safeguarding individual freedoms" (italics in original) .[17]

In implementation of this aim, Modinos noted, it was necessary *inter alia* "to establish a procedure of collective enforcement which would be applicable to individuals, who would thereby become subjects of international law."[18] The only realistic supranational hope for the Convention was of course that the individual's role would be enhanced vis-à-vis that of states in that individuals could appeal beyond their states to an independent international authority.[19] In fo-

---

[14] *Ibid.*, p. 450. The closing reference to the ICJ is not clear, for there is no jurisdictional similarity between it and the Court of Human Rights.

[15] "Summary of the Debates in the Consultative Assembly of the Council of Europe," *op. cit.,* p. 107.

[16] Lauterpacht, *op. cit.,* p. 449. There were, however, 17 abstentions, and 16 delegates were absent.

[17] Polys Modinos, "La Convention Européenne des Droits de l'Homme," *Annuaire Européen,* I (1953) , 155.

[18] *Ibid.*

[19] Modinos makes quite clear that the European Convention on Human Rights (with the possible exception of the new status of individuals) is strictly intergovernmental. He cites in this respect the views of Prof. Karl Joseph Partch: "a) that the Convention was signed by the representatives of governments, not so much as members of a common organization, but rather as representatives of their respective states, b) that the Convention does not contain any clause obliging the Members of the Council to present the ratification procedure before their national parliaments. He concludes from this that all the acts binding a State to the Convention fall exclusively within the internal juridical sphere of

cusing attention on the elevation of the individual, Modinos makes clear that "one should not lose sight of the fact that the Consultative Assembly had made the law of individual recourse the cornerstone of its edifice. It is in making the individual a subject of international law, it is in permitting him to be the guardian of his own political liberties that the founders of the Convention tried to create this new European juridical order."[20]

A. H. Robertson of the Council of Europe Secretariat corroborates these points. He points out that the two most important expectations concerning the Convention were: (1) the granting to individuals with denied rights direct access to an international organ capable of protecting them; and (2) the creation of a judicial body on the international plane competent to sit in judgment of national governments.[21]

The Convention and the assorted texts making up the constitutional basis of the Court show the specific form the above expectations have taken.

B. CONSTITUTIONAL BASIS

In the actual establishment of Human Rights organs the supranational goal of the drafters was eroded. A. H. Robertson writes: "It is interesting to compare these original proposals with the provisions that were finally adopted; in doing so one notes inevitably how the powers which were to be conferred on the international organs (the Commission and the Court) were gradually watered down and the traditional rights of sovereign States asserted. The result, of course, was to make the Convention a less effective instrument than had been originally envisaged."[22]

Although the Court is the main object of study here, a point that

---

the Member States of the Council." *Ibid.,* p. 162 (my translation). See Karl Joseph Partch, "Die Entstehung der europäischen Menschheitskonvention," *Zeitschrift für ausländisches öffentliches Recht und Völkerrecht,* XV, 4 (September, 1954), 631–660.

[20] Modinos, *op. cit.,* p. 167 (my translation).

[21] A. H. Robertson, "The European Convention for the Protection of Human Rights," *British Yearbook of International Law,* XXVII (1950), 162. See also in this connection "Beratende Versammlung [des Europarates] (3. Sitzungsperiode) 1951, Empfehlung betr. die Schaffung eines Europäischen Gerichtshofs," in Germany, Federal Republic, Auswärtiges Amt, Forschungsinstitut der deutschen Gesellschaft für Auswärtige Politik E.V., *Europa: Dokumente zur Frage der Europäischen Einigung,* Bd. 17 (München: R. Oldenbourg Verlag, 1962), pp. 502–503.

[22] A. H. Robertson, *Human Rights in Europe* (Dobbs Ferry, N.Y.: Oceana Publications, Inc., 1963), pp. 85–86. For an excellent discussion of the erosion of the supranational hopes of the drafters, see Chaps. 1 and 5 of Robertson's work.

needs restatement is that the Commission is the basic organ. Consequently, its functions require brief explanation.

The Commission

The functions of the two organs are not alternative, rather they are successive. Briefly, proceedings under the Convention begin when an alleged victim appeals to the Commission, which consists of a number of members equal to that of the high contracting parties.[23] The Commission may receive petitions from "any person, non-governmental organization or group of individuals claiming to be the victim of a violation by one of the High Contracting Parties" (Article 25 of the Convention) or from any high contracting party alleging a breach of the provisions of the Convention on the part of another high contracting party (Article 24 of the Convention).

The main qualification to the Commission's jurisdiction, making it clearly intergovernmental, is that "the High Contracting Party against which the complaint has been lodged has declared that it recognizes the competence of the Commission to receive such petitions" (Article 25).[24] After the acceptance of a petition, the Commission tries to effect a "friendly settlement."[25] Failing that, the Commission prepares a report which is transmitted to the states concerned and to the Committee of Ministers of the Council of Europe.[26]

At this point, as the President of the Court has noted, "the case may receive a judicial or political solution. . . ."[27] Article 32 of the Convention provides the political solution. By its terms, if the question has not been referred to the Court in accordance with Article 48 within a period of three months from the date the Committee of Ministers received the report, the Committee may, by a two-thirds

---

[23] Article 20 of the Convention for the Protection of Human Rights and Fundamental Freedoms (hereinafter referred to as Convention). The same article provides further that no two members of the Commission may be nationals of the same state. Commission members are elected by the Committee of Ministers from a list of names drawn up by the Bureau of the Consultative Assembly (Article 21). Articles of the Convention cited in this chapter are reprinted in Appendix H.

[24] Other qualifications concern exhaustion of domestic remedies, *rationae temporis* limitations, and various items such as a prohibition against anonymous petitioners. See Articles 26 and 27 of the Convention.

[25] Initial action is by a subcommission of seven members (Article 29).

[26] The report is prepared by the full Commission and includes its opinion and proposals (Article 31).

[27] Lord McNair, *The Expansion of International Law* (Jerusalem: Magnes Press of Hebrew University, 1962), p. 15.

vote, decide upon measures which are binding upon the high contracting parties. Article 48 of the Convention, which provides the judicial solution, is discussed below under "Access to the Court." First, however, the Court itself deserves description.

Composition of the Court

The Convention provides that the European Court of Human Rights "shall consist of a number of judges equal to that of the Members of the Council of Europe" and that no two judges may have the same nationality (Article 38). There is no direct national control over the election of judges. By the terms of Article 39, the judges are elected (majority vote) by the Consultative Assembly from a list of persons nominated by the members of the Council of Europe.[28] Judges are elected for a period of nine years and may be re-elected (Article 40).

For the consideration of a case, the Court meets in a chamber of seven judges. Unfortunately the *ad hoc* judge system has been reinstituted: for each state a party before the Court is entitled to have a judge of its nationality as an "ex officio" member of the chamber (Article 43). René Cassin, the Vice-President of the Court, has bitterly criticized this whole system:

> . . . the Court is not the "normal" instrument for settling actions involving violations of the Convention, as it does not sit permanently and, for example, the Judges are not paid an annual salary, but daily expenses.[29]
> . . . the Court is constituted as a Chamber composed of seven Judges, sitting not as a permanent tribunal but varying according to circumstances, one being the Judge national of the State involved, the others being drawn by lot. This avoids the summoning of fifteen Judges, or a Permanent Chamber of the same Judges, but involves the risk of the President or the Vice-President never being chosen.[30] Worse still, there is the danger of different interpretations of law on one question, according to the composition of the Court.[31]

Along these same lines, nothing can be said about possible political control of the Court. Since the Court is not the "normal instrument" for resolving conflicts arising under the Convention, and since it has had so little "business," there is simply no basis for studying these factors.

---

[28] According to Article 39 (1), each member nominates three candidates, of whom two at least shall be its nationals.

[29] See Article 42 of the Convention.

[30] These officers are selected according to the terms of Article 41.

[31] René Cassin, "La Cour Européenne des Droits de l'Homme," *Annuaire Européen*, VII (1959), 95–96.

Access to the Court

Article 48 of the Convention makes these specific provisions regarding parties before the Court:

The following may bring a case before the Court, provided that the High Contracting Party concerned, if there is only one, or the High Contracting Parties concerned, if there is more than one, are subject to the compulsory jurisdiction of the Court or, failing that, with the consent of the High Contracting Party concerned, if there is only one, or of the High Contracting Parties concerned if there is more than one:

(a) the Commission;
(b) a High Contracting Party whose national is alleged to be a victim;
(c) a High Contracting Party which referred the case to the Commission;
(d) a High Contracting Party against which the complaint has been lodged.

The most striking feature of this article is of course the fact that *individuals themselves have no standing before the Court.* They only have access through the offices of one of the four possible parties listed in Article 48. To make the matter even more specific, Article 44 further states, "Only the High Contracting Parties and the Commission shall have the right to bring a case before the Court." It is interesting that a tribunal supposedly catering to individuals does not allow individuals to appear before it. This would appear to be a step backward from the system of the Central American Court and the Court of the European Communities, both of which provided for direct access for individuals. On the other hand, the fact that the Commission handles the bulk of cases (where individuals do have direct access) probably justifies this diminished jurisdiction by the Court.

Jurisdiction

The Court's jurisdiction as provided for in the Convention is quite straightforward and clearly intergovernmental. *Ratione materiae,* Article 45 states that the Court's jurisdiction covers all cases "concerning the interpretation and application of the present Convention which the High Contracting Parties or the Commission shall refer to it in accordance with Article 48." This jurisdiction encompasses a violation of one's rights as spelled out in Articles 2 to 18 of the Convention.

Jurisdiction *ratione personae* has already been discussed. Only states and the Commission have standing before the Court. The important qualification is that states must give their consent. In this respect, jurisdiction is similar to that under the International Court of Justice.[32] Consent may either be given at the time of an appeal, or in a declaration recognizing "as compulsory *ipso facto* and without special agreement the jurisdiction of the Court in all matters concerning the interpretation and application of the . . . Convention" (Article 46). In terms of supranational potential, this provision is one of the more encouraging aspects of the Court.

Jurisdiction *ratione temporis* is only provided for in Article 47, which states that a case must be brought before the Court within three months of notification (by the Commission) of a failure to the Committee of Ministers, or else it lapses.

Judgments

The President of the European Court of Human Rights gives this cogent description of enforcement of judicial decisions: "The principal sanction for the execution of the Convention will always remain public opinion, for no Government—particularly a member of an intimate community such as is now being created by the Council of Europe—would like to be publicly convicted of a violation of a human right or a fundamental freedom."[33]

By the legal provisions of the Convention, the "High Contracting Parties undertake to abide by the decision of the Court in any case to which they are parties" (Article 53). Beyond this, only two general provisions provide for execution:

1. Article 54 states simply that the judgment of the Court shall be transmitted to the Committee of Ministers which shall supervise its execution.

2. Article 32 (2), (3), and (4) provides that the Committee of Ministers shall decide what measures the high contracting parties must take to give effect to the Court's judgment. These decisions are to be regarded as binding.

There is no machinery for actually enforcing Court decisions through coercive measures. Enforcement rests upon the strength of a state's attitude toward its legal obligations.

C. PRACTICE OF THE COURT

Jurisdiction

WORK OF THE COMMISSION The Commission has processed several thousand individual applications since its work

---

[32] Cf. Article 36 of the Statute of the International Court of Justice and Article 46 of the Convention.

[33] McNair, *op. cit.*, p. 15.

began.[34] Of these applications, however, the vast majority are for one reason or another declared inadmissible. Gordon Weil, who has studied the causes of this, finds that the high percentage of rejections is attributable to such factors as applications submitted by convicted criminals seeking freedom by any means, by mentally ill individuals, or other irresponsible applicants. Rejections on formal grounds are also numerous.[35] Table 11 shows the work of the Commission through 1967.

WORK OF THE COURT   As of May, 1968, the Court had rendered a judgment on the merits of only one case, *Lawless* v. *Ireland* in 1960 (see Table 12).[36] In another case, *DeBecker* v. *Belgium,* the Court voted to strike the case from the list in 1962 after the plaintiff withdrew his petition.[37] Further, the Court decided to join to the merits consideration of a preliminary objection in the *Belgian Linguistic Cases* on February 9, 1967,[38] and was seized of four other cases.[39]

There are at least four reasons for this lack of activity on the part of the Court: (1) the work of the Human Rights machinery is wholly grounded in national consent; (2) the Commission is a conciliatory body, whose task is really to keep controversies out of the Court; (3) individuals can only get to the Court indirectly; and (4) of the 18 members of the Council of Europe, only 11 have con-

---

[34] The work of the Commission has been likened to the minorities system set up by treaties at the Paris Peace Conference in 1919. See Denys P. Meyers, "The European Commission on Human Rights," *American Journal of International Law,* L, 4 (October, 1956), 949–951.

[35] Gordon Weil, "The Evolution of the European Convention on Human Rights," *American Journal of International Law,* LVII, 4 (October, 1963), 810–811.

[36] See judgment in *Annuaire Européen,* VIII (1960), 409–433.

[37] *Ibid.,* X (1962), 633–643.

[38] See Council of Europe, Registry of the Court, Publications of the European Court of Human Rights (Series A: Judgments and Decisions 1966–67), *Case "Relating to Certain Aspects of the Laws on the Use of Languages in Education in Belgium"* (preliminary objection). Judgment of February 9, 1967. The vote was unanimous. The case involved six applications against the Belgian government by French-speaking citizens (living in the Dutch-speaking part of the nation) for failure to provide adequate educational facilities in the French language.

[39] These four cases involved *K. H. Wemhoff* v. *Federal Republic of Germany* and respectively *F. Neumeister, E. Stögmüller,* and *O. Matznetter* v. *Austria.* Although differing from one another in various ways, these cases all have one feature in common. All are concerned with the interpretation of Article 5 (3) of the Convention, which guarantees that persons in custody shall be entitled to "trial within a reasonable time or to release pending trial." For details on the nature and status of these cases see Council of Europe, Directorate of Information, *Forward In Europe* (December, 1967, and February–March, 1968).

Table 11 Work of the European Commission of Human Rights[a]

	1955	56	57	58	59	60	61	62	63	64	65	66	Total on Sept. 3, 1967
Applications filed	138	104	101	96	233	291	344	442	346	293	310	303	3,305
Decisions taken	84	93	96	47	130	265	222	280	370	284	195	190	2,581
Applications rejected "de plano"	84	92	94	43	128	261	216	279	318	265	184	170	2,448
Applications rejected after communication to the respondent government	—	1	2	2	1	1	5	1	32	10	10	15	86
Applications declared admissible	—	—	—	2	1	3	1	—	20	9	1	5	47
Applications struck off the list	5	4	6	1	2	7	14	5	20	22	16	19	147

[a] Data from Council of Europe, Directorate of Information, *Forward in Europe* (December, 1967), p. 16.

Table 12 Work of the European Court of Human Rights[a]

Case[b]	Issue	Disposition	Judges' Vote
1. *Lawless v. Ireland*; *Annuaire Européen*, VIII (1960), 409–433; 14 Nov. 1960.	Detention without trial by the Irish government of an alleged member of the Irish Republican Army.	For Ireland.	6 to 1. The Greek judge dissented.
2. *DeBecker v. Belgium*; *Annuaire Européen*, X (1962), 633–643; 27 March 1962.	Raymond DeBecker, a journalist, had been condemned to death by the Brussels Conseil de Guerre in 1946 for collaboration with the Germans. Later this was changed, and he was only prohibited from exercising his profession of journalist.	For DeBecker. He withdrew his petition after the Belgian government came to an informal agreement with him.	6 to 1. The Court voted to strike the case from its list. The Danish judge dissented.

[a] Data derived from *Annuaire Européen*, VIII (1960), 409–433, and X (1962), 633–643.
[b] Column gives decision citation and date rendered. Total number of cases decided on merits as of March, 1968.

sented to individual applications (under Article 25 of the Convention), although it is encouraging that these 11 have accepted the compulsory jurisdiction of the Court provided for in Article 46 (see Table 13).

With only two cases disposed of, the jurisprudence of the Court regarding jurisdiction is necessarily sparse. Nevertheless, it has been significant. The most important question raised in a preliminary

Table 13 Ratifications and Declarations Concerning Human Rights Instruments[a]

Member of Council of Europe	Convention and Protocol	Individual Application	Compulsory Jurisdiction for Court
1. Austria	X	X	X
2. Belgium	X	X	X
3. Cyprus	X		
4. Denmark	X	X	X
5. France			
6. Fed. Rep. of Germany	X	X	X
7. Greece	X		
8. Iceland	X	X	X
9. Ireland	X	X	X
10. Italy	X		
11. Luxembourg	X	X	X
12. Malta	X		
13. Netherlands	X	X	X
14. Norway	X	X	X
15. Sweden	X	X	X
16. Switzerland			
17. Turkey	X		
18. United Kingdom	X	X	X

[a] Data taken from Council of Europe, Directorate of Information, *Council of Europe News*, No. 40 (January, 1966), p. 4, and from A. H. Robertson, "The European Convention on Human Rights," in Evan Luard (ed.), *The International Protection of Human Rights* (New York: Frederick A. Praeger, 1967), pp. 99–131. Current as of January, 1967.

objection occurred in the *Lawless* Case. It concerned the potential expansion of the Court's jurisdiction to include standing for individuals before the Court and is discussed below.

Parties Before the Court

The Convention makes clear that only states and the Commission have standing before the Court. In the *Lawless* Case, however, the way for individual access was opened. Lawless was appealing a conviction by the Irish government for his activities in the Irish Republican Army. During the course of the proceedings on his appeal the Commission also transmitted a copy of its report to Lawless, and later transmitted his observations on the report to the Court as part of the proceedings.

In the preliminary phase of the case the Irish government challenged *inter alia* these actions. It took "strong exception . . . to the right of the Commission to communicate to the Court the comments of the Applicant in regard to matters arising in the proceedings."[40] After noting that the Convention expressly states that *only* the high contracting parties and the Commission may bring a case before the Court, the Irish government continued:

The Commission . . . recognizes this as being the position, but it attempts by a subterfuge to bestow on the individual the quality of a party before the Court, by enabling the individual to make submissions to the Court in the form of a document which the Commission wishes to annex to its Memorial, and further by seeking directions as to the communication to the Court of the comments of the Applicant in regard to matters arising in the present proceedings. If this were permitted the Applicant would be enabled to play an active part in the proceedings before the Court in much the same way as if he were a party.

The Commission is in this way attempting to modify the Convention by an oblique procedure and without the approval of the High Contracting Parties who are the authors of the Convention.[41]

In its decision delivered November 14, 1960, the Court proceeded to define, and also expand, the standing of an individual before it. The Court noted that

Whereas, in the present case, G. R. Lawless, the Applicant, although he is not entitled to bring the case before the Court, to appear before the Court or even to make submissions through a representative appointed by him, *is nevertheless directly concerned with the proceedings before the Court* . . . whereas Article 38 of the Rules of the Court authorize it to hear any person whose deposition seems to it useful in the fulfilment of its task, as is admitted, moreover, both by the Irish Government and by the Commission . . . the Commission, in communicating its Report to G. R. Lawless, the Applicant, did not exceed its powers [italics mine].[42]

The Court further concluded that

Whereas, according to Article 44 of the Convention, Contracting States and the Commission are alone empowered to bring a case before the Court or to appear in Court; whereas, nevertheless, *the Court must bear in mind its duty to safeguard the interests of the individual, who may not be a party to any court proceedings,* and whereas *the whole of the proceedings*

---

[40] Cited in A. H. Robertson, "The First Case Before the European Court of Human Rights: *Lawless* v. *the Government of Ireland*," *British Yearbook of International Law*, XXXVI (1960) , 350.

[41] *Ibid.*, pp. 350–351.

[42] *Annuaire Européen*, VIII (1960) , 423.

in the Court, as laid down by the Convention and the Rules of the Court, *are upon issues which concern the Applicant;* whereas, *accordingly, it is in the interests of the proper administration of justice that the Court should have knowledge of and, if need be, take into consideration, the Applicant's point of view* . . . the Court rejects [by 6 to 1] the objections relating to procedure raised by the said Government [italics mine].[43]

In the lone dissent the Greek Judge G. Maridakis expressed concern that "the Applicant would be appearing before the Court *under cover of the Commission*" (italics in original).[44] He noted also that the wording of Article 44 of the Convention "means that the Court has not been set up to settle 'disputes' between the Applicant and the State which he is accusing of having violated, in his regard, its obligations under the Convention. It means that the Court is a high supervisory authority set up to guarantee the European order established by the Convention. (cf. Statute of the Council of Europe, Article 1b) " (italics in original).[45]

The net result of this case was to establish a precedent for limited individual access to the Court. Clearly individuals cannot appear as parties before the Court, but at least they may now present their views. This seems a worthwhile advance, for the individual's direct interest in the case is undeniable.

Disposition

In the two cases disposed of by the Court, an individual lost once against his state in the *Lawless* Case. Although there was no judicial solution in the *DeBecker* Case, DeBecker's action in seeking a Court solution was instrumental in prompting the Belgian government to act.[46] After the Court hearing of October 5, 1961, DeBecker addressed this memo to the Commission, in which he stated that he considered "that his Application to the Commission of Human Rights requesting the restitution of the right of free expression of which he was deprived under . . . the Belgian Penal Code has been met by the adoption in the Belgian Parliament of

---

[43] *Ibid.,* pp. 425–427.

[44] *Ibid.,* p. 429.

[45] *Ibid.*

[46] The counsel for Belgium "recognized that the opinion of the Commission had contributed to passage of the bill," and in an explanatory memorandum the Belgian government stated: "With a view to bringing our legislation into line with the European Convention on Human Rights, the Government have [*sic*] abolished the disabilities relating to intellectual and artistic media of expression, retaining only those of a political character." Quoted in Jack Greenberg and Anthony R. Shalit, "New Horizons for Human Rights: The European Convention, Court and Commission of Human Rights," *Columbia Law Review,* LXIII, 8 (December, 1963) , 1399.

the Act of 30th June, 1961" and that he recognized that it "gives everyone the possibility of regaining his or her full rights of free expression including that of political expression."[47]

For this reason DeBecker said at the end of his memo that he "now regards it as unnecessary further to proceed with this case and withdraws his Application."[48] The Commission transmitted the text of the memo to the Court on October 7, 1961.[49] The case was then struck from the list.[50] The evidence suggests that the Court is an instrumentality, even though indirect, whereby individuals can have complaints against their governments heard and disposed of. Little more than this can be said because of the limited experience of the Court.

Judicial Impartiality and Enforcement

In the two cases disposed of by the Court, no conclusion can be reached on impartiality and enforcement. The judges, nationals of the states before the Court, voted with the majority in both cases. The question of enforcement of the Court's decisions has not yet arisen.[51]

In summary, the European Court of Human Rights has fulfilled the two most important expectations of the drafters suggested above by A. H. Robertson.[52] The tribunal has provided an international appeal for the protection of individual rights and it does represent a judicial body capable of sitting in judgment of national governments. Disappointing to many, the Court does not reflect supranational power either in its constitution or its practice. Encouragingly, however, compulsory jurisdiction has found increasing acceptance, the very limited history and jurisprudence of the Court have been significant, and the right of individual appeal beyond the nationstate has been realized. Given the highly restrictive conditions under which access to the Court may be obtained, the body has been little used. Nevertheless, in terms of its mandate it seems a fair assessment to claim that the Court has had modest success. The value and meaning of this success will of course depend on the future

---

[47] *Annuaire Européen,* X (1962), 637.

[48] *Ibid.,* p. 639.

[49] *Ibid.*

[50] *Ibid.*

[51] For the official Irish reaction to the *Lawless* decision see Ireland, Department of External Affairs, *Iris Sheachtainiúil na Roinne Gnóthai Eachtracha (Weekly Bulletin of the Department of External Affairs),* VII, 536 (1961), 6–8. For Belgium see *supra,* footnote 46.

[52] See *supra,* p. 157.

development of the Court's role in the international protection of human rights.

The task at hand now is to re-examine briefly all five of the international tribunals covered in this study in an attempt to evaluate them in the light of one another's experience.

CHAPTER SEVEN

SUMMARY
AND CONCLUSIONS

Sovereignty and Supranationalism

The beginning chapter of this study attempted to make two basic points. First, sovereignty, while an elusive concept, is nevertheless a basic element of the nation-state and of the nation-state system. Second, while sovereignty implies the independence and equality of states within the international system, these qualities are subject to very real limitations—arising both through restrictions imposed by world politics and through voluntary submission to restrictions by the states themselves. A product certainly of both types of limitations, although particularly of the latter, is international integration through such international organizations as the European communities.

States are experiencing a need and a desire to seek cooperation beyond the nation-state. One manifestation of this condition has been the emergence of the new concept "supranationalism"—implying integration beyond the intergovernmental level yet still short of a federal system. On the assumption that law is a function of society rather than a constant, the international court presents itself as a possible measuring device for the minimum level of supranational integration sovereign states will tolerate. A full-scale examination of supranationalism, however, clearly requires a study of many other factors such as international executives and parliamentary bodies as well as of national foreign policies.

The preceding study has made one point especially clear. Nation-states alone are the main actors in international relations. Ultimate political power still resides in the nation-state. In the course of the judicial history of the five tribunals examined, states, while they have consented to limitations of sovereignty in varying degrees, have in no case handed over full judicial control of their affairs to an international tribunal. The extent to which states have submitted to supranational judicial control is reviewed in the following paragraphs.

Expectations

It is interesting to note that the creation of an organ with supranational power was given some consideration by the drafters of each of the five international tribunals. In the case of the League and the United Nations, as has been seen, attempts to move in this direction were quashed (although not without spirited debate), chiefly under the leadership of the Great Powers. The general reason for this is not hard to find. As Judge Charles DeVisscher notes, "every attempt to organize international relations is an attempt to redistribute power."[1] Since supranationalism proposes to redistribute power arrangements, DeVisscher would insist that it "must reckon with the social laws that govern all transformations of power," which are, namely, evolutionary development and adequate consensus among the participants.[2]

While a detailed inquiry into the specific meaning of "power" or the nature of these "social laws" is likely only to produce confusion, the general tenor of DeVisscher's remarks nevertheless makes sense. Nations will not give up any of their decision-making prerogatives unless they can see good reason for doing so. Larger nations are less likely to feel a need for supranational (or even international) authority simply because they are strong enough to guard their interests without it. Assuming, however, that the need is imminent, then it takes time for nations not only to adjust to this fact, but also to agree upon the institutional devices most apt to serve their need. The simple reality of both the Permanent Court of International Justice and the International Court of Justice was that the nations (especially the leading nations) were not ready to give them supranational decision-making powers.

DeVisscher's point is perhaps proved by the experience of the

---

[1] Charles DeVisscher, *Theory and Reality in Public International Law*, trans. P. E. Corbett (Princeton, N.J.: Princeton University Press, 1957), p. 365.
[2] *Ibid.*

Central American Court of Justice. The five Latin American republics were too impetuous in their attempt to create a supranational tribunal. They had tried to superimpose a legal institution on a hotbed of political dissension. With no sound foundation of political consensus, a condition undoubtedly made more acute by the role of the United States, the failure of the legal superstructure was preordained.

Further, the jurisdiction granted the Central American Court was too ambitious. To give a court, from one day to the next, jurisdiction over "all disputes" and compulsory jurisdiction as well is a temerarious act. A confrontation with political reality is simply a matter of time. When the inevitable occurred, a contemporary report sadly noted: "Confronted by this refusal of Nicaragua to acknowledge its jurisdiction in the case, the Court could only confess its helplessness to the world. . . ."[3]

Perhaps the two European courts studied herein are further evidence of the wisdom of DeVisscher's remarks. The claim can surely be made that they were "evolved." Consequently, their propensity for success is higher. The Europeans have had extensive experience (successful and unsuccessful) with regional international organizations. While the treaties creating these courts might not be the most perfect of documents, they were cautiously drafted. Great care was taken to outline the competence of the courts in minute detail. The result, particularly in the case of the Court of the European Communities, is a cumbersome mass of treaty provisions, protocols, and annexes. Yet the chances of gross misunderstanding and a political showdown, such as marked the demise of the Central American Court, are considerably lessened.

In retrospect, then, it appears that the supranational expectations of various statesmen, except in the case of the Central American Court of Justice, have invariably been modified by the political realities of the time. On the other hand, these "realities" have not prevented statesmen from trying to push back the frontiers of international cooperation. The compromise between the ideals of the supranationalists and the realities of national sovereignty has been most adequately reflected in the constitutional framework of each court.

Constitutional Basis

Of the international courts discussed in this study, only the Court of the European Communities is truly supranational ac-

---

[3] "Nicaragua Case," *Independent*, XC, 3571 (May 12, 1917), 274.

cording to the terms set forth in Chapter 1 (see p. 14). The essential traits of supranational power were held to be "common interests," "real powers," and the "autonomy of this power."[4] This implies enough interstate consensus to achieve agreement on the nature and function of an international organ. It also implies the delegation of certain actual decision-making powers—powers normally exercised only by the governmental organs of a sovereign state—to an international institution free from national control.

Of course, in all five cases there was enough "common interest" to result in the creation of an international institution. The strength of the institution created is proportionate to the level of shared interests. The key trait is the possession of "real powers"—the power to issue and enforce binding norms on the states and their inhabitants. Each of the courts is deficient (certainly not by accident) in some aspect of this trait. The strongest of the courts (constitutionally) in terms of the ability to issue binding norms, even over the protests of the parties, are the Central American Court and the Court of the European Communities. Given prior acceptance of compulsory jurisdiction, the other courts approximate them. The Central American Court and the Court of the European Communities, however, are weak in enforcement power.[5] Yet the International Court of Justice (and to a lesser extent the Permanent Court of International Justice) has a relatively strong enforcement mechanism, after initial consent to the Court's jurisdiction. Finally, all of the courts have (again constitutionally) been autonomous in the exercise of what power they did have (e.g., in provisions for judicial impartiality and freedom from national control). In practice, of course, a flagrant example of the breakdown of this autonomy occurred with the Central American Court. Further, the apparent link between the nationality of a judge and his vote on the Permanent Court of International Justice and the International Court of Justice has been less than exemplary.

Constitutionally then, all of the courts examined were based on common interests, and what power they did possess was basically autonomous. Nevertheless, it is quite obvious that the degree of real power given to the courts (with the exception of the Central American Court) has been carefully controlled by the participant states. The complexity of the jurisdictional instruments (again with the ex-

---

[4] These characteristics are perhaps more applicable to non-judicial international organs like the High Authority or the commissions.

[5] This statement requires some modification with the Court of the European Communities, depending upon the parties to the case. See Section B of Chapter 5.

ception of the Central American Court) reflected this. As a final note, the constitutional basis of the five courts examined has been a rather valid indicator of the limits of their power in practice. At least there are few cases of a court taking an expansive view of its jurisdiction. The most notable examples of such cases have been with the Court of the European Communities (cf. the *Humblet* and *Costa* decisions) and perhaps with the European Court of Human Rights (cf. the *Lawless* Case). Yet even in these few instances, neither the impact nor the permanency of the court's actions are yet fully clear.

Practice

JURISDICTION Sir Hersch Lauterpacht has noted that "there are few rules of modern international law which are more widely acknowledged than the rule that the jurisdiction of international tribunals is derived from the will of the parties. . . ."[6] The jurisprudence of especially the Permanent Court of the League and the United Nations International Court of Justice has clearly emphasized the element of consent. When consent has not been on an *ad hoc* basis, it has either been built into the basic document establishing the court (as with the Central American Court and the Court of the European Communities) or provided for in advance through declarations accepting compulsory jurisdiction under an optional clause (as with the PCIJ, the ICJ, and the European Court of Human Rights).

As already suggested above, when jurisdiction is provided for in advance through the basic document, care must be taken in its drafting to define jurisdiction explicitly. One of the leading contemporary assessments of the Central American Court of Justice labeled the Convention simply "une oeuvre imparfaite," the result of impetuousness.[7] There is little question that the Court was hastily founded in an atmosphere of idealism, which as Chapter 2 has indicated was largely an offshoot of the then current "Hague spirit." The unwillingness, or the inability, of the Court's drafters to take proper account of the traditional reluctance of sovereign states to submit to international controls (judicial or otherwise) undoubtedly set the stage for the Court's demise. Not only was the jurisdic-

---

[6] Hersch Lauterpacht, *The Development of International Law by the International Court* (London: Stevens & Sons Ltd., 1958), p. 338. Lauterpacht's view is illustrative of the attitude toward jurisdiction. See, for example, the collection of authorities in Kenneth S. Carlston, *The Process of International Arbitration* (New York: Columbia University Press, 1946), Chap. 3.

[7] Jean Eyma, *La Cour de Justice Centre-Américaine* (Paris: Ernest Sagot & Cie., 1928), p. 54.

tion they gave the Court too large, but worse in terms of a challenge to the five sovereign republics, the Court was free to define for itself the limits of its jurisdiction.

Added to all this was the failure of the drafters to establish other international machinery to supplement the Court's task. The Court stood as the sole arbiter of the squabbles of five unstable states, with little or no actual power at its command. As the preceding chapters have suggested, one has little reason to expect an international court to be in the forefront of supranational integration. As a final point explaining the failure of the Court, the contemporary study cited above notes that, given the bold innovations the Court represented, "one can only be astonished that its Founders had not dreamed of giving it a sanction for its decisions."[8]

The Court of the European Communities has avoided these problems, as has the World Court (and to a certain extent the European Court of Human Rights) simply through the reluctance of member states to accede to compulsory jurisdiction. Referring to the League Court, Judge Hudson made this initial optimistic appraisal:

In view of the actual developments with respect to the Court's compulsory jurisdiction, it may be thought that some of the framers of the Statute were too timid. The proposal of the 1920 Committee of Jurists [for the general adoption of compulsory jurisdiction] may have been too broad, and it was not well explained; yet it can hardly be said to have been premature, and those who so stoutly opposed compulsory jurisdiction in 1920 have not been vindicated. The willingness of so many States to confer compulsory jurisdiction on the Court in the subsequent years marks a substantial advance in the history of the law of pacific settlement of disputes.[9]

As seen in Chapter 3, and to some extent in Chapter 4, there was some basis for Hudson's optimism. There was a growing acceptance of compulsory jurisdiction under the League and even substantial acceptance in the larger community of the United Nations. Further, there has been gratifying acceptance by many of the Great Powers. Chapter 6 indicated the growing acceptance of compulsory jurisdiction for the European Court of Human Rights.

The Institute of International Law has even indicated that compulsory jurisdiction should be taken for granted in an international community such as that established under the United Nations. In a

---

[8] *Ibid.*, p. 57 (my translation). Judge Ramirez (El Salvador) puts the blame for failure more directly on the states, attributing it "a la soberania, honor nacional y a los interesses vitales." See Manuel Castro Ramirez, *Cinco Años en la Corte de Justicia Centroamericana* (San José, Costa Rica: Imprenta Lehmann, Sauter & Co., 1918), p. 174.

[9] Manley O. Hudson, *The Permanent Court of International Justice, 1920–1942: A Treatise* (New York: The Macmillan Company, 1943), p. 482.

1959 resolution, the Institute proclaimed that recourse to the International Court of Justice, or to any other international tribunal, should be standard procedure among friendly states and should never be regarded as an unfriendly act toward the respondent state.[10]

Chapters 3 and 4 have shown, however, that nation-states have in fact neither accepted the logic of the Institute's resolution nor fully justified Hudson's hopes. The majority of nations have not accepted compulsory jurisdiction. Of the acceptances, most are fraught with reservations, many of which rob the original acceptance of any meaning. Further, there is no reason to expect any noteworthy change in this state of affairs.

The most startling jurisdictional advance among the modern international tribunals is found in the Court of the European Communities. It most completely fulfills the requirements for supranationality. Etzioni has written that "even if [the European Community] does not progress beyond the point it has already reached, it is probably the most integrated union ever to have been formed among nation-states."[11]

This supranational strength suggests a similarity between the Court and a federal court.[12] The federal nature of the Court can be seen in at least three areas: (1) controversies between the "central government" (i.e., the Community organs) and the governments of the member states;[13] (2) controversies between member states;[14] and (3) uniform interpretation of Community law.[15]

---

[10] Reprinted in C. Wilfred Jenks, *The Prospects of International Adjudication* (London: Stevens & Sons Ltd., 1964), p. 114.

[11] Amitai Etzioni, "European Unification: A Strategy of Change," *World Politics,* XVI, 1 (October, 1963), 32.

[12] One leading proponent of this similarity is Werner Feld. See, for example, Werner Feld, "The European Community Court: Its Role in the Federalizing Process," *Minnesota Law Review,* L, 3 (January, 1966), 423–442. Another author notes: "The most highly developed federal aspect of the Communities is the judicial function exercised by the Court of Justice." See Peter Hay, *Federalism and Supranational Organizations: Patterns for New Legal Structures* (Urbana: University of Illinois Press, 1966), p. 101. See particularly Professor Hay's discussion of the federal nature of the Court and community law in Chaps. 4 and 5.

[13] See, for example, *Gouvernement de la République Italienne* v. *Haute Autorité,* VI *Rec* 663 (July 15, 1960) or *Gouvernement de la République Fédérale d'Allemagne* v. *Haute Autorité,* VI *Rec* 117 (March 8, 1960).

[14] A federal court has the power to adjudicate disputes among the component members of the federal system. The Community Court has this power (*ECSC Treaty,* Article 87; *EEC Treaty,* Article 219; and *Euratom Treaty,* Article 193), but as noted in Table 10, footnote a, this function has not yet been used.

[15] The leading case in this area is of course *M. Flaminio Costa* v. *E.N.E.L.,* X *Rec* 1141 (July 15, 1964).

That this similarity between the Community Court and a federal court exists must be admitted, but the similarity should not be pushed too far—nor should the traditional reluctance of nation-states to transfer decision-making powers to an international organ be underestimated. One of the most important qualifications, which indicates this similarity is illusory, is that the Court's competence is highly restricted to carefully delimited and rather technical areas of the economy. Not even the entire economic field has been turned over to the Community, but more significant, the political realm (including such elements as foreign policy, defense, and police) remains under the control of the member states.

Further, it should not be overlooked that ultimate political influence (as well as a monopoly of physical force) is retained by the six member states. This is most noticeable in the role of the Council of Ministers, in the carefully specified competence of not only the Court but of the whole Community, and in the ultimate dependence on the states for enforcement of Community decisions.[16] Chapter 5 showed that the Court has been expansive in the interpretation of its role, but while an expanded jurisdiction for an international tribunal may speed the "federalizing process"—to borrow a phrase from Carl Friedrich—it is no substitute for the integrative impetus that must ultimately come from the political sphere.[17] There is little reason to expect any further political impetus if one is to believe such a fascinating analysis as that offered by Don Cook in *Floodtide in Europe*.[18] He argues that the zenith of the postwar European integrative movement was reached when General de Gaulle vetoed British entry into the Common Market for it marked the re emergence (and triumph) of age-old nationalism.

One can readily conclude from the foregoing that Lauterpacht's view of an international court's jurisdiction has been completely substantiated. The jurisdiction granted an international tribunal is totally and unconditionally derived from the will of the parties. Given the supranational potential of compulsory jurisdiction (of the type found in the International Court of Justice, the European Court of Human Rights, and the Court of the European Communities), however, this will need not necessarily be present in a given

---

[16] For a discussion of why the Community is not federal see the argument of Michel Gaudet, Director-General of the Legal Service of the European Executives, in "The Legal Framework of the Community," *International and Comparative Law Quarterly*, Supplementary Publication No. 1 (1961), pp. 8–22.

[17] See Carl Friedrich, "International Federalism in Theory and Practice," in Elmer Plischke (ed.), *Systems of Integrating the International Community* (New York: D. Van Nostrand Company, Inc., 1964), pp. 126–137.

[18] See Don Cook, *Floodtide in Europe* (New York: G. P. Putnam's Sons, 1965).

case. Difficulty only arises when a state finds itself brought before an international court against its will (as would be common with compulsory jurisdiction), but in a case it feels it cannot tolerate. Then, of course, the will of a state, tempered only by its sense of legal obligation or perhaps by international public opinion, would ultimately prevail.

Although unfortunate, this condition is nevertheless a fact of international politics. This study has shown, however, that states are generally rather careful not to commit themselves to a greater jurisdiction (which is at the same time a restriction of their sovereign prerogatives) than they could ultimately accept. The Court of the European Communities is encouraging in this respect because it demonstrates that the limits of an international court's jurisdiction can indeed be quite broad.

PARTIES   Three of the tribunals in this study have allowed access by individuals, or by entities other than nation-states—the Central American Court of Justice, the Court of the European Communities, and the European Court of Human Rights (in the restricted sense discussed in Chapter 6). One can say that only with the latter two courts has this right of individual access been given practical reality.

At least two points need to be made regarding parties other than states. First, Georges Kaeckenbeeck raises this provocative question:

> Even when, as a result of what is almost a fiction, a State and a private person stand side by side as parties before an international tribunal—a new and still quite exceptional departure—it is essential that the impartiality of the judge should not be affected by the difference in the importance of the parties . . . and in this connection it is essential that the judge should treat the parties as equals.
>
> But from another standpoint, if we are not to lose touch with reality, it must be admitted that the interests of a State and the interests of an individual are not on the same level, and further, that the feelings of a nation, with their consequences, both national and international, are not commensurate with the psychological and material satisfaction which an individual receives when his strict rights are recognized.[19]

The drafters of the two European tribunals have generally avoided any unbalanced or embarrassing "showdown" between a sovereign nation-state and a "lesser" entity through a careful deline-

---

[19] Georges Kaeckenbeeck, *The International Experiment of Upper Silesia* (London: Oxford University Press, 1942), p. 78. Kaeckenbeeck served as President of the Mixed Commission and Arbitral Tribunal that functioned from 1922 to 1937 under the Upper Silesian Convention between Germany and Poland (which was one of the earliest international judicial bodies to hear individuals).

ation of jurisdiction. The Court of the European Communities serves primarily as an administrative tribunal for individuals (the *Humblet* Case notwithstanding) . The Court of Human Rights only has jurisdiction after the Commission has thoroughly considered a case, and then only if a defendant state accepts the jurisdiction of the Court. The net result of both these tribunals has been to provide one extra appeal for those suffering administrative or political wrongs—an appeal which only existed in token measure under the Central American Court and not at all under the World Court.

A second point that deserves consideration, should one entertain any hopes that new vistas have been opened for the supranational protection of individual rights, is the following. It is true that the two European tribunals mark a great advance in judicial recourse for the impairment of individual rights. Yet one can presume that nations willing to trouble themselves with the creation of international machinery for the protection of rights, and at the same time willing to give this machinery some degree of real power, are the nations most likely to protect these rights anyway. One of the tragic aspects of modern international relations is that only a handful of nations seem genuinely concerned with individual rights. The main hope is perhaps that the European courts will serve as a model for eventual imitation on a broader scale.

OTHER CONSIDERATIONS   A fact evident in the foregoing chapters is that the Court of the European Communities is the only one of the tribunals not suffering from lack of use.[20] One can surmise that the reluctance of states to resort to international adjudication is due to a number of causes, the main ones of which are undoubtedly: (a) the simple fear that sovereign states have of losing a case (an event they can easily avoid by refusing to submit to adjudication) ; (b) distrust of the "real impartiality" of the judges; and perhaps (c) the distrust held by the Communist bloc and the developing countries of a "capitalist" or "colonial" court.[21]

---

[20] It is probably not fair to include the Court of Human Rights in this generalization because of its special role.

[21] For a more detailed discussion of these and other related issues, see, for example, J. H. W. Verzijl, "The Present Stagnation of Interstate Adjudication: Causes and Possible Remedies," *International Relations* (London) , II, 8 (October, 1963) , 480–492. Other perceptive studies that deal with this same question are R. P. Anand, "Role of the New Asian African Countries in the Present International Legal Order," *American Journal of International Law,* LVI, 2 (April, 1962) , 383–406; and Ibrahim F. I. Shihata, "The Attitude of New States Toward the International Court of Justice," *International Organization,* XIX, 2 (Spring, 1965) , 203–222.

The innovation suggested earlier, whereby *ad hoc* judges would be abolished and the judges' vote would be secret (i.e., not determinable through the publishing of separate opinions) as in the Court of the European Communities, stands a good chance of alleviating problem b. Difficulties a and c concern broader issues of world politics and the role of international adjudication therein. Shabtai Rosenne sadly voices the confusion and despair found in efforts to grapple with these problems. Although he feels that international adjudication has made some contribution to peace, "the general picture," he writes, "is not encouraging and indicates some general malaise not yet fully diagnosed."[22]

The point is that no degree of procedural inventiveness with international courts will camouflage the basic need for political and social consensus. It is upon this area after all, as has been noted, that the international tribunal must rely for the enforcement of its decisions. While, as one author notes, "the viability of the nation-states [may] be judged precarious,"[23] the court can only *assist* in an integrative movement or even in the bare maintenance of peace. A comment made by Kaeckenbeeck years ago is quite relevant today —and it will be so in the future. He writes: "law requires supplementing by other methods. . . . Judicial settlement is not an end in itself, but only a means to an end. . . . Other good and acceptable means to the same end . . . are the manifold exertions of goodwill which, in such forms as mediation, conciliation, round table discussions, compromise settlement, and many others may contrive a *modus vivendi* acceptable to all, and are therefore conducive to happiness and stability."[24]

Acknowledging this requirement, three final points should be made. First, international courts have existed throughout this century. This continued experimentation with international tribunals must be evidence of a conviction that they indeed have value. Second, in the creation of each of the five tribunals in this study the designers gave some consideration to building a court with some supranational powers. Finally, although only the Court of the European Communities is truly supranational, the existence of all these courts has shown that nation-states can and will relinquish some of

---

[22] Shabtai Rosenne, "The Court and the Judicial Process," *International Organization,* XIX, 3 (Summer, 1965), p. 536.

[23] Karl W. Deutsch, *Political Community at the International Level: Problems of Definition and Measurement* (Garden City, N.Y.: Doubleday and Company, Inc., 1954), p. 25.

[24] Kaeckenbeeck, *op. cit.,* p. 538.

their sovereign decision-making prerogative, although indeed reluctantly. This existence has also shown that it is possible, however hesitantly, to go beyond the nation-state, not only in the creation of a higher judicial authority but also in the recognition of the rights of other entities—such as the individual. It is to be hoped that history will show the eventual acceptance of this fact.

APPENDIX A

SELECTED ARTICLES FROM THE CONVENTION ESTABLISHING THE CENTRAL AMERICAN COURT OF JUSTICE

Article I.

The High Contracting Parties agree by the present Convention to constitute and maintain a permanent tribunal which shall be called the "Central American Court of Justice," to which they bind themselves to submit all controversies or questions which may arise among them, of whatsoever nature and no matter what their origin may be, in case the respective Departments of Foreign Affairs should not have been able to reach an understanding.

Article II.

This court shall also take cognizance of the questions which individuals of one Central American country may raise against any of the other contracting Governments, because of the violation of treaties or conventions, and other cases of an international character; no matter whether their own Government supports said claim or not; and provided that the remedies which the laws of the respective country provide against such violation shall have been exhausted or that denial of justice shall have been shown.

Article III.[a]

The Central American Court of Justice shall also have jurisdiction over the conflicts which may arise between the Legislative, Executive, and Judicial Powers, and when as a matter of fact the judicial decisions and resolutions of the National Congress are not respected.

Article IV.

The Court can likewise take cognizance of the international questions which by special agreement any one of the Central American Governments and a foreign Government may have determined to submit to it.

Article VI.

The Central American Court of Justice shall consist of five Justices, one being appointed by each Republic and selected from among the jurists who possess the qualifications which the laws of each country prescribe for the exercise of high judicial office, and who enjoy the highest consideration, both because of their moral character and their professional ability.

---

[a] As amended.

Vacancies shall be filled by substitute Justices, named at the same time and in the same manner as the regular Justices, and who shall unite the same qualifications as the latter.

The attendance of the five Justices who constitute the Tribunal is indispensable in order to make a legal quorum in the decisions of the Court.

Article VII.

The Legislative Power of each one of the five contracting Republics shall appoint their respective Justices, one regular and two substitutes.

The salary of each Justice shall be eight thousand dollars, gold, per annum, which shall be paid them by the Treasury of the Court. The salary of the Justice of the country where the Court resides shall be fixed by the Government thereof. Furthermore each State shall contribute two thousand dollars, gold, annually toward the ordinary and extraordinary expenses of the Tribunal. The Governments of the contracting Republics bind themselves to include their respective contributions in their estimates of expenses and to remit quarterly in advance to the Treasury of the Court the share they may have to bear on account of such services.

Article VIII.

The regular and substitute Justices shall be appointed for a term of five years, which shall be counted from the day on which they assume the duties of their office, and they may be reelected.

In case of death, resignation, or permanent incapacity of any of them, the vacancy shall be filled by the respective Legislature, and the Justice elected shall complete the term of his predecessor.

Article X.

Whilst they remain in the country of their appointment the regular and substitute Justices shall enjoy the personal immunity which the respective laws grant to the magistrates of the Supreme Court of Justice, and in the other contracting Republics they shall have the privileges and immunities of Diplomatic Agents.

Article XIII.

The Central American Court of Justice represents the national conscience of Central America, wherefore the Justices who compose the Tribunal shall not consider themselves barred from the discharge of their duties because of the interest which the Republics, to which they owe their appointment, may have in any case or question. With regard to allegations of personal interest, the rules of procedure which the Court may fix shall make proper provision.

Article XIV.

When differences or questions subject to the jurisdiction of the Tribunal arise, the interested party shall present a complaint which shall comprise all the points of fact and law relative to the matter and all pertinent evidence. The Tribunal shall communicate without loss of time a copy of the complaint to the Governments or individuals interested, and shall invite them to furnish their allegations and evidence within the term that it may designate to them, which, in no case, shall exceed sixty days counted from the date of notice of the complaint.

Article XV.

If the term designated shall have expired without answer having been made to the complaint, the Court shall require the complainant or complainants to do so within a further term not to exceed twenty days, after the expiration of which and in view of the evidence presented and of such evidence as it may *ex officio* have seen fit to obtain, the Tribunal shall render its decision in the case, which decision shall be final.

Article XVII.

Each one of the Governments or individuals directly concerned in the questions to be considered by the Court has the right to be represented before it by a trustworthy person or persons, who shall present evidence, formulate arguments, and shall, within the terms fixed by this Convention and by the rules of the Court of Justice do everything that in their judgment shall be beneficial to the defense of the rights they represent.

Article XIX.

For all the effects of this Convention the Central American Court of Justice may address itself to the Governments or tribunals of justice of the contracting States, through the medium of the Ministry of Foreign Relations or the office of the Supreme Court of Justice of the respective country, according to the nature of the requisite proceeding, in order to have the measures that it may dictate within the scope of its jurisdiction carried out.

Article XX.

It may also appoint special commissioners to carry out the formalities above referred to, when it deems it expedient for their better fulfillment. In such case, it shall ask of the Government where the proceeding is to be had, its cooperation and assistance, in order that the Commissioner may fulfill his mission. The contracting Governments formally bind themselves to obey and to enforce the orders of the Court, furnishing all the assistance that may be necessary for their best and most expeditious fulfillment.

Article XXII.

The Court is competent to determine its jurisdiction, interpreting the Treaties and Conventions germane to the matter in dispute, and applying the principles of international law.

Article XXV.

The judgments of the Court shall be communicated to the five Governments of the contracting Republics. The interested parties solemnly bind themselves to submit to said judgments, and all agree to lend all moral support that may be necessary in order that they may be properly fulfilled, thereby constituting a real and positive guarantee of respect for this Convention and for the Central American Court of Justice.

APPENDIX B

SELECTED ARTICLES FROM THE COVENANT OF THE LEAGUE OF NATIONS

Article 13. Arbitration or Judical Settlement

1. The Members of the League agree that, whenever any dispute shall arise between them which they recognize to be suitable for submission to arbitration or judicial settlement, and which can not be satisfactorily settled by diplomacy, they will submit the whole subject-matter to arbitration or judicial settlement.

2. Disputes as to the interpretation of a treaty, as to any question of international law, as to the existence of any fact which, if established, would constitute a breach of any international obligation, or as to the extent and nature of the reparation to be made for any such breach, are declared to be among those which are generally suitable for submission to arbitration or judicial settlement.

3. For the consideration of any such dispute, the court to which the case is referred shall be the Permanent Court of International Justice, established in accordance with Article 14, or any tribunal agreed on by the parties to the dispute or stipulated in any convention existing between them.

4. The Members of the League agree that they will carry out in full good faith any award or decision that may be rendered, and that they will not resort to war against a Member of the League which complies therewith. In the event of any failure to carry out such an award or decision, the Council shall propose what steps should be taken to give effect thereto.

Article 14. Permanent Court of International Justice

The Council shall formulate and submit to the Members of the League for adoption plans for the establishment of a Permanent Court of International Justice. The Court shall be competent to hear and determine any dispute of an international character which the parties thereto submit to it. The Court may also give an advisory opinion upon any dispute or question referred to it by the Council or by the Assembly.

Article 16. Sanctions of Pacific Settlement

1. Should any Member of the League resort to war in disregard of its covenants under Articles 12, 13, or 15, it shall *ipso facto* be deemed to have committed an act of war against all other Members of the League, which hereby undertake immediately to subject it to the severance of all trade or financial relations, the prohibition of all intercourse between their nationals and the nationals of the covenant-breaking State, and the prevention of all financial, commercial or personal intercourse

between the nationals of the covenant-breaking State and the nationals of any other State, whether a Member of the League or not.

2. It shall be the duty of the Council in such case to recommend to the several Governments concerned what effective military, naval or air force the Members of the League shall severally contribute to the armed forces to be used to protect the covenants of the League.

3. The Members of the League agree, further, that they will mutually support one another in the financial and economic measures which are taken under this Article, in order to minimize the loss and inconvenience resulting from the above measures, and that they will mutually support one another in resisting any special measures aimed at one of their number by the covenant-breaking State, and that they will take the necessary steps to afford passage through their territory to the forces of any Members of the League which are cooperating to protect the covenants of the League.

4. Any Member of the League which has violated any covenant of the League may be declared to be no longer a Member of the League by a vote of the Council concurred in by the Representatives of all the other Members of the League represented thereon.

Article 17. Disputes Involving Non-Members

1. In the event of a dispute between a Member of the League and a State which is not a Member of the League, or between States not Members of the League, the State or States not Members of the League shall be invited to accept the obligations of membership in the League for the purposes of such dispute, upon such conditions as the Council may deem just. If such invitation is accepted, the provisions of Articles 12 to 16, inclusive, shall be applied with such modifications as may be deemed necessary by the Council.

2. Upon such invitation being given, the Council shall immediately institute an inquiry into the circumstances of the dispute and recommend such action as may seem best and most effectual in the circumstances.

3. If a State so invited shall refuse to accept the obligations of membership in the League for the purposes of such dispute, and shall resort to war against a Member of the League, the provisions of Article 16 shall be applicable as against the State taking such action.

4. If both parties to the dispute when so invited refuse to accept the obligations of Membership in the League for the purposes of such dispute, the Council may take such measures and make such recommendations as will prevent hostilities and will result in the settlement of the dispute.

APPENDIX C

SELECTED ARTICLES FROM THE STATUTE OF THE
PERMANENT COURT OF INTERNATIONAL JUSTICE

Article 2.

The Permanent Court of International Justice shall be composed of a body of independent judges, elected regardless of their nationality from amongst persons of high moral character, who possess the qualifications required in their respective countries for appointment to the highest judicial offices, or are jurisconsults of recognized competence in international law.

Article 9.

At every election, the electors shall bear in mind that not only should all the persons appointed as members of the Court possess the qualifications required, but the whole body also should represent the main forms of civilization and the principal legal systems of the world.

Article 10.

Those candidates who obtain an absolute majority of votes in the Assembly and in the Council shall be considered as elected.

In the event of more than one national of the same Member of the League being elected by the votes of both the Assembly and the Council, the eldest of these only shall be considered as elected.

Article 16.

The members of the Court may not exercise any political or administrative function, nor engage in any other occupation of a professional nature.

Any doubt on this point is settled by the decision of the Court.

Article 17.

No member of the Court may act as agent, counsel or advocate in any case.

No member may participate in the decision of any case in which he has previously taken an active part as agent, counsel or advocate for one of the contesting parties, or as a member of a national or international Court, or of a commission of enquiry, or in any other capacity.

Any doubt on this point is settled by the decision of the Court.

Article 19.

The members of the Court, when engaged on the business of the Court, shall enjoy diplomatic privileges and immunities.

Article 20.

Every member of the Court shall, before taking up his duties, make a solemn declaration in open Court that he will exercise his powers impartially and conscientiously.

Article 31.

Judges of the nationality of each of the contesting parties shall retain their right to sit in the case before the Court.

If the Court includes upon the Bench a judge of the nationality of one of the parties, the other party may choose a person to sit as judge. Such person shall be chosen preferably from among those persons who have been nominated as candidates as provided in Articles 4 and 5.

If the Court includes upon the Bench no judge of the nationality of the contesting parties, each of these parties may proceed to select a judge as provided in the preceding paragraph. [Paragraphs 4, 5, and 6 of the article omitted.]

Article 34.

Only States or Members of the League of Nations can be parties in cases before the Court.

Article 35.

The Court shall be open to the Members of the League and also to States mentioned in the Annex to the Covenant.

The conditions under which the Court shall be open to other States shall, subject to the special provisions contained in treaties in force, be laid down by the Council, but in no case shall such provisions place the parties in a position of inequality before the Court.

When a State which is not a Member of the League of Nations is a party to a dispute, the Court will fix the amount which that party is to contribute towards the expenses of the Court. This provision shall not apply if such State is bearing a share of the expenses of the Court.

Article 36.

The jurisdiction of the Court comprises all cases which the parties refer to it and all matters specially provided for in treaties and conventions in force.

The Members of the League of Nations and the States mentioned in the Annex to the Covenant may, either when signing or ratifying the Protocol to which the present Statute is adjoined, or at a later moment, declare that they recognize as compulsory *ipso facto* and without special agreement, in relation to any other Member or State accepting the same obligation, the jurisdiction of the Court in all or any of the classes of legal disputes concerning:

(a) the interpretation of a treaty;

(b) any question of international law;

(c) the existence of any fact which, if established, would constitute a breach of an international obligation;

(d) the nature or extent of the reparation to be made for the breach of an international obligation.

The declaration referred to above may be made unconditionally or on condition of reciprocity on the part of several or certain Members or States, or for a certain time.

In the event of a dispute as to whether the Court has jurisdiction, the matter shall be settled by the decision of the Court.

APPENDIX D

SELECTED ARTICLES FROM THE UNITED NATIONS
CHARTER

Article 1.

The Purposes of the United Nations are:

1. To maintain international peace and security, and to that end: to take effective collective measures for the prevention and removal of threats to the peace, and for the suppression of acts of aggression or other breaches of the peace, and to bring about by peaceful means, and in conformity with the principles of justice and international law, adjustment or settlement of international disputes or situations which might lead to a breach of the peace;

2. To develop friendly relations among nations based on respect for the principle of equal rights and self-determination of peoples, and to take other appropriate measures to strengthen universal peace;

3. To achieve international cooperation in solving international problems of an economic, social, cultural, or humanitarian character, and in promoting and encouraging respect for human rights and for fundamental freedoms for all without distinction as to race, sex, language, or religion; and;

4. To be a center for harmonizing the actions of nations in the attainment of these common ends.

Article 2.

The Organization and its Members, in pursuit of the Purposes stated in Article 1, shall act in accordance with the following Principles.

1. The Organization is based on the principle of the sovereign equality of all its Members.

2. All Members, in order to ensure to all of them the rights and benefits resulting from membership, shall fulfil in good faith the obligations assumed by them in accordance with the present Charter.

3. All Members shall settle their international disputes by peaceful means in such a manner that international peace and security, and justice, are not endangered.

4. All Members shall refrain in their international relations from the threat or use of force against the territorial integrity or political independence of any state, or in any other manner inconsistent with the Purposes of the United Nations.

5. All Members shall give the United Nations every assistance in any action it takes in accordance with the present Charter, and shall refrain from giving assistance to any state against which the United Nations is taking preventive or enforcement action.

6. The Organization shall ensure that states which are not Members of the United Nations act in accordance with these Principles so far as may be necessary for the maintenance of international peace and security.

7. Nothing contained in the present Charter shall authorize the United Nations to intervene in matters which are essentially within the domestic jurisdiction of any state or shall require the Members to submit such matters to settlement under the present Charter; but this principle shall not prejudice the application of enforcement measures under Chapter VII.

Article 35.

1. Any Member of the United Nations may bring any dispute, or any situation of the nature referred to in Article 34, to the attention of the Security Council or of the General Assembly.

2. A state which is not a Member of the United Nations may bring to the attention of the Security Council or of the General Assembly any dispute to which it is a party if it accepts in advance, for the purposes of the dispute, the obligations of pacific settlement provided in the present Charter.

3. The proceedings of the General Assembly in respect of matters brought to its attention under this Article will be subject to the provisions of Articles 11 and 12.

Article 39.

The Security Council shall determine the existence of any threat to the peace, breach of the peace, or act of aggression and shall make recommendations, or decide what measures shall be taken in accordance with Articles 41 and 42, to maintain or restore international peace and security.

Article 40.

In order to prevent an aggravation of the situation, the Security Council may, before making the recommendations or deciding upon the measures provided for in Article 39, call upon the parties concerned to comply with such provisional measures as it deems necessary or desirable. Such provisional measures shall be without prejudice to the rights, claims, or position of the parties concerned. The Security Council shall duly take account of failure to comply with such provisional measures.

Article 41.

The Security Council may decide what measures not involving the use of armed force are to be employed to give effect to its decisions, and it may call upon the Members of the United Nations to apply such measures. These may include complete or partial interruption of economic relations and of rail, sea, air, postal, telegraphic, radio, and other means of communication, and the severance of diplomatic relations.

Article 42.

Should the Security Council consider that measures provided for in Article 41 would be inadequate or have proved to be inadequate, it may take such action by air, sea, or land forces as may be necessary to maintain or restore international peace and security. Such action may include demonstrations, blockade, and other operations by air, sea, or land forces of Members of the United Nations.

Article 43.

1. All Members of the United Nations, in order to contribute to the maintenance of international peace and security, undertake to make

available to the Security Council, on its call and in accordance with a special agreement or agreements, armed forces, assistance, and facilities, including rights of passage, necessary for the purpose of maintaining international peace and security.

2. Such agreement or agreements shall govern the numbers and types of forces, their degree of readiness and general location, and the nature of the facilities and assistance to be provided.

3. The agreement or agreements shall be negotiated as soon as possible on the initiative of the Security Council. They shall be concluded between the Security Council and Members or between the Security Council and groups of Members and shall be subject to ratification by the signatory states in accordance with their respective constitutional processes.

Article 44.

When the Security Council has decided to use force it shall, before calling upon a Member not represented on it to provide armed forces in fulfillment of the obligations assumed under Article 43, invite that Member, if the Member so desires, to participate in the decisions of the Security Council concerning the employment of contingents of that Member's armed forces.

Article 45.

In order to enable the United Nations to take urgent military measures, Members shall hold immediately available national air-force contingents for combined international enforcement action. The strength and degree of readiness of these contingents and plans for their combined action shall be determined, within limits laid down in the special agreement or agreements referred to in Article 43, by the Security Council with the assistance of the Military Staff Committee.

Article 46.

Plans for the application of armed force shall be made by the Security Council with the assistance of the Military Staff Committee.

Article 48.

1. The action required to carry out the decisions of the Security Council for the maintenance of international peace and security shall be taken by all the Members of the United Nations or by some of them, as the Security Council may determine.

2. Such decisions shall be carried out by the Members of the United Nations directly and through their action in the appropriate international agencies of which they are members.

Article 49.

The Members of the United Nations shall join in affording mutual assistance in carrying out the measures decided upon by the Security Council.

Article 92.

The International Court of Justice shall be the principal judicial organ of the United Nations. It shall function in accordance with the annexed Statute, which is based upon the Statute of the Permanent Court of International Justice and forms an integral part of the present Charter.

Article 93.

1. All Members of the United Nations are *ipso facto* parties to the Statute of the International Court of Justice.

2. A state which is not a Member of the United Nations may become a party to the Statute of the International Court of Justice on conditions to be determined in each case by the General Assembly upon the recommendation of the Security Council.

Article 94.

1. Each Member of the United Nations undertakes to comply with the decision of the International Court of Justice in any case to which it is a party.

2. If any party to a case fails to perform the obligations incumbent upon it under a judgment rendered by the Court, the other party may have recourse to the Security Council, which may, if it deems necessary, make recommendations or decide upon measures to be taken to give effect to the judgment.

APPENDIX E

Article 2.

The Court shall be composed of a body of independent judges, elected regardless of their nationality from among persons of high moral character, who possess the qualifications required in their respective countries for appointment to the highest judicial offices, or are jurisconsults of recognized competence in international law.

Article 3.

1. The Court shall consist of fifteen members, no two of whom may be nationals of the same state.

2. A person who for the purposes of membership in the Court could be regarded as a national of more than one state shall be deemed to be a national of the one in which he ordinarily exercises civil and political rights.

Article 9.

At every election, the electors shall bear in mind not only that the persons to be elected should individually possess the qualifications required, but also that in the body as a whole the representation of the main forms of civilization and of the principal legal systems of the world should be assured.

Article 16.

1. No member of the Court may exercise any political or administrative function, or engage in any other occupation of a professional nature.

2. Any doubt on this point shall be settled by the decision of the Court.

Article 17.

1. No member of the Court may act as agent, counsel, or advocate in any case.

2. No member may participate in the decision of any case in which he has previously taken part as agent, counsel, or advocate for one of the parties, or as a member of a national or international court, or of a commission of enquiry, or in any other capacity.

3. Any doubt on this point shall be settled by the decision of the Court.

Article 18.

1. No member of the Court can be dismissed unless, in the unanimous opinion of the other members, he has ceased to fulfil the required conditions.

2. Formal notification thereof shall be made to the Secretary-General by the Registrar.

3. This notification makes the place vacant.

Article 19.

The members of the Court, when engaged on the business of the Court, shall enjoy diplomatic privileges and immunities.

Article 20.

Every member of the Court shall, before taking up his duties, make a solemn declaration in open court that he will exercise his powers impartially and conscientiously.

Article 31.

1. Judges of the nationality of each of the parties shall retain their right to sit in the case before the Court.

2. If the Court includes upon the Bench a judge of the nationality of one of the parties, any other party may choose a person to sit as judge. Such person shall be chosen preferably from among those persons who have been nominated as candidates as provided in Articles 4 and 5.

3. If the Court includes upon the Bench no judge of the nationality of the parties, each of these parties may proceed to choose a judge as provided in paragraph 2 of this Article.

4. The provisions of this Article shall apply to the case of Articles 26 and 29. In such cases, the President shall request one or, if necessary, two of the members of the Court forming the chamber to give place to the members of the Court of the nationality of the parties concerned, and, failing such, or if they are unable to be present, to the judges specially chosen by the parties.

5. Should there be several parties in the same interest, they shall, for the purpose of the preceding provisions, be reckoned as one party only. Any doubt upon this point shall be settled by the decision of the Court.

6. Judges chosen as laid down in paragraphs 2, 3, and 4 of this Article shall fulfil the conditions required by Articles 2, 17 (paragraph 2), 20, and 24 of the present Statute. They shall take part in the decision on terms of complete equality with their colleagues.

Article 34.

1. Only states may be parties in cases before the Court.

2. The Court, subject to and in conformity with its Rules, may request of public international organizations information relevant to cases before it, and shall receive such information presented by such organizations on their own initiative.

3. Whenever the construction of the constituent instrument of a public international organization or of an international convention adopted thereunder is in question in a case before the Court, the Registrar shall so notify the public international organization concerned and shall communicate to it copies of all the written proceedings.

Article 35.

1. The Court shall be open to the states parties to the present Statute.

2. The conditions under which the Court shall be open to other states shall, subject to the special provisions contained in treaties in force, be laid down by the Security Council, but in no case shall such conditions place the parties in a position of inequality before the Court.

3. When a state which is not a Member of the United Nations is a party to a case, the Court shall fix the amount which that party is to contribute towards the expenses of the Court. This provision shall not apply if such state is bearing a share of the expenses of the Court.

Article 36.

1. The jurisdiction of the Court comprises all cases which the parties refer to it and all matters specially provided for in the Charter of the United Nations or in treaties and conventions in force.

2. The states parties to the present Statute may at any time declare that they recognize as compulsory *ipso facto* and without special agreement, in relation to any other state accepting the same obligation, the jurisdiction of the Court in all legal disputes concerning:

a. the interpretation of a treaty;

b. any question of international law;

c. the existence of any fact which, if established, would constitute a breach of an international obligation;

d. the nature or extent of the reparation to be made for the breach of an international obligation.

3. The declarations referred to above may be made unconditionally or on condition of reciprocity on the part of several or certain states, or for a certain time.

4. Such declarations shall be deposited with the Secretary-General of the United Nations, who shall transmit copies thereof to the parties to the Statute and to the Registrar of the Court.

5. Declarations made under Article 36 of the Statute of the Permanent Court of International Justice and which are still in force shall be deemed, as between the parties to the present Statute, to be acceptances of the compulsory jurisdiction of the International Court of Justice for the period which they still have to run and in accordance with their terms.

6. In the event of a dispute as to whether the Court has jurisdiction, the matter shall be settled by the decision of the Court.

Article 40.

1. Cases are brought before the Court, as the case may be, either by the notification of the special agreement or by a written application addressed to the Registrar. In either case the subject of the dispute and the parties shall be indicated.

2. The Registrar shall forthwith communicate the application to all concerned.

3. He shall also notify the Members of the United Nations through the Secretary-General, and also any other states entitled to appear before the Court.

Article 41.

1. The Court shall have the power to indicate, if it considers that circumstances so require, any provisional measures which ought to be taken to preserve the respective rights of either party.

2. Pending the final decision, notice of the measures suggested shall forthwith be given to the parties and to the Security Council.

Article 59.

The decision of the Court has no binding force except between the parties and in respect of that particular case.

Article 60.

The judgment is final and without appeal. In the event of dispute as to the meaning or scope of the judgment, the Court shall construe it upon the request of any party.

Article 61.

1. An application for revision of a judgment may be made only when it is based upon the discovery of some fact of such a nature as to be a decisive factor, which fact was, when the judgment was given, unknown to the Court and also to the party claiming revision, always provided that such ignorance was not due to negligence.

2. The proceedings for revision shall be opened by a judgment of the Court expressly recording the existence of the new fact, recognizing that it has such a character as to lay the case open to revision, and declaring the application admissible on this ground.

3. The Court may require previous compliance with the terms of the judgment before it admits proceedings in revision.

4. The application for revision must be made at latest within six months of the discovery of the new fact.

5. No application for revision may be made after the lapse of ten years from the date of the judgment.

APPENDIX F

SELECTED ARTICLES FROM THE TREATIES ESTABLISHING THE EUROPEAN COMMUNITIES[a]

A. EUROPEAN COAL AND STEEL COMMUNITY

Article 2.

The mission of the European Coal and Steel Community is to contribute to economic expansion, the development of employment and the improvement of the standard of living in the participating countries through the institution, in harmony with the general economy of the member States, of a common market as defined in Article 4.

The Community must progressively establish conditions which will in themselves assure the most rational distribution of production at the highest possible level of productivity, while safeguarding the continuity of employment and avoiding the creation of fundamental and persistent disturbances in the economies of the member States.

Article 3.

Within the framework of their respective powers and responsibilities and in the common interest, the institutions of the Community shall:

(a) see that the common market is regularly supplied, taking account of the needs of third countries;

(b) assure to all consumers in comparable positions within the common market equal access to the sources of production;

(c) seek the establishment of the lowest prices which are possible without requiring any corresponding rise either in the prices charged by the same enterprises in other transactions or in the price-level as a whole in another period, while at the same time permitting necessary amortization and providing normal possibilities of remuneration for capital invested;

(d) see that conditions are maintained which will encourage enterprises to expand and improve their ability to produce and to promote a policy of rational development of natural resources, avoiding inconsiderate exhaustion of such resources;

(e) promote the improvement of the living and working conditions of the labor force in each of the industries under its jurisdiction so as to make possible the equalization of such conditions in an upward direction;

(f) further the development of international trade and see that equitable limits are observed in prices charged on external markets;

(g) promote the regular expansion and the modernization of produc-

---

[a] English versions from *United Nations Treaty Series*, CCLXI, 3229 (1957), 140–319; CCXCVIII, 4300 (1958), 1–165; and CCXCVIII, 4301 (1958), 167–266.

tion as well as the improvement of its quality, under conditions which preclude any protection against competing industries except where justified by illegitimate action on the part of such industries or in their favor.

Article 4.

The following are recognized to be incompatible with the common market for coal and steel, and are, therefore, abolished and prohibited within the Community in the manner set forth in the present Treaty:

(a) import and export duties, or charges with an equivalent effect, and quantitative restrictions on the movement of coal and steel;

(b) measures or practices discriminating among producers, among buyers or among consumers, specifically as concerns prices, delivery terms and transportation rates, as well as measures or practices which hamper the buyer in the free choice of his supplier;

(c) subsidies or state assistance, or special charges imposed by the state, in any form whatsoever;

(d) restrictive practices tending towards the division of markets or the exploitation of the consumer.

Article 5.

The Community shall accomplish its mission, under the conditions provided for in the present Treaty, with limited direct intervention.

To this end, the Community will:

—enlighten and facilitate the action of the interested parties by collecting information, organizing consultations and defining general objectives;

—place financial means at the disposal of enterprises for their investments and participate in the expenses of readaptation;

—assure the establishment, the maintenance and the observance of normal conditions of competition and take direct action with respect to production and the operation of the market only when circumstances make it absolutely necessary;

—publish the justification for its action and take the necessary measures to ensure observance of the rules set forth in the present Treaty.

The institutions of the Community shall carry out these activities with as little administrative machinery as possible and in close cooperation with the interested parties.

Article 14.

In the execution of its responsibilities under the present Treaty and in accordance with the provisions thereof, the High Authority shall issue decisions, recommendations and opinions.

Decisions shall be binding in all their details.

Recommendations shall be binding with respect to the objectives which they specify but shall leave to those to whom they are directed the choice of appropriate means for attaining these objectives.

Opinions shall not be binding.

When the High Authority is empowered to issue a decision, it may limit itself to making a recommendation.

Article 31.

The function of the Court is to ensure the rule of law in the interpretation and application of the present Treaty and of its implementing regulations.

Article 32.

The Court shall be composed of seven judges, appointed for six years by agreement among the governments of the member States from among persons of recognized independence and competence.

A partial change in membership of the Court shall occur every three years, affecting alternatively three members and four members. The three members whose terms expire at the end of the first period of three years shall be designated by lot.

Judges shall be eligible for reappointment.

The number of judges may be increased by unanimous vote of the Council on proposal by the Court.

The judges shall designate one of their number as President for a three-year term.

Article 33.

The Court shall have jurisdiction over appeals by a member State or by the Council for the annulment of decisions and recommendations of the High Authority on the grounds of lack of legal competence, substantial procedural violations, violation of the Treaty or of any rule of law relating to its application, or abuse of power. However, the Court may not review the conclusions of the High Authority, drawn from economic facts and circumstances, which formed the basis of such decisions or recommendations, except where the High Authority is alleged to have abused its powers or to have clearly misinterpreted the provisions of the Treaty or of a rule of law relating to its application.

The enterprises, or the associations referred to in Article 48, shall have the right of appeal on the same grounds against individual decisions and recommendations concerning them, or against general decisions and recommendations which they deem to involve an abuse of power affecting them.

The appeals provided for in the first two paragraphs of the present article must be taken within one month from the date of the notification or the publication, as the case may be, of the decision or recommendation.

Article 35.

In the cases where the High Authority is required by a provision of the present Treaty or of implementing regulations to issue a decision or recommendation, and fails to fulfill this obligation, such omission may be brought to its attention by the States, the Council or the enterprises and associations, as the case may be.

The same shall be true if the High Authority refrains from issuing a decision or recommendation which it is empowered to issue by a provision of the present Treaty or implementing regulations, where such failure to act constitutes an abuse of power.

If at the end of a period of two months the High Authority has not issued any decision or recommendation, an appeal may be brought before the Court, within a period of one month, against the implicit negative decision which is presumed to result from such failure to act.

Article 36.

Prior to assessing a pecuniary sanction or fixing a daily penalty payment provided for in the present Treaty, the High Authority shall give the interested enterprise an opportunity to present its views.

An appeal to the general jurisdiction of the Court may be taken from the pecuniary sanctions and daily penalty payments imposed under the provisions of the present Treaty.

In support of such an appeal, and under the terms of the first paragraph of Article 33 of the present Treaty, the petitioners may contest the regularity of the decisions and recommendations which they are charged with violating.

Article 38.

On the petition of a member State or of the High Authority, the Court may annul the acts of the Assembly or of the Council.

The petition must be submitted within one month from the publication of such act of the Assembly or of the notification of such act of the Council to the member States or to the High Authority.

Such an appeal may be based only on the grounds of lack of legal competence or substantial procedural violations.

Article 41.

When the validity of acts of the High Authority or the Council is contested in litigation before a national tribunal, such issue shall be certified to the Court, which shall have exclusive jurisdiction to rule thereon.

Article 44.

The judgments of the Court shall be executory on the territory of the member States under the terms of Article 92 below.

Article 86.

The member States bind themselves to take all general and specific measures which will assure the execution of their obligations under the decisions and recommendations of the institutions of the Community, and facilitate the accomplishment of the Community's purposes.

The member States bind themselves to refrain from any measures which are incompatible with the existence of the common market referred to in Articles 1 and 4.

To the extent of their competence, the member States will take all appropriate measures to assure the international payments arising out of trade in coal and steel within the common market; they will lend assistance to each other to facilitate such payments.

Officials of the High Authority charged with verifying information shall enjoy on the territories of the member States, to the extent necessary for the accomplishment of their mission, such rights and powers as are granted by the laws of such States to officials of its own tax services. The missions and the status of the officials charged with them shall be duly communicated to the State in question. Officials of such State may, at the request of such State or of the High Authority, assist those of the High Authority in carrying out their mission.

Article 88.

If the High Authority deems that a State is delinquent with respect to one of the obligations incumbent upon it by virtue of the present Treaty, it will, after permitting the State in question to present its views, take note of the delinquency in a decision accompanied by a justification. It will allow the State in question a period of time within which to provide for the execution of its obligation.

Such State may appeal to the Court's plenary jurisdiction within a period of two months from the notification of the decision.

If the State has not taken steps for the fulfillment of its obligation within the period fixed by the High Authority, or if its appeal has been rejected, the High Authority may, with the concurrence of the Council acting by a two-thirds majority:

(a) suspend the payment of sums which the High Authority may owe to the State in question under the present Treaty;

(b) adopt measures or authorize the other member States to adopt measures involving an exception to the provisions of Article 4, so as to correct the effects of the delinquency in question.

An appeal to the Court's plenary jurisdiction may be brought against the decisions taken in application of paragraphs (a) and (b) within two months following their notification.

If these measures should prove inoperative, the High Authority will lay the matter before the Council.

Article 89.

Any dispute among member States concerning the application of the present Treaty, which cannot be settled by another procedure provided for in the present Treaty, may be submitted to the Court at the request of one of the States parties to the dispute.

The Court shall also have jurisdiction to settle any dispute among member States related to the purpose of the present Treaty, if such dispute is submitted to it by virtue of an agreement to arbitrate.

Article 92.

The decisions of the High Authority imposing financial obligations on enterprises are executory.

They shall be enforced on the territory of member States through the legal procedures in effect in each of these States, after the writ of execution in use in the State on the territory of which the decision is to be carried out has been placed upon them; this shall be done with no other formality than the certification of the authenticity of such decisions. The execution of these formalities shall be the responsibility of a Minister which each of the governments shall designate for this purpose.

Enforcement of such decisions can be suspended only by a decision of the Court.

Article 95.

In all cases not expressly provided for in the present Treaty in which a decision or a recommendation of the High Authority appears necessary to fulfill, in the operation of the common market for coal and steel and in accordance with the provisions of Article 5 above, one of the purposes of the Community as defined in Articles 2, 3 and 4, such decision or recommendation may be taken subject to the unanimous concurrence of the Council and after consultation with the Consultative Committee.

The same decision or recommendation, taken in the same manner, shall fix any sanctions to be applied.

If, following the expiration of the transition period provided for by the Convention containing the transitional provisions, unforeseen difficulties which are brought out by experience in the means of application of the present Treaty, or a profound change in the economic or technical conditions which affects the common coal and steel market directly, should make necessary an adaptation of the rules concerning the exercise by the High Authority of the powers which are conferred upon it, appropriate modifications may be made provided that they do not modify the provisions of Articles 2, 3 and 4, or the relationship among the powers of the High Authority and the other institutions of the Community.

These modifications will be proposed jointly by the High Authority and the Council acting by a five-sixths majority. They shall then be submitted to the opinion of the Court. In its examination, the Court may look into all elements of law and fact. If the Court should recognize that they conform to the provisions of the preceding paragraph, such proposals shall be transmitted to the Assembly. They will enter into force if they are approved by the Assembly acting by a majority of three-quarters of the members present and voting comprising two-thirds of the total membership.

B. EUROPEAN ECONOMIC COMMUNITY

Article 5.

Member States shall take all general or particular measures which are appropriate for ensuring the carrying out of the obligations arising out of this Treaty or resulting from the acts of the institutions of the Community. They shall facilitate the achievement of the Community's aims.

They shall abstain from any measures likely to jeopardise the attainment of the objectives of this Treaty.

Article 164.

The Court of Justice shall ensure observance of law and justice in the interpretation and application of this Treaty.

Article 166.

The Court of Justice shall be assisted by two advocates-general.

The duty of the advocate-general shall be to present publicly, with complete impartiality and independence, reasoned conclusions on cases submitted to the Court of Justice, with a view to assisting the latter in the performance of its duties as laid down in Article 164.

Should the Court of Justice so request, the Council may, by means of a unanimous vote, increase the number of advocates-general and make the requisite amendments to Article 167, third paragraph.

Article 167.

The judges and the advocates-general shall be chosen from among persons of indisputable independence who fulfil the conditions required for the holding of the highest judicial office in their respective countries or who are jurists of a recognised competence; they shall be appointed for a term of six years by the Governments of Member States acting in common agreement.

A partial renewal of the Court of Justice shall take place every three years. It shall affect three and four judges alternately. The three judges whose terms of office are to expire at the end of the first period of three years shall be chosen by lot.

A partial renewal of the advocates-general shall take place every three years. The advocate-general whose term of office is to expire at the end of the first period of three years shall be chosen by lot.

The retiring judges and advocates-general shall be eligible for reappointment.

The judges shall appoint from among their members the President of the Court of Justice for a term of three years. Such term shall be renewable.

Article 169.

If the Commission considers that a Member State has failed to fulfil any of its obligations under this Treaty, it shall give a reasoned opinion on the matter after requiring such State to submit its comments.

If such State does not comply with the terms of such opinion within the period laid down by the Commission, the latter may refer the matter to the Court of Justice.

Article 170.

Any Member State which considers that another Member State has failed to fulfil any of its obligations under this Treaty may refer the matter to the Court of Justice.

Before a Member State institutes, against another Member State, proceedings relating to an alleged infringement of the obligations under this Treaty, it shall refer the matter to the Commission.

The Commission shall give a reasoned opinion after the States concerned have been required to submit their comments in written and oral pleadings.

If the Commission, within a period of three months after the date of reference of the matter to it, has not given an opinion, reference to the Court of Justice shall not hereby be prevented.

Article 171.

If the Court of Justice finds that a Member State has failed to fulfil any of its obligations under this Treaty, such State shall take the measures required for the implementation of the judgment of the Court.

Article 172.

The regulations laid down by the Council pursuant to the provisions of this Treaty may confer on the Court of Justice full jurisdiction in respect of penalties provided for in such regulations.

Article 173.

The Court of Justice shall review the lawfulness of acts other than recommendations or opinions of the Council and the Commission. For this purpose, it shall be competent to give judgment on appeals by a Member State, the Council or the Commission on grounds of incompetence, of errors of substantial form, of infringement of this Treaty or of any legal provision relating to its application, or of abuse of power.

Any natural or legal person may, under the same conditions, appeal against a decision addressed to him or against a decision which, although in the form of a regulation or a decision addressed to another person, is of direct and specific concern to him.

The appeals provided for in this Article shall be lodged within a period of two months dating, as the case may be, either from the publication of the act concerned or from its notification to the appellant or, failing that, from the day on which the latter had knowledge of that act.

Article 175.

In the event of the Council or the Commission in violation of this Treaty failing to act, the Member States and the other institutions of the Community may refer the matter to the Court of Justice with a view to establishing such violation.

Such appeal shall only be admissible if the institution concerned has previously been invited to act. If, at the expiry of a period of two months after such invitation that institution has not stated its attitude, the appeal may be lodged within a further period of two months.

Any natural or legal person may submit to the Court of Justice, under the conditions laid down in the preceding paragraphs, a complaint to the effect that one of the institutions of the Community has failed to address to him an act other than a recommendation or an opinion.

Article 177. .

The Court of Justice shall be competent to make a preliminary decision concerning:

(a) the interpretation of this Treaty;

(b) the validity and interpretation of acts of the institutions of the Community; and

(c) the interpretation of the statutes of any bodies set up by an act of the Council, where such statutes so provide.

Where any such question is raised before a court or tribunal of one of the Member States, such court or tribunal may, if it considers that its judgment depends on a preliminary decision on this question, request the Court of Justice to give a ruling thereon.

Where any such question is raised in a case pending before a domestic court or tribunal from whose decisions no appeal lies under municipal law, such court or tribunal shall refer the matter to the Court of Justice.

Article 180.

The Court of Justice shall be competent, within the limits laid down below, to hear cases concerning:

(a) the fulfilment by Member States of the obligations arising under the Statute of the European Investment Bank. The Board of Directors of the Bank shall, in this respect, dispose of the powers conferred upon the Commission by Article 169;

(b) the conclusions of the Board of Governors of the Bank. Any Member State, the Commission or the Board of Directors of the Bank may lodge an appeal in this matter under the conditions laid down in Article 173; and

(c) the conclusions of the Board of Directors of the Bank. Appeals against such conclusions may be lodged, under the conditions laid down in Article 173, provided that they may only be lodged by a Member State or by the Commission, and only on the grounds of an infringement of formal procedures laid down in Article 21, paragraph 2 and paragraphs 5 to 7 inclusive of the Statute of the Bank.

Article 182.

The Court of Justice shall be competent to decide in any dispute between Member States in connection with the object of this Treaty, where such dispute is submitted to it under the terms of a compromise.

Article 187.

The judgments of the Court of Justice shall be enforceable under the conditions laid down in Article 192.

Article 192.

Decisions of the Council or of the Commission which contain a pecuniary obligation on persons other than States shall be enforceable.

Forced execution shall be governed by the rules of civil procedure in force in the State in whose territory it takes place. The writ of execution shall be served, without other formality than the verification of the authenticity of the written act, by the domestic authority which the Government of each Member State shall designate for this purpose and of which it shall give notice to the Commission and to the Court of Justice.

After completion of these formalities at the request of the party concerned, the latter may, in accordance with municipal law, proceed with such forced execution by applying directly to the authority which is competent.

Forced execution may only be suspended pursuant to a decision of the Court of Justice. Supervision as to the regularity of the measures of execution shall, however, be within the competence of the domestic courts or tribunals.

Article 228.

1. Where this Treaty provides for the conclusion of agreements between the Community and one or more States or an international organization, such agreements shall be negotiated by the Commission. Subject to the powers conferred upon the Commission in this field, such agreements shall be concluded by the Council after the Assembly has been consulted in the cases provided for by this Treaty.

The Council, the Commission or a Member State may, as a preliminary, obtain the opinion of the Court of Justice as to the compatibility of the contemplated agreements with the provisions of this Treaty. An agreement which is the subject of a negative opinion of the Court of Justice may only enter into force under the conditions laid down, according to the case concerned, in Article 236.

2. Agreements concluded under the conditions laid down above shall be binding on the institutions of the Community and on Member States.

C. EUROPEAN ATOMIC ENERGY COMMUNITY[b]

Article 2.

For the attainment of its aims the Community shall, in accordance with the provisions set out in this Treaty:

(a) develop research and ensure the dissemination of technical knowledge,

(b) establish, and ensure the application of, uniform safety standards to protect the health of workers and of the general public,

(c) facilitate investment and ensure, particularly by encouraging business enterprise, the construction of the basic facilities required for the development of nuclear energy within the Community,

(d) ensure a regular and equitable supply of ores and nuclear fuels to all users in the Community,

(e) guarantee, by appropriate measures of control, that nuclear materials are not diverted for purposes other than those for which they are intended,

(f) exercise the property rights conferred upon it in respect of special fissionable materials,

(g) ensure extensive markets and access to the best technical means by the creation of a common market for specialised materials and equipment, by the free movement of capital for nuclear investment, and by freedom of employment for specialists within the Community,

(h) establish with other countries and with international organisations any contacts likely to promote progress in the peaceful uses of nuclear energy.

Article 3.

Same as *EEC* Article 4.

Article 18.

An Arbitration Committee shall hereby be established for the purposes stated in this Section; its members shall be appointed and its rules of procedure laid down by the Council acting on a proposal of the Court of Justice.

Decisions of the Arbitration Committee may, within a period of one month after their notification, be the subject of appeals brought by the parties before the Court of Justice to stay execution. The Court may decide only upon the regularities of form of the decision and upon the interpretation given by the Arbitration Committee to the provisions of this Treaty.

The final decisions of the Arbitration Committee shall have the force of *res judicata* as between the parties. They shall be enforceable under the provisions laid down in Article 164.

---

[b] Much of the Euratom Treaty, with minor stylistic changes, is similar to the EEC Treaty. Also, some articles are the same. These are indicated below.

Article 38.
Similar to *EEC* Article 169.

Article 82.
Similar to *EEC* Article 173.

Article 103.
Similar to *EEC* Article 228.

Article 138.
Similar to *EEC* Article 166.

Article 139.
Same as *EEC* Article 167.

Article 141.
Same as *EEC* Article 169.

Article 142.
Same as *EEC* Article 170.

Article 143.
Same as *EEC* Article 171.

Article 145.
Similar to *EEC* Article 169.

Article 146.
Same as *EEC* Article 173.

Article 148.
Same as *EEC* Article 175.

Article 150.
Same as *EEC* Article 177.

Article 154.
Same as *EEC* Article 182.

Article 159.
Similar to *EEC* Article 187.

Article 164.
Similar to *EEC* Article 192.

Article 192.
Similar to *EEC* Article 5.

APPENDIX G

NATURE AND SOLUTION OF CONTENTIOUS CASES BEFORE THE COURT OF THE EUROPEAN COMMUNITIES[a]

Case	Parties[b]	Issue	Disposition
1. 1–54. *Gouvernement de la République Française* v. *Haute Autorité de la CECA* (I, 7; 21 Dec. 1954)[c]	S/IO	The French government sought annulment of HA Decisions 1, 2, & 3–54 (allowing steel producers to sell at a price different from their published lists) on the grounds of violation of the Treaty (Art. 60, par. 2) and *détournement de pouvoir*.	Substantially for France. Art. 1 of Decision 2–54 was annulled. An appeal for annulment of Decisions 1 & 3–54 & 2–54 (2) was rejected.
2. 2–54. *Gouvernement de la République Italienne* v. *Haute Autorité de la CECA* (I, 73; 21 Dec. 1954)	S/IO	The Italian government sought annulment of HA Decisions 1, 2, & 3–54. In addition to the reasons listed in the prior case, the Italian government claimed a violation of the Treaty (Art. 15) and the convention containing the transitional provisions and of *détournement de pouvoir*.	Substantially for Italy. The Court annulled Decision 2–54 (1), but rejected all other appeals.

[a] Data derived from Cour de la Communauté Européenne du Charbon et de l'Acier, *Recueil de la Jurisprudence de la Cour*, Vols. I–V (Luxembourg: Villa Vauban, 1954–59) and from Cour de Justice des Communautés Européennes, *Recueil de la Jurisprudence de la Cour*, Vols. VI–XIII (Luxembourg, 1960–67). Both series form a single, continuous unit. Also used were European Coal and Steel Community, High Authority, *General Report*, 1st–15th (1954–67) and European Economic Community, Commission, *General Report*, 1st–10th (1958–67).

[b] S—State; I—Individual; IO—International Organ; E—Enterprise.

[c] The numbers preceding each case refer to folio number (*affaire n°*). As the French series of the Court reports were used in obtaining this data, the French case titles have been retained, both for continuity and to avoid possible misinterpretation through translation. The figures in parentheses refer to the volume and page number of the *Recueil de la Jurisprudence de la Cour* where the decision is to be found. The date in parentheses indicates when judgment was rendered.

[d] The explanation for this series of actions all challenging the same decisions is that the Court in 1954 did not make public the fact that appeals had been introduced. A Court *avis* of July 20, 1954, decided that future appeals would be published in the *Journal Officiel*.

No.	Case	Class	Description	Outcome
3.	3–54. *Associazione Industrie Siderurgiche Italiane (ASSIDER) v. Haute Autorité de la CECA* (I, 123; 11 Feb. 1955)	E/IO	An association of Italian steel companies sought annulment of HA Decisions 1, 2, & 3–54.ᵈ	Unclear. The Court ruled the case *res judicata*, but High Authority lost on its principal submission that the case was inadmissible.
4.	4–54. *Industrie Siderurgiche Associate (ISA) v. Haute Autorité de la CECA* (I, 177; 11 Feb. 1955)	E/IO	Same as above (appeal filed same day).	Same as above.
5.	6–54. *Gouvernement du Royaume des Pays-Bas v. Haute Autorité de la CECA* (I, 201; 21 March 1955)	S/IO	The Dutch government claimed that HA Decision 18–54, freeing all coal prices in the Community except in the Ruhr, Nord, and Pas-de-Calais, meant that the Ruhr monopoly would determine coal prices and thus should be annulled.	For High Authority. Dutch appeal rejected.
6.	5–55. *Associazione Industrie Siderurgiche Italiane (ASSIDER) v. Haute Autorité de la CECA* (I, 263; 28 June 1955)	E/IO	An appeal for interpretation of Judgment 3–54, which plaintiffs felt did not apply to them.	Substantially for plaintiff.
7.	1–55. *Antoine Kergall v. Assemblée Commune* (II, 9; 19 July 1955)	I/IO	Plaintiff claimed that the Assembly was abolishing his post as a "mere pretext" for dismissing him, which could only be done for cause and with a severance allowance.	For Mr. Kergall. He was granted damages amounting to 16 months of his salary.
8.	7 & 9–54. *Groupement des Industries Sidérurgiques Luxembourgeoises v. Haute Autorité de la CECA* (II, 53; 23 April 1956)	E/IO	Plaintiff contested the legality of the *Caisse de Compensation* set up by the Luxembourg government and its ability to impose a levy on all coal and coke imports. The *Caisse* was abolished before judgment, but plaintiff continued the case on the basis of principle.	Unclear. The Court held there was no need for a ruling on part of the appeal and rejected the remainder.
9.	8 & 10–54. *Association des Utilisateurs de Charbon du grand-duché de Luxembourg v. Haute Autorité de la CECA* (II, 157; 23 April 1956)	E/IO	Cases substantially the same as 7 & 9–54. The HA protested admissibility because plaintiff was a "consumer" association rather than a "producer" as specified by Arts. 48 & 80 of the Treaty.	For High Authority. Complaint inadmissible.

Case	Parties	Issue	Disposition
10. 8–55. *Fédération Charbonnière de Belgique v. Haute Autorité de la CECA* (II, 199; 16 July 1956)	E/IO	An association of all the collieries of Belgium challenged the validity of HA Decision 22–55 and letter of 28 May 1955, fixing terms and conditions of ECSC subsidies to the Belgian coal industry.	For High Authority. Decision upheld.
11. 9–55. *Société des Charbonnages de Beeringen, Société des Charbonnages de Houthalen, Société des Charbonnages de Helchteren et Zolder v. Haute Autorité de la CECA* (II, 323; 29 Nov. 1956)	E/IO	Three enterprises of the Campine coal field in Belgium presented the same arguments as Case 8–55, and also protested the withdrawal of compensation payments by the HA.	For High Authority. Appeal dismissed.
12. 10–55. *Miranda Mirossevich v. Haute Autorité de la CECA* (II, 365; 12 Dec. 1956)	I/IO	Plaintiff claimed she was dismissed on grounds of incompetence as a translator without a proper trial period.	For Miss Mirossevich. The Court ordered her rehired for a probationary period of six months.
13. 1–56. *René Bourgaux v. Assemblée Commune* (II, 421; 17 Dec. 1956)	I/IO	Plaintiff challenged his release through abolishment of his post as improper dismissal.	For Common Assembly. Appeal dismissed.
14. 2–56. *Sociétés Minières du Bassin de la Ruhr Groupées au Sein du Comptoir de Vente du Charbon de la Ruhr "Geitling" et Comptoir de Vente du Charbon de la Ruhr "Geitling" v. Haute Autorité de la CECA* (III, 421; 17 Dec. 1956)	E/IO	Nineteen coal-mining enterprises and "Geitling" (one of three sales agencies replacing GEORG) sought annulment of Art. 8 of HA Decision 5–56, which refused to authorize restrictive sales practices.	For High Authority. Appeal dismissed.
15. 7–56, 3 to 7–57. *Dineke Algera, Giacomo Cicconardi, Simone Couturand, Ignazio Gennardi, et Félicie Steichen v. Assemblée Commune* (III, 81; 12 July 1957)	I/IO	Plaintiffs challenged various administrative acts degrading their status as civil servants.	For plaintiffs.

No.		E/IO	Description	Result
16.	8-56. *Acciaierie Laminatoi Magliano Albi (ALMA) v. Haute Autorité de la CECA* (III, 179; 10 Dec. 1957)	E/IO	An Italian steel works appealed a fine of 800,-000 *lire* (about $1,300) levied by the HA on the grounds that they weren't aware they were being fined and that they had no chance to present their case to the HA. The HA claimed that the company was notified.	For High Authority. Fine upheld.
17.	1 & 14-57. *Société des Usines à Tubes de la Sarre v. Haute Autorité de la CECA* (III, 201; 10 Dec. 1957)	E/IO	Plaintiffs appealed against an HA letter rejecting certain of their investment proposals.	For High Authority. Appeals inadmissible.
18.	9-56. *Meroni & Co., Industrie Metallurgiche, S.p.A. v. Haute Autorité de la CECA* (IV, 9; 13 Jan. 1958)	E/IO	An Italian steel-producing enterprise challenged the validity of HA Decision 14-55 establishing a subsidy for imported scrap iron.	For Meroni & Co. Decision annulled.
19.	10-56. *Meroni & Co, Industrie Metallurgiche, Società in Accomandita Semplice v. Haute Autorité de la CECA* (IV, 51; 13 June 1958)	E/IO	An Italian steel firm refused to pay a pre-existing debt.	For Meroni & Co. Decision annulled.
20.	2-57. *Compagnie des Hauts Fourneaux de Chasse v. Haute Autorité de la CECA* (IV, 129; 13 June 1958)	E/IO	A French firm sought annulment of an HA decision levying a uniform tax on purchased scrap iron because it discriminated against purchasers of cheaper grades of scrap.	For High Authority. Appeal dismissed.
21.	15-57. *Compagnie des Hauts Fourneaux de Chasse v. Haute Autorité de la CECA* (IV, 155; 13 June 1958)	E/IO	A French firm refused to pay a pre-existing levy debt on the grounds that the money would help competitors.	For High Authority. Appeal rejected.
22.	8-57. *Groupement des Hauts Fourneaux et Aciéries Belges v. Haute Autorité de la CECA* (IV, 223; 21 June 1958)	E/IO	A non-profit organization in Brussels challenged HA Decision 2-57 as it was adversely affected by a supplementary tax on scrap consumption.	For High Authority. Action admissible but not well-founded.

Case	Parties	Issue	Disposition
23. 13–57. *Wirtschaftsvereinigung Eisen- und Stahlindustrie, Gußstahlwerk Carl Bönnhoff, Gußstahlwerk Witten, Ruhrstahl, et Eisenwerk Annahütte Alfred Zeller v. Haute Autorité de la CECA* (IV, 261; 21 June 1958)	E/IO	A group of German steel producers challenged HA Decision 2–57.	For High Authority. Appeals dismissed.
24. 9–57. *Chambre Syndicale de la Sidérurgie Française v. Haute Autorité de la CECA* (IV, 363; 26 June 1958)	E/IO	A syndicate of French iron and steel producers challenged certain financial arrangements (concerning levies on scrap iron) under HA Decision 2–57.	For High Authority. Action admissible but not well-founded.
25. 10–57. *Société des Anciens Établissements Anbert et Duval v. Haute Autorité de la CECA* (IV, 399; 26 June 1958)	E/IO	A French steel mill contested the levy and resulting production restriction of HA Decision 2–57.	For High Authority. Appeal dismissed as not well-founded.
26. 11–57. *Société d'Electro-chimie d'Electro-metallurgie et des Aciéries Électriques d'Ugine v. Haute Autorité de la CECA* (IV, 435; 26 June 1958)	E/IO	French steel producers challenged the validity of HA Decision 2–57.	For High Authority. Appeal dismissed.
27. 12–57. *Syndicat de la Sidérurgie du Centre-midi v. Haute Autorité de la CECA* (IV, 471; 26 June 1958)	E/IO	A syndicate of French steel producers challenged the validity of HA Decision 2–57.	For High Authority. Appeal dismissed.
28. 17–57. *De Gezamenlijke Steenkolenmijnen in Limburg v. Haute Autorité de la CECA* (V, 9; 4 Feb. 1959)	E/IO	A Dutch firm challenged an HA decision approving a subsidy by the German government to certain German coal mines.	For High Authority. Appeal inadmissible.
29. 1–58. *Enterprise Friedrich Stork et Cie., Kohlengroßhandlung v. Haute Autorité de la CECA* (V, 43; 4 Feb. 1959)	E/IO	A German firm sought annulment of an HA decision of 27 Nov. 1957 allowing the coal producer GEORG to refuse to trade with the plaintiff.	For High Authority. Appeal dismissed.

30. 18–57. *Firma I. Nold KG, Kohlen- und Baustoffgroßhandlung v. Haute Autorité de la CECA* (V, 89; 17 July 1959)	E/IO	A German coal-distributing firm sought a court order suspending, and eventual judgment annulling, HA Decisions 16 to 18–57, prohibiting them from acting as a direct trading wholesaler.	For Nold. Both the order and the annulment were granted.
31. 20–58. *Phoenix-Rheinrohr AG, Vereinigte Hütten- und Röhrenwerke v. Haute Autorité de la CECA* (V, 163; 17 July 1959)	E/IO	A German steel firm challenged the validity of certain technical definitions in an HA letter of 18 Dec. 1957.	For High Authority. Appeal inadmissible.
32. 21–58. *Felten und Guilleaume Carlswerk Eisen- und Stahl AG et Walzwerke AG, Anciennement E. Böking et Cie. v. Haute Autorité de la CECA* (V, 211; 17 July 1959)	E/IO	Two German steel firms challenged the validity of certain technical definitions in an HA letter of 18 Dec. 1957. Substantially the same case as 20–58.	For High Authority. Appeal inadmissible.
33. 22–58. *Bochumer Verein für Gußstahlfabrikation AG, Niederrheinische Hütte AG, et Stahlwerke Südwestfalen AG v. Haute Autorité de la CECA* (V, 231; 17 July 1959)	E/IO	Three German steel firms challenged the validity of certain technical definitions in an HA letter of 18 Dec. 1957. Substantially the same case as the two foregoing cases.	For High Authority. Appeal inadmissible.
34. 23–58. *Mannesmann AG, Hoeschwerke AG, Klöcknerwerke AG, Rheinische Stahlwerke AG, et Aktiengesellschaft für Berg- und Hüttenbetriebe v. Haute Autorité de la CECA* (V, 253; 17 July 1959)	E/IO	Five German steel firms challenged the validity of certain technical definitions in an HA letter of 18 Dec. 1957. Substantially the same case as the three foregoing cases.	For High Authority. Appeal inadmissible.
35. 32 & 33–58. *Société Nouvelle des Usines de Pont-lieue—Aciéries du Temple (SNUPAT) v. Haute Autorité de la CECA* (V, 275; 17 July 1959)	E/IO	Two French steel firms challenged the validity of certain technical definitions in HA letters and of certain aspects of scrap iron levies.	For High Authority. Case 33–58 inadmissible and 32–58 not well-founded.

Case	Parties	Issue	Disposition
36. 36, 37, 38, 40, & 41–58. *Società Industriale Metallurgica di Napoli (SIMET), Meroni & Co., Industrie Metallurgiche à Erba, Meroni & Co., Metallurgiche à Milan, FerRo (Ferriere Rossi), et Acciaierie San Michele v. Haute Autorité de la CECA* (V, 331; 17 July 1959)	E/IO	Italian firms challenged the validity of HA Decision 13–58 (amending portions of Decisions 14–55 and 2–57, declared illegal by the Court) empowering the HA to tax scrap iron consumption.	For High Authority. Cases 40 & 41 inadmissible; other cases dismissed as not well-founded.
37. 42–58. *Société des Aciers Fin de l'Est (SAFE) v. Haute Autorité de la CECA* (V, 381; 17 July 1959)	E/IO	A French steel enterprise challenged an HA decision and a letter of 31 July 1958 refusing to exempt them from a scrap levy.	For High Authority. Appeal against decision dismissed; appeal against letter inadmissible.
38. 1–59. *Macchiorlatti Dalmas & Figli v. Haute Autorité de la CECA* (V, 413; 17 Dec. 1959)	E/IO	An Italian firm appealed a fine of 2,500,000 *lire* (about $4,000) levied by the HA because the firm had deviated from its price lists and discriminated against customers. The firm claimed the deviation was justified by differences in product quality.	For High Authority. Fine upheld.
39. 14–59. *Société des Fonderies de Pont-a-Mousson v. Haute Autorité de la CECA* (V, 445; 17 Dec. 1959)	E/IO	A French enterprise challenged an HA decision to tax scrap used in processing molten pig-iron.	For High Authority. Appeal rejected.
40. 23–59. *Acciaieria Ferriera di Roma (FERAM) v. Haute Autorité de la CECA* (V, 501; 18 Nov. 1959)	E/IO	An Italian company demanded a scrap iron rebate on a subsidy wrongly paid out in Cases 4 to 13–59.	For High Authority. Appeal dismissed.
41. 15 & 29–59. *Société Métallurgique de Knutange v. Haute Autorité de la CECA* (VI, 9; 12 Feb. 1960)	E/IO	A French firm contested a supplementary tax upon any increased consumption of scrap iron.	For High Authority. Appeal dismissed.

No. / Case	Type	Description	Outcome
42. 16, 17 & 18–59. "Geitling" et Autres v. Haute Autorité de la CECA (VI, 45; 12 Feb. 1960)	E/IO	Plaintiffs sought annulment of certain provisions of a covering letter of 31 March 1960 sent out by the HA along with Decision 17–59.	Substantially for High Authority. The appeal was declared inadmissible because the letter had no binding force, but the High Authority was ordered to pay one-third of court costs because the "imperative manner" of the letter forced the suit.
43. 3–59. Gouvernement de la République Fédérale d'Allemagne v. Haute Autorité de la CECA (VI, 117; 8 March 1960)	S/IO	The German government appealed an HA decision of 1 Dec. 1958 giving effect to Court Judgment 19–58.	For High Authority. Appeal dismissed.
44. 31–59. Acciaieria e Tubificio di Brescia v. Haute Autorité de la CECA (VI, 151; 14 April 1960)	E/IO	An Italian steel producer contested the HA's power to collect information from enterprises and to verify it.	For High Authority. Appeal dismissed.
45. 34–59. Raymond Elz v. Haute Autorité de la CECA (VI, 215; 4 April 1960)	I/IO	Plaintiff contested his civil service classification.	For High Authority. Appeal inadmissible.
46. 4 to 13–59. Mannesmann AG et Autres v. Haute Autorité de la CECA (VI, 241; 4 April 1960)	E/IO	Plaintiffs refused to pay back a scrap iron subsidy wrongly paid out by Hansa Rohstoffverwertung, a middle man handling disbursements for the Caisse. They appealed the HA order to repay.	For High Authority. Case dismissed.
47. 1–60. Acciaieria Ferriera di Roma v. Haute Autorité de la CECA (VI, 351; 10 May 1960)	E/IO	A request for revision of Judgment 23–59 on procedural grounds (language of submitted documents).	For High Authority. Case inadmissible.
48. 3 to 18, 25, & 26–58. Barbara Erzbergbau AG et Autres v. Haute Autorité de la CECA (VI, 367; 10 May 1960)	E/IO	A group of German firms challenged an HA decision revoking their special freight rates, granted by the German government, for coal and other ores.	For High Authority. All appeals dismissed.

Case	Parties	Issue	Disposition
49. 19–58. *Gouvernement de la République Fédérale d'Allemagne v. Haute Autorité de la CECA* (VI, 469; 10 May 1960)	S/IO	The German government challenged the validity of HA decisions embodied in a letter of 12 Feb. 1958, regulating *Bundesbahn* tariffs. Germany claimed this interference would "provoke fundamental and persistent disturbances in the economy."	For High Authority. Appeal dismissed.
50. 27, 28, & 29–58. *Compagnie des Hauts Fourneaux et Fonderies de Givors et Autres v. Haute Autorité de la CECA* (VI, 501; 10 May 1960)	E/IO	Three French firms sought annulment of an HA decision contained in a letter of 12 Feb. 1958, which revoked their special freight concessions.	For High Authority. Appeals dismissed.
51. 24 & 34–58. *Chambre Syndicale de la Sidérurgie de l'Est de la France et Autres v. Haute Autorité de la CECA* (VI, 573; 15 July 1960)	E/IO	French firms challenged an HA decision approving special freight rates for certain German firms as discriminatory.	Unclear. Substantial portions of the decision were annulled in Case 24–58, but the remainder of that case and all of Case 34–58 were declared inadmissible.
52. 20–59. *Gouvernement de la République Italienne v. Haute Autorité de la CECA* (VI, 663; 15 July 1960)	S/IO	Italy challenged HA Decision 18–59 ordering ECSC members to publish or notify the HA of transport rates.	For Italy. Decision annulled because of procedural violations.
53. 25–59. *Gouvernement du Royaume des Pays-Bas v. Haute Autorité de la CECA* (VI, 723; 15 July 1960)	S/IO	The Dutch government presented the same case as Italy in the previous case.	For the Netherlands.
54. 27 & 39–59. *Alberto Campolongo v. Haute Autorité de la CECA* (VI, 795; 15 July 1960)	I/IO	Procedure for termination of contract by an employee and monetary allowances resulting therefrom.	Substantially for plaintiff. Much of this case was settled out of Court, of which the Court took judicial notice. The High Authority was condemned for costs; the plaintiff won most of his main points but lost his claim for damages.

55. 36, 37, 38, & 40–59. *Comptoirs de Vente du Charbon de la Ruhr "Präsident," "Geitling," "Mausegatt," Entreprise I. Nold KG v. Haute Autorité de la CECA* (VI, 857; 15 July 1960)	E/IO	Plaintiffs contested HA Decision 36–59 (a re-enacted version of 17–59).	Substantially for plaintiffs.
56. 43, 45, & 48–59. *Eva von Lachmüller, Bernard Peurrier, et Roger Ehrhardt v. Commission de la CEE* (VI, 933; 15 July 1960)	I/IO	Plaintiffs protested their dismissal as civil servants as improper.	Unclear. Plaintiffs lost their main appeal for employment security but were awarded damages anyway.
57. 41 & 50–59. *Hamborner Bergbau AG et Friedrich Thyssen Bergbau AG v. Haute Autorité de la CECA* (VI, 989; 16 Dec. 1960)	E/IO	Plaintiffs sought exemption from the HA steel and coal production levy.	For High Authority. Case 41–59 rejected and 50–59 inadmissible.
58. 44–59. *Rudolf Pieter Marie Fiddelaar v. Commission de la CEE* (VI, 1077; 16 Dec. 1960)	I/IO	Plaintiff protested his dismissal as a civil servant as improper.	Unclear. Plaintiff lost his main appeal for employment security but was awarded damages anyway.
59. 6–60. *Jean-E. Humblet v. État Belge* (VI, 1125; 16 Dec. 1960)	I/S	Plaintiff, a Belgian national, protested Belgium's tax on his income, which was exempt on the basis of Art. 11 (b) of the ECSC Protocol on Privileges and Immunities (exempting salaries paid by the Community).	For Humblet. A significant historical precedent of an individual successfully prosecuting a case against his state by appealing to an outside legal authority.
60. 30–59. *De Gezamenlijke Steenkolenmijnen in Limburg v. Haute Autorité de la CECA* (VII, 1; 23 Feb. 1961)	E/IO	Plaintiff challenged the government subsidy to the German coal-mining industry.	For plaintiff.
61. 42 & 49–59. *Société Nouvelle des Usines de Pont-lieue—Aciéries du Temple (SNUPAT) v. Haute Autorité de la CECA* (VII, 99; 22 March 1961)	E/IO	Challenge of an HA decision of 7 Aug. 1959 exempting certain enterprises from paying contributions under the scrap compensation scheme.	Unclear. First case disallowed; part of decision annulled in second.
62. 5, 7, & 8–60. *Meroni & Co., Acciaieria Ferriera di Roma (FERAM), et Società Industriale Metallurgica di Napoli (SIMET) v. Haute Autorité de la CECA* (VII, 199; 1 June 1961)	E/IO	Certain Italian steel works appealed against HA decisions setting out how much they owed by virtue of a particular levy on tons of scrap purchased.	For firms, although firms were awarded court costs because they had continued the suit even after the High Authority had rescinded its decisions.

Case	Parties	Issue	Disposition
63. 15–60. *Gabriel Simon v. Cour de Justice des Communautés Européennes* (VII, 223; 1 June 1961)	I/IO	A staff member appealed concerning entitlement to the separation allowance payable under Art. 47 (3) of the Staff Rules and Regulations.	For plaintiff.
64. 2 & 3–60. *Niederrheinische Bergwerks-Aktiengesellschaft, Unternehmensverband des Aachener Steinkohlenbergbaues v. Haute Autorité de la CECA* (VII, 259; 13 July 1961)	E/IO	Plaintiff sought annulment of HA Decision 40–59 (as amended by 1–60) granting aid to the Belgian coal-mining industry.	For High Authority. Appeal dismissed.
65. 14, 16, 17, 20, 24, 26, & 27–60, 1–61. *Meroni & Co. et Autres v. Haute Autorité de la CECA* (VII, 319; 13 July 1961)	E/IO	Firms sought damages from the HA through alleged negligence in failing to notify them promptly on the amount of scrap compensation contribution payable, resulting in a profit loss.	For High Authority. Appeals dismissed.
66. 22 & 23–60. *Raymond Elz v. Haute Autorité de la CECA* (VII, 357; 13 July 1961)	I/IO	A staff member challenged his grading by the HA.	For High Authority. Case dismissed.
67. 9 & 12–60. *Société Commerciale Antoine Vloeberghs S.A. v. Haute Autorité de la CECA* (VII, 391; 14 July 1961)	E/IO	Plaintiff sought damages from the HA for adverse effects suffered because the HA hadn't compelled the French government to recognize free movement of third-country products within the Community.	For High Authority. Appeals dismissed.
68. 12–61. *Wilhelmus Severinus et Antoine Nannes Gorter v. Conseils de la CEE et de la CEEA* (VII, 535; 14 Dec. 1961)	I/IO	A suit for damages brought by an official of the Secretariat of the Councils, who had, he claimed, been compelled to resign by "moral pressure."	For Councils. Case dismissed.

No.	Case	Code	Description	Result
69.	19 & 21–60, 2 & 3–61. *Société Fives Lille Cail et Autres v. Haute Autorité de la CECA* (VII, 559; 15 Dec. 1961)	E/IO	Firms sought annulment of an HA decision regarding the price compensation scheme for imported and internal scrap.	For High Authority. Appeals dismissed.
70.	7–61. *Commission de la CEE v. Gouvernement de la République Italienne* (VII, 633; 19 Dec. 1961)	IO/S	An action against Italy concerning the suspension of imports of pig meat in violation of Art. 31 (2) of the EEC Treaty.	For Commission.
71.	10–61. *Commission de la CEE v. Gouvernement de la République Italienne* (VIII, 1; 27 Feb. 1962)	IO/S	Concerning customs duties imposed by Italy on radio tubes, valves, and lamps from other member states in violation of Arts. 12 & 14 (1) of the EEC Treaty.	For Commission.
72.	25–60. *Leda De Bruyn v. Assemblée Parlementaire Européenne* (VIII, 39; 1 March 1962)	I/IO	A personnel matter appealed under the EEC Treaty, Art. 179, and the Euratom Treaty, Art. 152.	For Mrs. De Bruyn. She was awarded damages of 40,000 Bfr.
73.	21 to 26–61. *Meroni & Co. et Cinq Autres Requérantes v. Haute Autorité de la CECA* (VIII, 143; 6 April 1962)	E/IO	Plaintiffs appealed HA inaction in removing certain scrap levies.	For High Authority. Case inadmissible.
74.	13–60. *Comptoirs de Vent du Charbon de la Ruhr "Geitling," "Mausegatt," et "Präsident" Soutenus par le Gouvernement du Land de Rhénanie-du-Nord-Westphalie v. Haute Autorité de la CECA* (VIII, 165; 18 May 1962)	E/IO	Firms appealed against HA Decision 16–60 refusing to authorize the establishment of one over-all joint sales organization for the collieries of the Ruhr.	For High Authority. Appeal dismissed.
75.	42 & 49–59. *Breedband N.V. v. Société des Aciéries du Temple, Haute Autorité de la CECA, Koninklijke Nederlandsche Hoogovens en Staalfabrieken N.V., et Società Breda Siderurgica* (VIII, 275; 12 July 1962)	E/E & IO	Plaintiff sought modification of the Court's decision of 22 March 1961 in a joint case.	For defendants. Case inadmissible.
76.	9 & 12–60. *Gouvernement du Royaume de Belgique v. Société Commerciale Antoine Vloeberghs et Haute Autorité de la CECA* (VIII, 331; 12 July 1962)	S/E & IO	Belgium sought modification of the Court's decision of 14 July 1961 in Joint Cases 9 & 12–60.	For defendants. Case inadmissible.

Case	Parties	Issue	Disposition
77. 18–60. *Louis Worms* v. *Haute Autorité de la CECA* (VIII, 377; 12 July 1962)	I/IO	An application for damages under Art. 40 of the Treaty.	For High Authority. Appeal dismissed.
78. 9–61. *Gouvernement du Royaume des Pays-Bas* v. *Haute Autorité de la CECA, Soutenue par les Charbonnages de France et Deux Autres Intervenants* (VIII, 413; 12 July 1962)	S/IO	An appeal against the HA concerning publication or notification of rates and conditions of carriage in respect to consignments of coal and steel.	For High Authority. Appeal dismissed.
79. 14–61. *Koninklijke Nederlandsche Hoogovens en Staalfabrieken N.V.* v. *Haute Autorité de la CECA, Soutenue par la Société des Aciéries du Temple* (VIII, 485; 12 July 1962)	E/IO	An appeal against scrap price compensation assessments.	For High Authority. Appeal dismissed.
80. 16–61. *Acciaierie Ferrière e Fonderie di Modena* v. *Haute Autorité de la CECA* (VIII, 547; 12 July 1962)	E/IO	An Italian firm appealed an HA decision fining it for four infringements of Art. 60 of the Treaty.	Substantially for High Authority. First three counts of appeal dismissed; fourth upheld.
81. 17 & 20–61. *Klöcknerwerke AG et Hoesch AG* v. *Haute Autorité de la CECA* (VIII, 615; 13 July 1962)	E/IO	An appeal against scrap price compensation assessments.	For High Authority. Appeal dismissed.
82. 19–61. *Mannesmann AG* v. *Haute Autorité de la CECA, Soutenue par Phoenix-Rheinrohr AG* (VIII, 675; 13 July 1962)	E/IO	An appeal against scrap price compensation assessments.	For High Authority. Appeal dismissed.
83. 33–59. *Compagnie des Hauts Fourneaux de Chasse* v. *Haute Autorité de la CECA* (VIII, 719; 14 Dec. 1962)	E/IO	An application under Art. 40 of the Treaty (negligence) for damages against the HA in respect to injuries suffered as a consequence of the improper admission of scrap tonnages for compensation.	For High Authority. Appeal dismissed.

Case	Type	Subject	Outcome
84. 46 & 47–59. *Meroni & Co., Erba, et Meroni & Co., Milan* v. *Haute Autorité de la CECA* (VIII, 750; 14 Dec. 1962)	E/IO	Same as above.	Same as above.
85. 2 & 3–62. *Commission de la CEE* v. *Grand-duché de Luxembourg et Royaume de Belgique* (VIII, 813; 14 Dec. 1962)	IO/S	Concerning increased duties imposed by Belgium and Luxembourg on honey bread (*pain d'épice*) in violation of Art. 12 of the EEC Treaty.	For Commission.
86. 5 to 11 & 13 to 15–62. *Società Industriale San Michele et Neuf Autres Requérantes* v. *Haute Autorité de la CECA* (VIII, 859; 14 Dec. 1962)	E/IO	A protest against an HA decision requiring firms to send their electricity bills to Luxembourg (for the purpose of checking leviable scrap tonnage).	For High Authority. Case dismissed.
87. 16 & 17–62. *Confédération Nationale des Producteurs de Fruits et légumes et Trois Autres Requérantes, Soutenues par l'Assemblée Permanente des Présidents de Chambres d'Agriculture* v. *Conseil de la CEE* (VIII, 901; 14 Dec. 1962)	E/IO	Plaintiff sought annulment of Council Regulation 23, which established a common organization of the fruit and vegetable market and especially Art. 9 thereof.	For Council. Case inadmissible.
88. 19 to 22–62. *Fédération Nationale de la Boucherie en Gros et du Commerce en Gros des Viandes et Trois Autres Requérantes* v. *Conseil de la CEE* (VIII, 943; 14 Dec. 1962)	E/IO	The Court was asked to annul Art. 2 (1), second sentence, of Council Regulation 26, which made certain rules of competition applicable to production of and trade in farm products.	For Council. Case inadmissible.
89. 31 & 33–62. *Milchwerke Heinz Wöhrmann & Sohn et Alfons Lütticke GmbH* v. *Commission de la CEE* (VIII, 965; 14 Dec. 1962)	E/IO	Plaintiffs asked the Court to quash or declare inapplicable Art. 3 of the Commission's 15 March 1961 decision fixing a countervailing charge on imports of whole milk powder into West Germany pursuant to Art. 46 of the Treaty.	For Commission. Applications inadmissible.
90. 32–62. *Maurice Alvis* v. *Conseil de la CEE* (IX, 99; 4 July 1963)	I/IO	A personnel appeal concerning dismissal.	For Council. Case unfounded.

Case	Parties	Issue	Disposition
91. 24–62. *Gouvernement de la République Fédérale d'Allemagne v. Commission de la CEE* (IX, 129; 4 July 1963)	S/IO	Germany asked the Court, under Art. 25 (3) of the EEC Treaty, to quash a Commission decision of 11 May 1962 fixing a tariff quota on distilling wines.	For Germany. The decision was annulled for lack of supporting reasons by the Commission; but the Commission's power to act was upheld.
92. 12–63. *Marca Schlieker, née Diepenbruck v. Haute Autorité de la CECA* (IX, 173; 4 July 1963)	I/IO	Frau Schlieker appealed against HA failure to act in voiding certain contracts between the Schlieker group, in which she was a partner, and certain ECSC enterprises.	For High Authority. Case dismissed.
93. 25–62. *Plaumann & Co. v. Commission de la CEE* (IX, 197; 15 July 1963)	E/IO	Plaintiff appealed a Commission decision of 22 May 1962 refusing to let Germany suspend the duties or open up a quota for importing clementines.	For Commission. Case inadmissible.
94. 34–62. *Gouvernement de la République Fédérale d'Allemagne v. Commission de la CEE* (IX, 269; 15 July 1963)	S/IO	Germany sued for the annulment of a decision of 30 July 1962, in which the Commission rejected a request to suspend import duties on oranges.	For Commission. Suit dismissed as not well-founded.
95. 13–63. *Gouvernement de la République Italienne v. Commission de la CEE* (IX, 335; 17 July 1963)	S/IO	The Italian government appealed a Commission decision of 17 June 1963 authorizing the French government to levy a special charge on electric refrigerators from Italy.	For Commission. Appeal rejected.
96. 35–62, 16–63. *André Leroy v. Haute Autorité de la CECA* (IX, 399; 5 Dec. 1963)	I/IO	Plaintiff sought annulment of a personnel decision refusing integration.	For High Authority. First appeal inadmissible; second dismissed as not well-founded.
97. 23, 24, & 52–63. *Société Anonyme Usines Émile Henricot et Deux Autres Requérantes v. Haute Autorité de la CECA* (IX, 439; 5 Dec. 1963)	E/IO	An appeal against HA letters addressed to plaintiffs requesting payment of certain sums in respect to scrap price compensation.	For High Authority. Cases dismissed.

No. / Case	Type	Description	Outcome
98. 28–63. *Koninklijke Nederlandsche Hoogovens en Staalfabrieken N.V. v. Haute Autorité de la CECA* (IX, 467; 5 Dec. 1963)	E/IO	Same as above.	For High Authority. Case dismissed.
99. 53 & 54–63. *Lemmerzwerke GmbH et Trois Autres Requérantes v. Haute Autorité de la CECA* (IX, 487; 5 Dec. 1963)	E/IO	Same as above.	For High Authority. Cases dismissed.
100. 18–62. *Emilia Barge, Veuve de Vitorio Leone v. Haute Autorité de la CECA* (IX, 529; 16 Dec. 1963)	I/IO	An appeal against HA Decisions 2 & 16–59, specifically employment of officials of a trust company to gather information and conduct check-ups under Art. 47 of the Treaty and use of the electric bill to calculate the amount of leviable scrap consumed.	For High Authority. However, specific portions of the contested decisions were reversed after the appellant had produced vouchers showing the exact consumption of electric current.
101. 36–62. *Société des Aciéries du Temple v. Haute Autorité de la CECA* (IX, 583; 16 Dec. 1963)	E/IO	A French enterprise brought a damage suit (negligence) against the HA in connection with the issuance and application of the basic decisions instituting the scrap compensation scheme.	For High Authority.
102. 1–63. *Macchiorlati Dalmas e Figli v. Haute Autorité de la CECA* (IX, 613; 16 Dec. 1963)	E/IO	An appeal against an HA decision requiring plaintiffs to pay interest on arrears of levy under Art. 50 of the Treaty.	For plaintiff. Decision reversed.
103. 2 to 10–63. *Società Industriale Acciaierie San Michele et Huit Autres Requérantes v. Haute Autorité de la CECA* (IX, 661; 16 Dec. 1963)	E/IO	Italian firms appealed against HA decisions imposing fines and daily penalty payments for refusing to furnish evidence concerning their consumption of imported scrap.	For High Authority. Appeals dismissed.
104. 14–63. *Forges de Clabecq S.A. v. Haute Autorité de la CECA* (IX, 719; 16 Dec. 1963)	E/IO	A Belgian enterprise contested an HA decision calculating its leviable tonnage of scrap.	For High Authority. Appeals dismissed.
105. 15–63. *Claude Lassalle v. Parlement Européen* (X, 57; 4 March 1964)	I/IO	Plaintiff sought annulment of a personnel decision by the Parliament Secretariat.	For plaintiff. Decision annulled.

Case	Parties	Issue	Disposition
106. 11–63. *Robert Lepape v. Haute Autorité de la CECA* (X, 121; 19 March 1964)	I/IO	An appealed personnel matter against the HA.	For High Authority. Case inadmissible.
107. 18–63. *Estelle Schmitz, Épouse Roland Wollast v. Communauté Économique Européenne* (X, 163; 19 March 1964)	I/IO	An appeal against Commission personnel action.	For plaintiff. Commission decision quashed.
108. 20 & 21–63. *Jean Maudet v. Commission de la CEE* (X, 213; 19 March 1964)	I/IO	An appeal against Commission personnel action.	For plaintiff. Commission decision quashed.
109. 27–63. *Goffredo Raponi v. Commission de la CEE* (X, 247; 19 March 1964)	I/IO	An appeal against Commission personnel action.	For plaintiff. Commission decision quashed.
110. 67–63. *Société Rhénane d' Exploitation et de Manutention "Sorema" v. Haute Autorité de la CECA* (X, 293; 19 March 1964)	E/IO	Plaintiff sought annulment of HA Decision 8–63 ordering "Sorema" to cease participation in the O.K.U. (Oberrheinische Kohlenunion).	For plaintiff. Decision annulled as groundless.
111. 55 to 59 & 61 to 63–63. *Acciaierie Fonderie Ferriere di Modena et Sept Autres Requérantes v. Haute Autorité de la CECA* (X, 413; 9 June 1964)	E/IO	Appellants sought reversal of HA Decision 7–63 in respect to matters relating to the scrap compensation scheme.	For High Authority. Case inadmissible.
112. 69–63. *Anne-Marie Capitaine, Épouse de Gérard Marcillat v. Commission de la CEEA* (X, 471; 9 June 1964)	I/IO	Plaintiff sought reversal of personnel decisions canceling her separation allowance following her marriage.	For Commission. Appeal dismissed as not well-founded.
113. 79 & 82–63. *Jean Reynier et Piero Erba v. Commission la CEE* (X, 511; 9 June 1964)	I/IO	An appeal concerning grading.	For plaintiffs. Commission decision quashed.
114. 94 & 96–63. *Pierre Bernusset v. Commission de la CEE* (X, 587; 9 June 1964)	I/IO	An appeal of cancellation of announcement of vacancy.	For plaintiffs. Commission decision annulled.

115.	84–63. *J.A.G. Baron de Vos van Steenwijk v. Commission de la CEEA* (X, 633; 25 June 1964)	I/IO	A personnel appeal concerning non-integration.	For Commission. Appeal dismissed as not well-founded.
116.	26–63. *Piergiovanni Pistoj v. Commission de la CEE* (X, 673; 1 July 1964)	I/IO	An appeal concerning establishment.	For Commission. Appeal dismissed.
117.	78–63. *Rémy Huber v. Commission de la CEE* (X, 721; 1 July 1964)	I/IO	An appeal concerning establishment.	For Commission. Appeal dismissed.
118.	80–63. *Robert Degreef v. Commission de la CEE* (X, 767; 1 July 1964)	I/IO	An appeal concerning establishment.	For plaintiff. Commission decision quashed.
119.	1–64. *Glucoseries Réunies v. Commission de la CEE* (X, 811; 2 July 1964)	E/IO	Plaintiff sought annulment of a Commission decision of 28 Nov. 1963 authorizing France to impose countervailing charges on imports of glucose from certain member states.	For Commission. Case inadmissible.
120.	103–63. *Société Rhenania et Deux Autres Requérants v. Commission de la CEE* (X, 839; 2 July 1964)	E/IO	German firms filed a complaint, under Art. 179 of the Treaty, alleging failure of the Commission to take action against the German government for the fixing of intervention prices on certain cereal products.	For Commission. Case dismissed.
121.	70–63. *Umberto Collotti v. Cour de Justice des Communautés Européennes* (X, 861; 7 July 1964)	I/IO	A personnel appeal concerning grading.	For plaintiff. Personnel decision annulled.
122.	87–63. *Jacqueline Georges v. Commission de la CEEA* (X, 921; 7 July 1964)	I/IO	Plaintiff sought damages and annulment of decisions concerning non-integration.	For Commission. Appeal dismissed as not well-founded.
123.	93–63. *Simone Van Nuffel, Épouse Minet v. Commission de la CEEA* (X, 959; 7 July 1964)	I/IO	Plaintiff sought damages and annulment of decisions concerning non-integration.	For Commission. Appeal dismissed as not well-founded.
124.	97–63. *Luigi de Pascale v. Commission de la CEE* (X, 1011; 7 July 1964)	I/IO	An appeal concerning grading.	For plaintiff. Commission decision annulled.

Case	Parties	Issue	Disposition
125. 66–63. *Gouvernement du Royaume des Pays-Bas v. Haute Autorité de la CECA* (X, 1047; 15 July 1964)	S/IO	The Dutch government protested HA Decisions 5 & 6–63 allowing two selling agencies in the Ruhr coalfield.	For High Authority. Complaints rejected.
126. 90 & 91–63. *Commission de la CEE v. Grand-duché de Luxembourg et Royaume de Belgique* (X, 1217; 13 Nov. 1964)	IO/S	The Commission sought a ruling that a special charge on the issue of import licenses for certain milk products by the two governments violated Art. 12 of the Treaty.	For Commission.
127. 109–63, 13–64. *Charles Muller v. Commission de la CEE* (X, 1293; 16 Dec. 1964)	I/IO	An appeal concerning grading.	For Commission. Case dismissed.
128. 102–63. *Jacques Boursin v. Haute Autorité de la CECA* (X, 1347; 17 Dec. 1964)	I/IO	A personnel appeal for the annulment of certain decisions affecting plaintiff's career.	For High Authority. Case dismissed.
129. 108–63. *Officine Elettro-meccaniche Ing. A. Merlini v. Haute Autorité de la CECA* (XI-1, 1; 21 Jan. 1965)	E/IO	An Italian firm sought annulment of an HA decision of 30 Aug. 1963 setting its scrap tonnage allotment.	For High Authority. Case dismissed.
130. 20–64. *S.A.R.L. Albatros v. Société des Pétroles et des Combustibles Liquides (SOPECO)* (XI-3, 1; 4 Feb. 1965)	E/E	The Italian firm Albatros sued the French firm SOPECO for breach of contract when the French government would not give SOPECO an import license for petrol. Both parties felt the treaties should prevent such action by the French government.	Unclear, though probably for SOPECO. The Court remanded the case to the Civil Court of Rome.
131. 14–64. *Dame Emilia Barge, Veuve Leone v. Haute Autorité de la CECA* (XI-4, 1; 16 Feb. 1965)	I/IO	Plaintiff sought annulment of an HA decision of 18 March 1964 asking her to pay an amount due on scrap imported by the former firm Acciaieria Leone.	For High Authority. Case dismissed.
132. 70–64. *René Jullien v. Commission de la CEE* (XI-5, 1; 24 Feb. 1965)	I/IO	An appeal concerning grading.	For Commission. Case dismissed.

No.	Type	Description	Result
133. 12 & 29–64. *Ernest Ley v. Commission de la CEE* (XI, 143; 31 March 1965)	I/IO	An appeal for annulment of "notice of vacancy" for post of Head of Division and of other Commission decisions concerning the appointment.	For Commission. First case dismissed as unfounded; second inadmissible.
134. 16–64. *Gertrud Rauch v. Commission de la CEE* (XI, 179; 31 March 1965)	I/IO	Miss Rauch appealed a decision concerning the admission of an auxiliary employee to an internal competitive exam.	For Commission. Case dismissed as unfounded.
135. 23–64. *Thérèse Marie-Louise Vandevyvere v. Parlement Européen* (XI, 205; 31 March 1965)	I/IO	A personnel appeal seeking annulment of competitive exam no. PE/1/B.	For Parliament. Case dismissed as not well-founded.
136. 21–64. *Macchiorlati Dalmas e Figli v. Haute Autorité de la CECA* (XI, 227; 31 March 1965)	E/IO	An Italian firm sought annulment of an HA decision of 14 April 1964 assessing it 1,000,000 *lire* for late estimates of its deductions.	For High Authority. Case dismissed.
137. 38–64. *Getreide-Import Gesellschaft v. Commission de la CEE* (XI, 263; 1 April 1965)	E/IO	An appeal for annulment of a Commission decision of 25 June 1964 establishing sorghum prices.	For Commission. Case inadmissible.
138. 40–64. *Marcello Sgarlata et Neuf Autres Requérants v. Commission de la CEE* (XI, 279; 1 April 1965)	I/IO	An appeal for annulment of Commission Regulations 65 & 74–64 establishing reference prices for certain citrus fruits and of Council Regulations 23 & 100 (lemons, mandarins and clementines, sweet potatoes).	For Commission. Case dismissed as not of "individual concern" to the appellants.
139. 28–64. *Richard Müller v. Conseil de la CEE et Conseil de la CEEA* (XI, 307; 7 April 1965)	I/IO	A personnel appeal concerning grading.	For Councils. Case dismissed as unfounded.
140. 35–64. *Cesare Alfieri v. Parlement Européen* (XI, 337; 7 April 1965)	I/IO	A personnel appeal concerning appointment of another to plaintiff's position as a result of a competitive exam in which plaintiff participated.	For Parliament. Case dismissed as unfounded.

Case	Parties	Issue	Disposition
141. 70–63. *Haute Autorité de la CECA v. Umberto Collotti et Cour de Justice des Communautés Européennes* (XI, 353; 7 April 1965)	IO/I & IO	An unusual case was an appeal by the HA for an interpretation of the Court's decision in Case 70–63 of 7 July 1964.	For defendants. Case inadmissible.
142. 11–64. *Kurt Weighardt v. Commission de la CEEA* (XI, 365; 7 April 1965)	I/IO	A personnel appeal concerning grading.	For Commission. Case part inadmissible and part unfounded.
143. 9 & 25–64. *Acciaieria Ferriera di Roma (FERAM) et Six Autres Requérantes v. Haute Autorité de la CECA* (XI, 401; 2 June 1965)	E/IO	Plaintiffs sought damages from the HA for negligence in the administration and control of the equalization scheme for imported scrap.	For High Authority. Appeals inadmissible.
144. 36–64. *Société Rhénane d'Exploitation et de Manutention (SOREMA) v. Haute Autorité de la CECA* (XI, 425; 2 June 1965)	E/IO	Plaintiff sought annulment of HA Decision 15–64 relating to plaintiff's participation in the common purchase of fuels.	For High Authority. Case dismissed.
145. 48–64, 1–65. *Claude Brus v. Commission de la CEE* (XI, 455; 16 June 1965)	I/IO	Both suits were filed by the same EEC Commission official seeking annulment of the Commission's decision concerning his grade.	For Commission. First suit inadmissible; second rejected as groundless.
146. 32–64. *Gouvernement de la République Italienne v. Commission de la CEE* (XI, 473; 17 June 1965)	S/IO	Italy sought annulment of a decision of 22 May 1964 concerning adoption of safeguard measures for certain products in Chap. 50 of the Italian customs tariff.	For Commission. Suit rejected.
147. 43–64. *Richard Müller v. Conseils de la CEE, CEEA, et CECA* (XI, 499; 17 June 1965)	I/IO	A personnel appeal concerning grading.	For Councils. Case inadmissible.

No.	Case	Type	Description	Outcome
148.	106 & 107–63. Alfred Töpfer et Getreide-Import Gesellschaft v. Commission de la CEE (XI, 525; 1 July 1965)	E/IO	Firms sought annulment of a Commission decision of 3 Oct. 1963 authorizing Germany to retain safeguard measures for imports of maize, millet, and sorghum.	For firms. Commission decision quashed.
149.	3 & 4–64. Chambre Syndicale de la Sidérurgie Française et 16 Autres Requérantes v. Haute Autorité de la CECA (XI, 567; 8 July 1965)	E/IO	An appeal against certain articles of HA Decisions 19, 20, & 21–63.	For High Authority. Case inadmissible.
150.	27 & 30–64. Fulvio Fonzi v. Commission de la CEEA (XI, 615; 8 July 1965)	I/IO	A personnel appeal concerning grading.	For Commission. Case inadmissible.
151.	49–64. Emmanuel Stipperger v. Haute Autorité de la CECA (XI, 661; 8 July 1965)	I/IO	A personnel appeal concerning grading.	For High Authority. Case dismissed as not well-founded.
152.	19 & 65–63. Satya Prakash v. Commission de la CEEA (XI, 677; 8 July 1965)	I/IO	A personnel appeal of refusal to reimburse moving and other costs.	For Commission. Appeals dismissed.
153.	68–63. Hartmut Luhleich v. Commission de la CECA (XI, 727; 8 July 1965)	I/IO	Plaintiff appealed his dismissal.	For plaintiff. The Court awarded him damages.
154.	83–63. Stefan Krawczynski v. Commission de la CEEA (XI, 773; 8 July 1965)	I/IO	Plaintiff contested his grading and the personal hostility of a superior.	For Commission. Case dismissed as not well-founded.
155.	110–63. Alfred Willame v. Commission de la CECA (XI, 803; 8 July 1965)	I/IO	An appeal against a personnel decision for dismissal and non-integration.	For individual. Decision annulled.
156.	111–63. Lemmerz-Werke GmbH v. Haute Autorité de la CECA (XI, 835; 13 July 1965)	E/IO	A German firm sought annulment of an HA decision of 6 Nov. 1963 concerning the financial obligations of the firm under the system of equalization on imported scrap.	For High Authority. Case dismissed as not well-founded.
157.	37–64. Mannesmann AG v. Haute Autorité de la CECA (XI, 893; 13 July 1965)	E/IO	A German firm sought annulment of an HA decision of 8 July 1964 concerning the financial obligations of the firm under the system of equalization or imported scrap.	For High Authority. Case dismissed as not well-founded.

Case	Parties	Issue	Disposition
158. 39–64. *Société des Aciéries du Temple v. Haute Autorité de la CECA* (XI, 937; 13 July 1965)	E/IO	Plaintiff sought annulment of an HA decision of 12 Oct. 1964.	For High Authority. Case dismissed as not well-founded.
159. 18 & 19–64. *Filippo Alvino et 21 Autres Requérants v. Commission de la CEE* (XI, 971; 14 July 1965)	I/IO	Applicants sought annulment of internal competitive exam no. 165 (reserve).	For applicants. Exam and resulting appointments annulled.
160. 46–64. *Götz Schoffer v. Commission de la CEE* (XI, 999; 14 July 1965)	I/IO	An appeal of a Commission decision concerning plaintiff's status.	For Commission. Case inadmissible.
161. 50, 51, 53, 54, & 57–64. *Ralph Loebisch et Quatre Autres Requérants v. Conseils de la CEE, CEEA, et CECA* (XI, 1015; 14 July 1965)	I/IO	A personnel appeal concerning grading.	For Councils. Case inadmissible.
162. 55–64. *Jean Lens v. Cour de Justice des Communautés Européennes* (XI, 1033; 17 Nov. 1965)	I/IO	A personnel appeal concerning grading.	For Court. Case inadmissible.
163. 20–65. *Umberto Collotti v. Cour de Justice des Communautés Européennes* (XI, 1045; 17 Nov. 1965)	I/IO	A personnel appeal concerning grading.	For Court. Case inadmissible.
164. 45–64. *Commission de la CEE v. République Italienne* (XI, 1057; 1 Dec. 1965)	IO/S	The Commission charged that Italy had allowed a drawback of taxes and charges on exports of certain engineering products not eligible under Art. 96 of the Treaty.	For Commission.
165. 29, 31, 36, 39 to 47, 50, & 51–63. *Société Anonyme des Laminoirs, Hauts Fourneaux, Forges, Fonderies et Usines de la Providence et 13 Autres Requérantes v. Haute Autorité de la CECA* (XI, 1123; 9 Dec. 1965)	E/IO	Firms sought damages, based on Art. 40 of the ECSC Treaty, charging the HA with *faute de service* in the functioning of the equalization system for imported scrap.	For plaintiffs. The Court ordered the parties to reach an accord on the amount of damages within three months; failing that, they would submit their figures to the Court for decision.

No.	Case	Type	Description	Outcome
166.	52-64. Fred Pfoeschner v. Commission de la CEE (XI, 1211; 14 Dec. 1965)	I/IO	A personnel appeal concerning grading.	For Commission. Case inadmissible.
167.	5-65. André Sandray v. Commission de la CEE (XI, 1227; 14 Dec. 1965)	I/IO	A personnel appeal concerning grading.	For Commission. Case inadmissible.
168.	12-65. Fred Bauer v. Commission de la CEE (XI, 1239; 14 Dec. 1965)	I/IO	A personnel appeal concerning grading.	For Commission. Case inadmissible.
169.	47-65. Edith Kalkuhl v. Parlement Européen (XI, 1251; 14 Dec. 1965)	I/IO	A personnel appeal concerning grading.	For Parliament. Case inadmissible.
170.	11-65. Domenico Morina v. Parlement Européen (XI, 1259; 14 Dec. 1965)	I/IO	A personnel appeal seeking annulment of internal exam no. B 10 and the appointment of a Mrs. Marie-Thérèse to a post.	For plaintiff. Annulment granted.
171.	21-65. Domenico Morina v. Parlement Européen (XI, 1279; 14 Dec. 1965)	I/IO	A personnel appeal seeking annulment of grades granted by exam no. B 10 and the promotion of a Mr. Pirano.	For plaintiff. Annulment granted.
172.	15-65. Werner Klaer v. Haute Autorité de la CECA (XI, 1295; 15 Dec. 1965)	I/IO	A personnel appeal concerning grading.	For plaintiff. Annulment granted.
173.	3-65. Société Anonyme Métallurgique d'Espérance-Longdoz v. Haute Autorité de la CECA (XI, 1321; 15 Dec. 1965)	E/IO	Plaintiff sought annulment of an HA decision of 13 Nov. 1964 assessing plaintiff under the equalization system for imported scrap.	For High Authority. Case dismissed as not well-founded.
174.	4-65. Société Anonyme Métallurgique Hainaut-Sambre v. Haute Autorité de la CECA (XI, 1363; 15 Dec. 1965)	E/IO	Plaintiff sought annulment of an HA decision of 13 Nov. 1964 concerning scrap tonnage allotment and levy.	For High Authority. Case dismissed as not well-founded.
175.	8-65. Acciaierie e Ferriere Pugliesi S.p.A. v. Haute Autorité de la CECA (XII, 1; 8 Feb. 1966)	E/IO	An appeal against an HA decision of 13 Nov. 1964 requiring payment of 39,329,539 lire.	For enterprise. Decision annulled.
176.	48-65. Alfons Lütticke GmbH et Deux Autres Requérantes v. Commission de la CEE (XII, 27; 1 March 1966)	E/IO	An application under Art. 173 against a Commission letter refusing to take action against Germany for the imposition of a countervailing charge on milk powder imports.	For Commission. Pleas inadmissible.

Case	Parties	Issue	Disposition
177. 30–65. *Macchiorlati Dalmas e Figli S.A.S.* v. *Haute Autorié de la CECA* (XII, 49; 22 March 1966)	E/IO	An appeal against two HA decisions of 7 April 1965 establishing tonnage requirements and fees.	For High Authority. Case dismissed as not well-founded.
178. 49–65. *Ferriere e Acciaierie Napoletane S.p.A.* v. *Haute Autorié de la CECA* (XII, 103; 28 April 1966)	E/IO	An appeal against an HA decision of 19 May 1965 concerning plaintiff's financial obligations in the equalization mechanism for imported scrap iron.	For plaintiff. Decision annulled.
179. 51–65. *ILFO—Industria Laminati Ferrosi Odolese S.R.L.* v. *Haute Autorié de la CECA* (XII, 125; 28 April 1966)	E/IO	An appeal against two HA decisions of 19 May 1965 fixing the quantity of taxable scrap iron and the equalization scale.	For High Authority. Case dismissed as not well-founded.
180. 18 & 35–65. *Max Gutmann* v. *Commission de la CEEA* (XII, 149; 5 May 1966)	I/IO	A personnel appeal.	For plaintiff. Commission decision and opinion annulled.
181. 29, 31, 36 to 47, 50, & 51–63. *Société Anonyme des Laminoirs, Hauts Fourneaux, Forges, Fonderies et Usines de la Providence et 13 Autres Requérantes* v. *Haute Autorié de la CECA* (XII, 199; 7 June 1966)	E/IO	An appeal for reparations under Art. 40 (concerning the equalization mechanism for scrap iron).	For plaintiff in part. The High Authority was ordered to pay damages, but Cases 31, 39 to 42, 44 to 46, & 51–63 were dismissed as not well-founded.
182. 50–65. *Acciaierie e Ferriere di Solbiate S.p.A.* v. *Haute Autorié de la CECA* (XII, 209; 16 June 1966)	E/IO	An appeal against two HA decisions of 19 May 1965 assessing plaintiff under the equalization system for imported scrap.	For High Authority. Case dismissed as not well-founded.
183. 52 & 55–65. *République Fédérale d'Allemagne* v. *Commission de la CEE* (XII, 227; 16 June 1966)	S/IO	Germany requested annulment of two Commission directives fixing the timetable for removing German levies on imported meat and farm products.	For Commission. Both cases dismissed as groundless.

No.	Case	Code	Description	Outcome
184.	54–65. *Compagnie des Forges de Châtillon Commentry et Neuves-Maison v. Haute Autorité de la CECA* (XII, 265; 16 June 1966)	E/IO	An appeal for annulment of an HA decision of 21 July 1965 concerning equalization on imported scrap.	For High Authority. Case dismissed as not well-founded.
135.	2–65. *Ferriera Ernesto Preo e Figli v. Haute Autorité de la CECA* (XII, 315; 30 June 1966)	E/IO	An appeal for annulment of two HA decisions of 13 Nov. 1964 concerning payment of duties under equalization for imported scrap.	For plaintiff. Decisions annulled.
186.	110–63 bis. *Alfred Willame v. Commission de la CEEA* (XII, 411; 13 July 1966)	I/IO	Plaintiff sought interpretation of Court Decision 110–63 of 8 July 1965.	For Commission. No grounds for reinterpretation.
187.	56 & 58–64. *Établissements Consten S.A.R.L. et Grundig-Verkaufs-GmbH, Soutenus par le Gouvernement de la République Italienne et le Gouvernement de la République Fédérale d'Allemagne v. Commission de la CEE, Soutenue par la Firme Willy Leissner et la Firme U.N.E.F.* (XII, 429; 13 July 1966)	E/IO	Suits sought annulment of a Commission decision of 23 Sept. 1964 finding that agreements between Consten and Grundig fell under Art. 85.	Unclear. The Court dismissed all plaintiffs' arguments to the effect that the import monopoly for the benefit of Consten was not prohibited by Art. 85 of the Treaty, but not all clauses of the agreement were affected by Art. 85.
188.	32–65. *Gouvernement de la République Italienne v. Conseil de la CEE et Commission de la CEE* (XII, 563; 13 July 1966)	S/IO	The Italian government sought annulment of Council Regulation 19–65 and a declaration that Council Regulation 17–62 and Commission Regulation 153–62 were inapplicable.	For Council and Commission. Suit inadmissible in respect to Council Regulation 17–62 and Commission Regulation 153–62; appeal against Council Regulation 19–65 dismissed on merits.
189.	3–66. *Cesare Alfieri v. Parlement Européen* (XII, 633; 14 Dec. 1966)	I/IO	A personnel appeal concerning retirement.	For Parliament. Case dismissed as not well-founded.
190.	15–64 & 60–65. *Jean Moreau v. Commission de la CEEA* (XII, 663; 15 Dec. 1966)	I/IO	A personnel appeal concerning grading.	For Commission. Case 15–64 without object; 60–65 not well-founded.

Case	Parties	Issue	Disposition
191. 28–65. *Fulvio Fonzi v. Commission de la CEEA* (XII, 689; 15 Dec. 1966)	I/IO	A personnel appeal.	For Commission. Case inadmissible.
192. 31–65. *Fulvio Fonzi v. Commission de la CEEA* (XII, 741; 15 Dec. 1966)	I/IO	A personnel appeal concerning promotion.	For Commission. Case inadmissible.
193. 34–65. *Hans Dieter Mosthaf v. Commission de la CEEA* (XII, 753; 15 Dec. 1966)	I/IO	A personnel appeal.	For Commission. Case inadmissible.
194. 59–65. *Heinrich Schreckenberg v. Commission de la CEEA* (XII, 785; 15 Dec. 1966)	I/IO	A personnel appeal concerning grading.	For Commission. Case inadmissible.
195. 62–65. *Manlio Serio v. Commission de la CEEA* (XII, 813; 15 Dec. 1966)	I/IO	A personnel appeal.	For plaintiff.
196. 9 & 58–65. *Faillite des Acciaierie San Michele S.p.A. v. Haute Autorité de la CECA* (XIII, 1; 2 March 1967)	E/IO	An appeal for annulment of HA decisions of 13 Nov. 1964 and 5 Oct. 1965 concerning the tonnage of taxable scrap iron.	For plaintiff. Decisions annulled.
197. 25 & 26–65. *Società Industriale Metallurgica di Napoli (SIMET) et Acciaierie e Ferriere di Roma (FERAM) v. Haute Autorité de la CECA* (XIII, 39; 2 March 1967)	E/IO	An appeal for annulment of an HA decision of 11 Feb. 1965 levying fees under the scrap iron equalization system.	Unclear. Decision in Case 25–65 annulled and in Case 26–65 inadmissible.
198. 18 & 35–65. *Max Gutmann v. Commission de la CEEA* (XIII, 75; 15 March 1967)	I/IO	A personnel appeal.	For plaintiff.
199. 8 to 11–66. *Société Anonyme Cimenteries C.B.R. Cementsbedrijven N.V. et 51 Autres Requérantes v. Commission de la CEE* (XIII, 93; 15 March 1967)	E/IO	Cases brought against letters sent by the Commission under Art. 15 (6) of Council Regulation 17, which deprived the enterprises of benefits under par. 5 of said article.	For plaintiffs. Letters annulled as insufficiently reasoned.

No.		Description	Outcome
200. 26–66. *Koninklijke Nederlandsche Hoogovens en Staalfabrieken N.V. v. Haute Autorité de la CECA* (XIII, 149; 14 June 1967)	E/IO	Appeal against an HA decision of 20 July 1956 levying fees under the imported scrap iron equalization system.	For High Authority. Case dismissed as not well-founded.
201. 28–64. *Richard Müller v. Conseil de la CEE et Conseil de la CEEA* (XIII, 183; 22 June 1967)	I/IO	A personnel appeal. Plaintiff sought revision of a Court decision in Case 28–64 of 7 April 1965.	For Council. Case inadmissible.
202. 10–67. *Johannes Coenraad Moulijn v. Commission de la CEE* (XIII, 191; 22 June 1967)	I/IO	A personnel appeal.	For Commission. Case inadmissible.
203. 12–66. *Alfred Willame v. Commission de la CEEA* (XIII, 199; 22 June 1967)	I/IO	A personnel appeal concerning integration.	Unclear. Appeal partially rejected; Commission required to pay damages.
204. 5, 7, & 13 to 24–66. *Firma E. Kampffmeyer et 13 Autres Requérantes v. Commission de la CEE* (XIII, 331; 14 July 1967)	E/IO	Claims for losses and deprival of potential profits arising from a Commission decision of 3 Oct. 1963 confirming the safeguard measures taken by Germany against imports of maize.	Unsettled. Interim ruling on Cases 5, 7, 13 to 15, 19, & 21–66 called for more evidence in Court by 31 Dec. 1967; claims 17, 18, 20, 22 to 24–66 disallowed.
205. 30–66. *Firma Kurt A. Becher v. Commission des Communautés Européennes* (XIII, 369; 30 Nov. 1967)	E/IO	An appeal for damages under Art. 215 (2) of the EEC Treaty.	Unclear. Plaintiff was required to transmit to the Court proof of a series of actions. Court costs were reserved.

APPENDIX H

SELECTED ARTICLES FROM THE CONVENTION FOR THE PROTECTION OF HUMAN RIGHTS AND FUNDAMENTAL FREEDOMS

Article 20.

The Commission shall consist of a number of members equal to that of the High Contracting Parties. No two members of the Commission may be nationals of the same State.

Article 21.

(1) The members of the Commission shall be elected by the Committee of Ministers by an absolute majority of votes, from a list of names drawn up by the Bureau of the Consultative Assembly; each group of the Representatives of the High Contracting Parties in the Consultative Assembly shall put forward three candidates, of whom two at least shall be its nationals.

(2) As far as applicable, the same procedure shall be followed to complete the Commission in the event of other States subsequently becoming Parties to this Convention, and in filling casual vacancies.

Article 24.

Any High Contracting Party may refer to the Commission, through the Secretary-General of the Council of Europe, any alleged breach of the provisions of the Convention by another High Contracting Party.

Article 25.

(1) The Commission may receive petitions addressed to the Secretary-General of the Council of Europe from any person, non-governmental organization or group of individuals claiming to be the victim of a violation by one of the High Contracting Parties of the rights set forth in this Convention, provided that the High Contracting Party against which the complaint has been lodged has declared that it recognises the competence of the Commission to receive such petitions. Those of the High Contracting Parties who have made such a declaration undertake not to hinder in any way the effective exercise of this right.

(2) Such declarations may be made for a specific period.

(3) The declarations shall be deposited with the Secretary-General of the Council of Europe who shall transmit copies thereof to the High Contracting Parties and publish them.

(4) The Commission shall only exercise the powers provided for in this Article when at least six High Contracting Parties are bound by declarations made in accordance with the preceding paragraphs.

Article 26.

The Commission may only deal with the matter after all domestic remedies have been exhausted, according to the generally recognised rules of international law, and within a period of six months from the date on which the final decision was taken.

Article 29.

(1) The Commission shall perform the function set out in Article 28 by means of a Sub-Commission consisting of seven members of the Commission.

(2) Each of the parties concerned may appoint as members of this Sub-Commission a person of its choice.

(3) The remaining members shall be chosen by lot in accordance with arrangements prescribed in the Rules of Procedure of the Commission.

Article 30.

If the Sub-Commission succeeds in effecting a friendly settlement in accordance with Article 28, it shall draw up a Report which shall be sent to the States concerned, to the Committee of Ministers and to the Secretary-General of the Council of Europe for publication. This Report shall be confined to a brief statement of the facts and of the solution reached.

Article 31.

(1) If a solution is not reached, the Commission shall draw up a Report of the facts and state its opinion as to whether the facts found disclose a breach by the State concerned of its obligations under the Convention. The opinions of all the members of the Commission on this point may be stated in the Report.

(2) The Report shall be transmitted to the Committee of Ministers. It shall also be transmitted to the States concerned, who shall not be at liberty to publish it.

(3) In transmitting the Report to the Committee of Ministers the Commission may make such proposals as it thinks fit.

Article 32.

(1) If the question is not referred to the Court in accordance with Article 48 of this Convention within a period of three months from the date of the transmission of the Report to the Committee of Ministers, the Committee of Ministers shall decide by a majority of two-thirds of the members entitled to sit on the Committee whether there has been a violation of the Convention.

(2) In the affirmative case the Committee of Ministers shall prescribe a period during which the High Contracting Party concerned must take the measures required by the decision of the Committee of Ministers.

(3) If the High Contracting Party concerned has not taken satisfactory measures within the prescribed period, the Committee of Ministers shall decide by the majority provided for in paragraph (1) above what effect shall be given to its original decision and shall publish the Report.

(4) The High Contracting Parties undertake to regard as binding on them any decision which the Committee of Ministers may take in application of the preceding paragraphs.

Article 38.

The European Court of Human Rights shall consist of a number of judges equal to that of the Members of the Council of Europe. No two judges may be nationals of the same State.

Article 39.

(1) The members of the Court shall be elected by the Consultative Assembly by a majority of the votes cast from a list of persons nominated by the Members of the Council of Europe; each Member shall nominate three candidates, of whom two at least shall be its nationals.

(2) As far as applicable, the same procedure shall be followed to complete the Court in the event of the admission of new Members of the Council of Europe, and in filling casual vacancies.

(3) The candidates shall be of high moral character and must either possess the qualifications required for appointment to high judicial office or be jurisconsults of recognised competence.

Article 40.

(1) The members of the Court shall be elected for a period of nine years. They may be re-elected. However, of the members elected at the first election the terms of four members shall expire at the end of three years, and the terms of four more members shall expire at the end of six years.

(2) The members whose terms are to expire at the end of the initial periods of three and six years shall be chosen by lot by the Secretary-General immediately after the first election has been completed.

(3) A member of the Court elected to replace a member whose term of office has not expired shall hold office for the remainder of his predecessor's term.

(4) The members of the Court shall hold office until replaced. After having been replaced, they shall continue to deal with such cases as they already have under consideration.

Article 41.

The Court shall elect its President and Vice-President for a period of three years. They may be re-elected.

Article 43.

For the consideration of each case brought before it the Court shall consist of a Chamber composed of seven judges. There shall sit as an ex officio member of the Chamber the judge who is a national of any State party concerned, or, if there is none, a person of its choice who shall sit in the capacity of judge; the names of the other judges shall be chosen by lot by the President before the opening of the case.

Article 44.

Only the High Contracting Parties and the Commission shall have the right to bring a case before the Court.

Article 45.

The jurisdiction of the Court shall extend to all cases concerning the interpretation and application of the present Convention which the High Contracting Parties or the Commission shall refer to it in accordance with Article 48.

Article 46.

(1) Any of the High Contracting Parties may at any time declare that it recognises as compulsory *ipso facto* and without special agreement the jurisdiction of the Court in all matters concerning the interpretation and application of the present Convention.

(2) The declarations referred to above may be made unconditionally or on condition of reciprocity on the part of several or certain other High Contracting Parties or for a specified period.

(3) These declarations shall be deposited with the Secretary-General of the Council of Europe who shall transmit copies thereof to the High Contracting Parties.

Article 47.

The Court may only deal with a case after the Commission has acknowledged the failure of efforts for a friendly settlement and within the period of three months provided for in Article 32.

Article 48.

The following may bring a case before the Court, provided that the High Contracting Party concerned, if there is only one, or the High Contracting Parties concerned, if there is more than one, are subject to the compulsory jurisdiction of the Court or, failing that, with the consent of the High Contracting Party concerned, if there is only one, or of the High Contracting Parties concerned if there is more than one:

(a) the Commission;

(b) a High Contracting Party whose national is alleged to be a victim;

(c) a High Contracting Party which referred the case to the Commission;

(d) a High Contracting Party against which the complaint has been lodged.

Article 53.

The High Contracting Parties undertake to abide by the decision of the Court in any case to which they are parties.

Article 54.

The judgment of the Court shall be transmitted to the Committee of Ministers which shall supervise its execution.

REFERENCES

A. SOVEREIGNTY AND SUPRANATIONALISM

Public Documents

League of Nations, Permanent Court of International Justice. *Collection of Judgments, Orders and Advisory Opinions,* Series A/B, No. 41 (*Customs Regime Between Germany and Austria*).

"Report of Rapporteur of Committee 1 to Commission I," in United Nations Conference on International Organization, *Documents,* Vol. VI, Doc. 944 (English), I/1/34 (1).

The Schooner Exchange v. *McFaddon,* 7 Cranch (U.S.), 116 (1812).

"Treaty Between the Federal Republic of Germany, the Kingdom of Belgium, the French Republic, the Italian Republic, the Grand Duchy of Luxembourg and the Kingdom of the Netherlands Instituting the European Coal and Steel Community," Signed at Paris on 18 April 1951. *United Nations Treaty Series,* CCLXI, 3229 (1957), 140–319.

United Nations, General Assembly. "Draft Declaration of the Rights and Duties of States," *Official Records.* 4th Sess., Supp. No. 10, A/925, June 24, 1949.

Books

Bishop, William. *International Law: Cases and Materials.* 2nd ed. Boston: Little, Brown and Company, 1962.

Bourquin, Maurice. *L'Etat Souverain et l'Organisation Internationale.* New York: Manhattan Publishing Company, 1959.

Brierly, J. L. *The Law of Nations.* Oxford: Clarendon Press, 1963.

Carlston, Kenneth S. *Law and Organization in World Society.* Urbana: University of Illinois Press, 1962.

———. *Law and Structures of Social Action.* New York: Columbia University Press, 1956.

Cook, Don. *Floodtide in Europe.* New York: G. P. Putnam's Sons, 1965.

Coplin, William D. *The Functions of International Law: An Introduction to the Role of International Law in the Contemporary World.* Chicago: Rand McNally and Company, 1966.

De Jouvenel, Bertrand. *Sovereignty: An Enquiry into the Political Good.* Chicago: University of Chicago Press, 1957.

Deutsch, Karl W. *Political Community at the International Level: Problems of Definition and Measurement.* Garden City, N.Y.: Doubleday and Company, Inc., 1954.

——— et al. *Political Community and the North Atlantic Area: International Organization in the Light of Historical Experience.* Princeton, N.J.: Princeton University Press, 1957.

De Vattel, Emerich. *The Law of Nations.* London: New Edition by Joseph Chitty, 1834.

DeVisscher, Charles. *Theory and Reality in Public International Law.*

Translated by P. E. Corbett. Princeton, N.J.: Princeton University Press, 1957.

Dickenson, E. D. *The Equality of States in International Law.* Princeton, N.J.: Princeton University Press, 1920.

Eagleton, Clyde. *International Government.* Rev. ed. New York: The Ronald Press Company, 1948.

Feld, Werner. *The Court of the European Communities: New Dimension in International Adjudication.* The Hague: Martinus Nijhoff, 1964.

Fenwick, Charles. *International Law.* 4th ed. New York: Appleton-Century-Crofts, Inc., 1965.

Friedmann, Wolfgang. *The Changing Structure of International Law.* New York: Columbia University Press, 1964.

Goodspeed, Stephen S. *The Nature and Function of International Organization.* New York: Oxford University Press, 1967.

Haas, Ernst B. *The Uniting of Europe: Political, Social, and Economic Forces, 1950–1957.* Stanford, Calif.: Stanford University Press, 1958.

Haines, C. Grove (ed.). *European Integration.* Baltimore: The Johns Hopkins Press, 1957.

Hay, Peter. *Federalism and Supranational Organizations: Patterns for New Legal Structures.* Urbana: University of Illinois Press, 1966.

Herz, John. *International Politics in the Atomic Age.* New York: Columbia University Press, 1959.

Hobbes, Thomas. *Leviathan.* Reprinted from the edition of 1651. Oxford: Clarendon Press, 1958.

Jacobini, H. B. *International Law.* Homewood, Ill.: The Dorsey Press, 1968.

Jenks, C. Wilfred. *The Prospects of International Adjudication.* London: Stevens & Sons Ltd., 1964.

Jessup, Philip C. *A Modern Law of Nations.* New York: The Macmillan Company, 1948.

——— et al. *International Organization.* New York: Carnegie Endowment for International Peace, 1955.

Kaeckenbeeck, Georges. *The International Experiment of Upper Silesia.* London: Oxford University Press, 1942.

Kooijmans, P. H. *The Doctrine of the Legal Equality of States.* Leyden: A. W. Sythoff, 1964.

Korowicz, Marek. *Introduction to International Law: Present Conceptions of International Law in Theory and Practice.* The Hague: Martinus Nijhoff, 1959.

Lawson, Ruth (ed.). *International Regional Organizations: Constitutional Foundations.* New York: Frederick A. Praeger, 1962.

Lauterpacht, Hersch. *The Development of International Law by the International Court.* London: Stevens & Sons Ltd., 1958.

Liska, George. *Europe Ascendant: The International Politics of Unification.* Baltimore: The Johns Hopkins Press, 1964.

Mark, Max. *Beyond Sovereignty.* Washington, D.C.: Public Affairs Press, 1965.

Mason, Henry L. *The European Coal and Steel Community: Experiment in Supranationalism*. The Hague: Martinus Nijhoff, 1955.

Reuter, Paul. *La Communauté Européenne du Charbon et de l'Acier*. Paris: Librairie Générale de Droit et de Jurisprudence, 1953.

————. *International Institutions*. London: George Allen & Unwin Ltd., 1958.

Rölling, B. V. A. *International Law in an Expanded World*. Amsterdam: Djambatan, 1960.

Schlochauer, Hans-Jürgen. *Der Rechtsschutz gegenüber der Tätigkeit Internationaler und Übernationaler Behörden*. Frankfurt/M: Vittorio Klostermann, 1952.

Schwarzenberger, Georg. *International Law as Applied by International Courts and Tribunals*. London: Stevens & Sons Ltd., 1950.

Shihata, Ibrahim F. I. *The Power of the International Court to Determine Its Own Jurisdiction: Compétence de la Compétence*. The Hague: Martinus Nijhoff, 1965.

Stoessinger, John G. *The Might of Nations: World Politics in Our Time*. Rev. ed. New York: Random House, 1965.

Wheare, K. C. *Federal Government*. New York: Oxford University Press, 1964.

Wright, Quincy. *Contemporary International Law: A Balance Sheet*. Garden City, N.Y.: Doubleday and Company, Inc., 1955.

————. *The Study of War*. Vol. II. Chicago: University of Chicago Press, 1944.

Wynner, Edith, and Georgia Lloyd (eds.). *Searchlight on Peace Plans: Choose Your Road to World Government*. New York: E. P. Dutton and Company, Inc., 1944.

Articles and Periodicals

Anand, R. P. "Role of the New Asian African Countries in the Present International Legal Order," *American Journal of International Law*, LVI, 2 (April, 1962), 383–406.

Beloff, Max. "International Integration and the Modern State," *Journal of Common Market Studies*, II, 1 (September, 1963), 52–62.

Carlston, Kenneth S. "The Grasp of Jurisdiction," *Proceedings of the American Society of International Law* (1959), 170–173.

Dickinson, John. "A Working Theory of Sovereignty," *Political Science Quarterly*, LXII, 4 (December, 1927), 524–548.

Etzioni, Amitai. "The Dialectics of Supranational Unification," *American Political Science Review*, LVI, 4 (December, 1962), 927–935.

————. "European Unification: A Strategy of Change," *World Politics*, XVI, 1 (October, 1963), 32–51.

Feld, Werner. "The European Community Court: Its Role in the Federalizing Process," *Minnesota Law Review*, L, 3 (January, 1966), 423–442.

Friedrich, Carl. "International Federalism in Theory and Practice," in Elmer Plischke (ed.), *Systems of Integrating the International Community*. New York: D. Van Nostrand Company, Inc., 1964.

Garner, J. W. "Limitations on National Sovereignty in International

Relations," *American Political Science Review*, XIX, 1 (February, 1925), 1–24.

Haas, Ernst B. "International Integration: The European and the Universal Process," in *International Political Communities: An Anthology*. Garden City, N.Y.: Anchor Books, 1966.

Hahn, Hugo J. "Constitutional Limitations in the Law of the European Organizations," *Recueil des Cours*, CVIII, 1 (1963), 189–306.

Herz, John. "Rise and Demise of the Territorial State," *World Politics*, IX, 4 (July, 1957), 473–493.

Jaenicke, G. "Die Sicherung des übernationalen Charakters der Organe internationaler Organisationen," *Zeitschrift für ausländisches öffentliches Recht und Völkerrecht*, XIV, 1 (December–January, 1952–53), 46–67.

Korowicz, Marek. "Some Present Aspects of Sovereignty in International Law," *Recueil des Cours*, CII (1961), 1–120.

Kunz, Josef L. "Supra-national Organs," *American Journal of International Law*, XLVI, 4 (October, 1952), 690–698.

Lansing, Robert. "Notes on Sovereignty in a State," *American Journal of International Law*, I, 1 (January, 1907), 105–128, and I, 2 (April, 1907), 297–320.

Loewenstein, Karl. "Sovereignty and International Coöperation," *American Journal of International Law*, XLVIII, 2 (April, 1954), 222–244.

Pescatore, Pierre. "Les Relations Extérieures des Communautés Européennes: Contribution à la Doctrine de la Personnalité des Organisations Internationales," *Recueil des Cours*, CIII, 2 (1961), 1–244.

Reuter, Paul. "Le Plan Schuman," *Recueil des Cours*, LXXXI, 2 (1952), 523–629.

Rosenau, James N. "Compatibility, Consensus, and an Emerging Political Science of Adaptation," *American Political Science Review*, LXI, 4 (December, 1967), 983–988.

Rosenne, Shabtai. "The Court and the Judicial Process," *International Organization*, XIX, 3 (Summer, 1965), 518–536.

Schlochauer, Hans-Jürgen. "Rechtsformen der europäischen Ordnung," *Archiv des Völkerrechts*, V (1955–56), 40–50.

Shihata, Ibrahim F. I. "The Attitude of New States Toward the International Court of Justice," *International Organization*, XIX, 2 (Spring, 1965), 203–222.

Van Houtte, Albert. "La Cour de Justice de la Communauté du Charbon et de l'Acier," *Annuaire Européen*, II (1956), 183–222.

Van Raalte, E. "The Treaty Constituting the European Coal and Steel Community," *International and Comparative Law Quarterly*, I, 7 (January, 1952), 73–85.

Vernon, Raymond. "The Schuman Plan: Sovereign Powers of the European Coal and Steel Community," *American Journal of International Law*, XLVII, 2 (April, 1953), 183–202.

Verzijl, J. H. W. "The Present Stagnation of Interstate Adjudication: Causes and Possible Remedies," *International Relations* (London), II, 8 (October, 1963), 479–492.

Wright, Quincy. "Domestic Jurisdiction as a Limit on National and Supra-national Action," *Northwestern University Law Review,* LVI, 1 (March–April, 1961), 11–40.

———. "The Jural Personality of the United Nations," *American Journal of International Law,* XLIII, 3 (July, 1949), 509–516.

Zemanek, Karl. "Supranationale Institutionen," in *Staatslexikon: Recht, Wirtschaft, Gesellschaft.* Herausgegeben von der Görres-Gesellschaft. Sechste, völlig neu bearbeitete und erweiterte Auflage. Bd. 7. Freiburg im Breisgau: Verlag Herder, 1962.

B. CENTRAL AMERICAN COURT OF JUSTICE

Public Documents

American Journal of International Law. 1906–18. [Although not official, many of the court cases and other public documents relating to the Central American Court are reprinted. Such documents are generally unavailable elsewhere.]

Bulletin of the International Bureau of the American Republics. 1908–11.

Corte de Justicia Centroamericana. *Anales de la Corte de Justicia Centroamericana.*

U.S. *Congressional Record.* 58th Cong., 3rd Sess., 1904.

U.S. *Papers Relating to the Foreign Relations of the United States.* 1906–18.

Books

Anchisi, Juan. *La Corte de Justicia Centroamericana.* Guatemala: Universidad de San Carlos de Guatemala, 1951.

Bailey, Thomas A. *A Diplomatic History of the American People.* 6th ed. New York: Appleton-Century-Crofts, Inc., 1958.

Ball, M. Margaret. *The Problem of Inter-American Organization.* Stanford, Calif.: Stanford University Press, 1944.

Carlston, Kenneth S. *The Process of International Arbitration.* New York: Columbia University Press, 1946.

Crowther, Samuel. *The Romance and Rise of the American Tropics.* Garden City, N.Y.: Doubleday, Doran and Company, Inc., 1929.

Davis, Calvin DeArmond. *The United States and the First Hague Peace Conference.* Ithaca, N.Y.: Cornell University Press, 1962.

Eyma, Jean. *La Cour de Justice Centre-Américaine.* Paris: Ernest Sagot & Cie., 1928.

Hudson, Manley O. *International Legislation.* Vol. II. New York: Carnegie Endowment for International Peace, 1922–24.

———. *International Tribunals: Past and Future.* Washington, D.C.: Carnegie Endowment for International Peace and Brookings Institution, 1944.

Jones, Chester Lloyd. *Caribbean Interests of the United States.* New York: D. Appleton and Company, 1916.

Karnes, Thomas L. *The Failure of Union: Central America, 1824–1960.* Chapel Hill: University of North Carolina Press, 1961.

Lyons, F. S. L. *Internationalism in Europe: 1815–1914*. Leyden: A. W. Sythoff, 1963.

Martin, Ernesto. *La Labor del Pacifismo y la Corte de Justicia Centroamericana*. San José, Costa Rica: Tip. de A. Alsina, 1908.

Munro, Dana G. *The Five Republics of Central America: Their Political and Economic Development and Their Relations with the United States*. New York: Oxford University Press, 1918.

———. *The United States and the Caribbean Area*. Boston: World Peace Foundation, 1934.

Palmer, Frederick. *Central America and Its Problems*. New York: Moffat, Yard and Company, 1910.

Politis, Nicolas S. *La Justice Internationale*. Paris: Librairie Hachette, 1924.

Ramirez, Manuel Castro. *Cinco Años en la Corte de Justicia Centroamericana*. San José, Costa Rica: Imprenta Lehmann, Sauter & Co., 1918.

Scott, James Brown (ed.). *The Hague Conventions and Declarations of 1899 and 1907: Tables of Signatures, Ratifications and Adhesions of the Various Powers and Texts of Reservations*. 3rd ed. New York: Oxford University Press, 1918.

Stuart, Graham H. *Latin America and the United States*. New York: D. Appleton-Century Company, Inc., 1943.

Wilgus, A. Curtis (ed.). *The Caribbean Area*. Washington, D.C.: George Washington University Press, 1934.

Articles and Periodicals

Anderson, Luis. "The Peace Conference of Central America," *American Journal of International Law*, II, 1 (January, 1908), 144–151.

Bailey, Thomas A. "Interest in a Nicaraguan Canal, 1903–1931," *Hispanic American Historical Review*, XVI (February, 1936), 2–28.

Brown, Philip Marshall. *"Costa Rica v. Nicaragua,"* *American Journal of International Law*, XI, 1 (January, 1917), 156–160.

Carlston, Kenneth S. "Development and Limits of International Adjudication," *Proceedings of the American Society of International Law* (1965), pp. 182–189.

Finch, George A. "The Treaty with Nicaragua Granting Canal and Other Rights to the United States," *American Journal of International Law*, X, 2 (April, 1916), 344–351.

González, Salvador Rodriguez. "The Neutrality of Honduras and the Question of the Gulf of Fonseca," *American Journal of International Law*, X, 3 (July, 1916), 509–542.

Hudson, Manley O. "The Central American Court of Justice," *American Journal of International Law*, XXVI, 4 (October, 1932), 759–786.

"New Peace Palace of the Central American Court of Justice," *Bulletin of the Pan American Union*, XLIV (June 17, 1916), 734–739.

"Nicaragua Case," *Independent*, XC, 3571 (May 12, 1917), 274.

"One International Tribunal," *Nation*, CVI, 2752 (March 28, 1918), 339.

Scott, James Brown. "The Central American Peace Conference of 1907," *American Journal of International Law*, II, 1 (January, 1908), 121–143.

———. "The Closing of the Central American Court of Justice," *American Journal of International Law*, XII, 2 (April, 1918), 380–382.

Wheless, Joseph. "The Central American Court of Justice," *Case and Comment*, XXI, 7 (December, 1914), 551–557.

"Where We Let Justice Fail," *North American Review*, CCVII, 751 (June, 1918), 814–817.

C. PERMANENT COURT OF INTERNATIONAL JUSTICE

Public Documents

League of Nations. *Acts of the First Assembly, Plenary Meetings.* 1920.

———. *Covenant.*

———. *Official Journal.*

———. *Treaty Series.* 1920–44.

League of Nations, Assembly. *Records.*

League of Nations, P.C.I.J. Series A. *Collection of Judgments and Orders.*

———. Series A/B. *Collection of Judgments, Orders and Advisory Opinions.*

———. Series D. *Collection of Texts Governing the Jurisdiction of the Court.*

———. Series E. *Annual Reports.*

———. *Statute.*

League of Nations, Secretariat. *Documents Concerning the Action Taken by the Council of the League of Nations Under Article 14 of the Covenant and the Adoption by the Assembly of the Statute of the Permanent Court.* Geneva, 1921.

U.S. Department of State. *The Treaty of Versailles and After: Annotations of the Text of the Treaty.* Publication No. 2724, Conference Series 92, 1947.

———. *The United States and the Permanent Court of International Justice: Documents Relating to the Question of American Accession to the Court.* Publication No. 44, 1930.

U.S. Senate, Committee on Foreign Relations. *Hearings, Relative to the Protocols Concerning the Adherence of the United States to the Permanent Court of International Justice.* Part 2, 73rd Cong., 2nd Sess., May 16, 1934.

Books

Bustamente y Sirven, Antonio Sánchez de. *The World Court.* Translated by Elizabeth F. Read. New York: The Macmillan Company, 1925.

Cory, Helen May. *Compulsory Arbitration of International Disputes.* New York: Columbia University Press, 1932.

Fleming, D. F. *The United States and World Organization: 1920–1933.* New York: Columbia University Press, 1938.

————. *The United States and the World Court.* Garden City, N.Y.: Doubleday, Doran and Company, Inc., 1945.

Howard-Ellis, C. *The Origin, Structure and Working of the League of Nations.* Boston and New York: Houghton Mifflin Company, 1928.

Hudson, Manley O. *The Permanent Court of International Justice, 1920–1942: A Treatise.* New York: The Macmillan Company, 1943.

————. *The World Court: 1921–1938.* Boston: World Peace Foundation, 1938.

Marburg, Theodore. *Development of the League of Nations Idea: Documents and Correspondence of Theodore Marburg.* Edited and with an Introduction by John H. Latané. New York: The Macmillan Company, 1932.

Miller, David Hunter. *The Drafting of the Covenant.* 2 vols. New York: G. P. Putnam's Sons, 1928.

Morley, Felix. *The Society of Nations: Its Organization and Constitutional Development.* Washington, D.C.: Brookings Institution, 1932.

Politis, Nicolas S. *La Justice Internationale.* Paris: Librairie Hachette, 1924.

Rosenne, Shabtai. *The World Court: What It Is and How It Works.* Leyden: A. W. Sythoff, 1962.

Scott, James Brown. *The Project of a Permanent Court of International Justice and Resolutions of the Advisory Committee of Jurists.* Pamphlet Series of the Carnegie Endowment for International Peace, Division of International Law, No. 35. Washington, D.C.: Carnegie Endowment, 1920.

Shihata, Ibrahim F. I. *The Power of the International Court to Determine Its Own Jurisdiction: Compétence de la Compétence.* The Hague: Martinus Nijhoff, 1965.

Walters, F. P. *A History of the League of Nations.* 2 vols. London: Oxford University Press, 1952.

Articles and Periodicals

Baker, Philip. "The Making of the Covenant," in P. Munch (ed.), *Les Origines et l'Oeuvre de la Société des Nations.* Copenhagen: Rask-Örstedfonden, 1924.

"Conditions upon Which the United States Will Enter the World Court," *Congressional Digest,* V, 2 (February, 1926), 46.

"The First Assembly of the League of Nations," in *A League of Nations.* World Peace Foundation Pamphlets, Vol. IV, No. 1. Boston: World Peace Foundation, 1921.

"How the World Court Is Financed," *Congressional Digest,* V, 2 (February, 1926), 53.

Hudson, Manley O. "The First Year of the Permanent Court of International Justice," *American Journal of International Law,* XVII, 1 (January, 1923), 15–28.

"The Permanent Court of International Justice: Documents Establishing the Court," *Congressional Digest,* II, 8 (May, 1923), 234–235.

Pollock, Frederick. "The Permanent Court of International Justice," *British Yearbook of International Law* (1926), pp. 135–140.

"President Harding Presents World Court Proposal to Senate," *Congressional Digest,* II, 8 (May, 1923), 230.

"Senate Discusses U.S. Entry into World Court," *Congressional Digest,* V, 2 (February, 1926), 55–56.

"Three Months of the League of Nations," in *A League of Nations.* World Peace Foundation Pamphlets, Vol. III, Nos. 1 and 2. Boston: World Peace Foundation, 1920.

D. INTERNATIONAL COURT OF JUSTICE

Public Documents

United Nations. *Charter.*

United Nations Conference on International Organization. *Documents.* 15 vols. London and New York: United Nations Information Organizations, 1945.

United Nations, Department of Political and Security Council Affairs. *Repertoire of the Practice of the Security Council: 1946–1951.* New York: Department of Political and Security Council Affairs, 1954.

United Nations, General Assembly. *Official Records.*

United Nations, I.C.J. *Reports of Judgments, Advisory Opinions and Orders.*

————. *Statute.*

————. *Yearbook.*

United Nations, Office of Public Information. *The International Court of Justice.* 5th ed. United Nations Publication 65.I.5, May, 1965.

United Nations, Press Services, Office of Public Information. *Weekly News Summary.*

United Nations, Security Council. *Official Records.*

U.S. *Congressional Record.* 79th Cong., 1st Sess., 1945.

U.S. Department of State. *The International Court of Justice: Selected Documents Relating to the Drafting of the Statute.* Publication No. 2491, Conference Series 84, 1946.

————. *The United Nations Conference on International Organization: Selected Documents.* Publication No. 2490, Conference Series 83, 1946.

U.S. Senate. *A Report to Accompany S. Res. 196.* 79th Cong., 2nd Sess., 1946.

U.S. Senate, Subcommittee of the Committee on Foreign Relations. *Hearings, on S. Res. 196, a Resolution Proposing Acceptance of Compulsory Jurisdiction of the International Court of Justice by the United States Government.* 79th Cong., 2nd Sess., 1946.

Books

Bailey, Thomas A. *A Diplomatic History of the American People.* 7th ed. New York: Appleton-Century-Crofts, Inc., 1964, Chaps. 49 and 51.

Goodrich, Leland M., and Edvard Hambro. *Charter of the United Nations: Commentary and Documents.* Boston: World Peace Foundation, 1946.

Hambro, Edvard. *The Case Law of the International Court: A Repertoire of the Judgments, Advisory Opinions and Orders of the Permanent Court of International Justice and the International Court of Justice.* Leyden: A. W. Sijthoff, 1952.

————. *L'Exécution des Sentences Internationales.* Paris: Librairie de Recueil Sirey, 1936.

Hudson, Manley O. *International Tribunals: Past and Future.* Washington, D.C.: Carnegie Endowment for International Peace and Brookings Institution, 1944.

Kitchel, Denison. *Too Grave a Risk: The Connally Amendment Issue.* New York: William Morrow and Company, 1963.

Lissitzyn, Oliver J. *The International Court of Justice.* New York: Marstin Press, 1951.

O'Connell, D. P. *International Law.* London: Stevens & Sons Ltd., 1965.

Rosenne, Shabtai. *The International Court of Justice: An Essay in Political and Legal Theory.* Leyden: A. W. Sijthoff's Uitgeversmaatschappij N.V., 1957.

————. *The World Court: What It Is and How It Works.* Leyden: A. W. Sythoff, 1962.

Russell, Ruth B., and Jeannette E. Muther. *A History of the United Nations Charter: The Role of the United States, 1940–1945.* Washington, D.C.: Brookings Institution, 1958.

Schwarzenberger, Georg. *International Law.* Vol. I. London: Stevens & Sons Ltd., 1949.

Sohn, Louis B. (ed.). *Cases on United Nations Law.* Brooklyn: The Foundation Press, Inc., 1956.

Articles and Periodicals

Bloomfield, Lincoln. "Law, Politics and International Disputes," *International Conciliation,* No. 516 (January, 1958), pp. 257–316.

Briggs, Herbert W. "Reservations to the Acceptance of Compulsory Jurisdiction of the International Court of Justice," *Recueil des Cours,* XCIII (1958), 223–367.

————. "The United States and the International Court of Justice: A Re-examination," *American Journal of International Law,* LIII, 2 (April, 1959), 301–318.

Carlston, Kenneth S. "Development and Limits of International Adjudication," *Proceedings of the American Society of International Law* (1965), pp. 182–189.

Catudal, Honoré M. "Procedure for Accepting the Optional Clause of the Statute of the International Court of Justice," *American Journal of International Law,* XL, 3 (July, 1947), 634–637.

"Compulsory Jurisdiction of the International Court of Justice," *Department of State Bulletin,* XXIV, 616 (April 23, 1951), 664–669.

"Congress and the Ratification of Treaties," *International Conciliation,* No. 411 (May, 1945), pp. 363–378.

Couve de Murville, Maurice. "International Court of Justice: Optional

Clause—Withdrawal of Automatic Reservation by France," *International and Comparative Law Quarterly*, VIII, 4 (October, 1959), 735.

Gross, Leo. "Bulgaria Invokes the Connally Amendment," *American Journal of International Law*, LVI, 2 (April, 1962), 357–382.

Hackworth, Green H. "The International Court of Justice," *Department of State Bulletin*, XIII, 320 (August 12, 1945), 216.

Honig, F. "The Diminishing Role of the World Court," *International Affairs*, XXXIV, 2 (April, 1958), 184–194.

Hudson, Manley O. "The Twenty-fourth Year of the World Court," *American Journal of International Law*, XL, 1 (January, 1946), 1–52.

Hyde, Charles. "The United States Accepts the Optional Clause," *American Journal of International Law*, XL, 4 (October, 1946), 778–781.

"International Court of Justice Action on Cases Involving U.S. Claims," *Department of State Bulletin*, XXXIV, 874 (March 26, 1956), 513–514.

Jennings, R. Y. "The Progress of International Law," *British Yearbook of International Law*, XXXIV (1958), 334–355.

Jessup, Philip C. "Acceptance by the United States of the Optional Clause of the International Court of Justice," *American Journal of International Law*, XXXIX, 4 (October, 1945), 745–751.

Lawson, Ruth. "The Problem of the Compulsory Jurisdiction of the World Court," *American Journal of International Law*, XLVI, 2 (April, 1952), 219–238.

"New Declarations of Acceptance by France and India of the Jurisdiction of the World Court Under Article 36 (2) of Its Statute," *Duke Law Journal*, LVI, 1 (Winter, 1960), 84–87.

Potter, Pitman B. "As Determined by the United States," *American Journal of International Law*, XL, 4 (October, 1946), 792–794.

Preuss, Lawrence. "The International Court of Justice, the Senate, and Matters of Domestic Jurisdiction," *American Journal of International Law*, XL, 4 (October, 1946), 720–736.

"Recognition of Compulsory Jurisdiction of the International Court of Justice," *Department of State Bulletin*, XV, 375 (September 8, 1946), 452–453.

"Report of the Informal Inter-Allied Committee on the Future of the Permanent Court of International Justice," *American Journal of International Law Supplement: Official Documents*, XXXIX, 1 (January, 1945), 1–41.

"The Self-Judging Aspect of the U.S. Reservation on Jurisdiction of the International Court," *Department of State Bulletin*, XLII, 1077 (February 15, 1960), 227–232.

Stone, Julius. "The International Court and World Crisis," *International Conciliation*, No. 536 (January, 1962), 3–64.

"The United States and World Court Jurisdiction," *Congressional Digest*, XL, 1 (January, 1961), 1–32.

Waldock, C. H. M. "Decline of the Optional Clause," *British Yearbook of International Law,* XXXII (1955–56), 244–287.

Wilcox, Francis O. "The United States Accepts Compulsory Jurisdiction," *American Journal of International Law,* XL, 4 (October, 1946), 699–719.

E. COURT OF THE EUROPEAN COMMUNITIES

Public Documents

"Convention Relating to Certain Institutions Common to the European Communities," Done at Rome on 25 March 1957. *United Nations Treaty Series,* CCXCVIII, 4302 (1958), 267–274.

Cour de la Communauté Européenne du Charbon et de l'Acier. *Recueil de la Jurisprudence de la Cour.* Vols. I–V (1954–59).

Cour de Justice des Communautés Européennes. *Recueil de la Jurisprudence de la Cour.* Vols. VI–XIII (1960–67).

Europäische Gemeinschaft, Presse- und Informationsdienst. *Gerichtshof der Europäischen Gemeinschaften: Seine Aufgaben, seine Verfassung, sein Verfahren.* Bonn: Presse- und Informationsdienst der Europäischen Gemeinschaften, 1966.

———. "Zeittafel der europäischen Integration," in *Die Europäische Gemeinschaft: EWG-Montanunion-Euratom.* Brüssel: Presse- und Informationsdienst der Europäischen Gemeinschaften, 1963.

Europäische Gemeinschaften, Europäisches Parlament. *Verträge von Rom: Synoptische Ausgabe in den vier Amtssprachen,* 1964.

European Coal and Steel Community, High Authority. *General Report.* 1st–15th (1954–67).

European Community Information Service. *European Community.* 1960–68.

———. *The European Community.* London Office: Press and Information Office of the European Communities, 1961.

———. *The European Community at a Glance.* London Office: Press and Information Office of the European Communities, 1964.

———. *European Community: The Facts.* Washington Office: Press and Information Office of the European Communities, 1967.

European Economic Community, Commission. *General Report.* 1st–10th (1958–67).

European Parliament, General Directorate of Parliamentary Documentation and Information. *Monthly Bulletin of European Documentation.*

France. *Constitution* (1958), Preamble.

France, Assemblée Nationale. *Journal Officiel.* December 6 and 7, 1951.

Germany, Federal Republic. *Basic Law* (1949), Article 24, pars. 1–3.

Germany, Federal Republic, Bundestag. *Sitzungsbericht.* July 12, 1951, and January 10, 1952.

Germany, Federal Republic, Presse- und Informationsamt der Bundesregierung. *The Bulletin.*

Italy. *Constitution,* Article XI.

Netherlands. *Constitution,* Articles 63 and 67.

"Protocol and the Statute of Justice of the European Economic Community," Done at Brussels on 17 April 1957. *United Nations Treaty Series,* CCXCVIII, 4300 (1958), 147–156.

"Protocol on the Code of the Court of Justice," Signed at Paris on 18 April 1951. *United Nations Treaty Series,* CCLXI, 3729 (1957), 247–267.

"Protocol on the Privileges and Immunities of the EEC," reprinted in Alan Campbell and Dennis Thompson, *Common Market Law: Text and Commentaries.* London: Stevens & Sons Ltd., 1962.

"Protocol on the Statute of the Court of Justice of the European Atomic Energy Community," Done at Brussels on 17 April 1957. *United Nations Treaty Series,* CCXCVIII, 4301 (1958), 256–266.

"Summary of the Debates in the Consultative Assembly of the Council of Europe," *European Assembly,* I, 1 (August 7–11, 1950). Published by authority of the Council of Europe by the Hansard Society.

"Treaty Between the Federal Republic of Germany, the Kingdom of Belgium, the French Republic, the Italian Republic, the Grand Duchy of Luxembourg and the Kingdom of the Netherlands Instituting the European Coal and Steel Community," Signed at Paris on 18 April 1951. *United Nations Treaty Series,* CCLXI, 3229 (1957), 140–319.

"Treaty Establishing a Single Council and a Single Commission of the European Communities," *Annuaire Européen,* XIII (1967), 461–503.

"Treaty (with Annexes and Protocol) Establishing the European Atomic Energy Community (EURATOM)," Done at Rome on 25 March 1957. *United Nations Treaty Series,* CCXCVIII, 4301 (1958), 167–266.

"Treaty Establishing the European Economic Community (with Annexes and Protocols)," Done at Rome on 25 March 1957. *United Nations Treaty Series,* CCXCVIII, 4300 (1958), 1–165.

Books

Bebr, Gerhard. *Judicial Control of the European Communities.* New York: Frederick A. Praeger, 1962.

Curtis, Michael. *Western European Integration.* New York: Harper and Row, 1965.

Feld, Werner. *The Court of the European Communities: New Dimension in International Adjudication.* The Hague: Martinus Nijhoff, 1964.

Haas, Ernst B. *The Uniting of Europe: Political, Social and Economic Forces, 1950–1957.* Stanford, Calif.: Stanford University Press, 1958.

Haines, C. Grove (ed.). *European Integration.* Baltimore: The Johns Hopkins Press, 1957.

Hay, Peter. *Federalism and Supranational Organizations: Patterns for New Legal Structures.* Urbana: University of Illinois Press, 1966.

Junckerstorff, Henry Alfred (ed.). *International Manual on the EEC.* St. Louis: St. Louis University Press, 1963.

Kitzinger, Uwe W. *The Challenge of the Common Market.* Oxford: Basil Blackwell, 1962.

Mason, Henry L. *The European Coal and Steel Community: Experiment in Supranationalism.* The Hague: Martinus Nijhoff, 1955.

Mayne, Richard. *The Community of Europe: Past, Present and Future.* New York: W. W. Norton and Company, Inc., 1963.

Monnet, Jean. *Les États-Unis d'Europe Ont Commencé.* Paris: Robert Laffort, 1955.

Reuter, Paul. *La Communauté Européenne du Charbon et de l'Acier.* Paris: Librairie Générale de Droit et de Jurisprudence, 1953.

Scheingold, Stuart A. *The Rule of Law in European Integration: The Path of the Schuman Plan.* New Haven: Yale University Press, 1965.

Siegler, Heinrich. *Dokumentation der europäischen Integration.* Bonn: Siegler & Co. KG. Verlag für Zeitarchive, 1961.

Speier, Hans, and W. Phillips Davison (eds.). *West German Leadership and Foreign Policy.* Evanston, Ill.: Row, Peterson and Company, 1957.

Stein, Eric, and Thomas L. Nicholson (eds.). *American Enterprise in the European Common Market: A Legal Profile.* Ann Arbor: University of Michigan Law School, 1960.

Valentine, D. G. *The Court of Justice of the European Coal and Steel Community.* The Hague: Martinus Nijhoff, 1955.

———. *The Court of Justice of the European Communities.* 2 vols. London: Stevens & Sons Ltd., 1965.

Weil, Gordon (ed.). *A Handbook on the European Economic Community.* New York: Frederick A. Praeger, 1965.

Articles and Periodicals

Berlia, Georges. "Jurisprudence des Tribunaux Internationaux en Ce Qui Concerne Leur Compétence," *Recueil des Cours,* LXXXVI, 2 (1955), 105–157.

Donner, A. M. "The Court of Justice of the European Communities," *International and Comparative Law Quarterly,* Supplementary Publication No. 1 (1961), pp. 66–75.

———. "The Single Voice of the Court," *European Community,* No. 107 (November, 1967), 14–15.

Erades, L. "International Law, European Community Law and Municipal Law of Member States," *International and Comparative Law Quarterly,* XV, Part 1, 4th Series (January, 1966), 117–132.

Feld, Werner. "The European Community Court: Its Role in the Federalizing Process," *Minnesota Law Review,* L, 3 (January, 1966), 423–442.

Gaudet, Michel. "The Legal Framework of the Community," *International and Comparative Law Quarterly,* Supplementary Publication No. 1 (1961), 8–22.

Hay, Peter. "Federal Jurisdiction of the Common Market Court," *American Journal of Comparative Law,* XII, 1 (Winter, 1963), 21–40.

Martinez, Ruben A. Berrios. "The Nature and Functioning of Article 177 of the Rome Treaty," *Journal of Common Market Studies*, V, 2 (December, 1966), 113–139.

McMahon, J. F. "The Court of the European Communities: Judicial Interpretation and International Organization," *British Yearbook of International Law*, XXXVII (1961), 320–350.

Ostroff, Nathan. "Treaty of Rome Establishes a New Supranational Legal Order Which Is Superior to the Municipal Laws of the Individual Member States," *Texas International Law Forum*, I, 2 (June, 1965), 121–145.

Reuter, Paul. "Aspects de la Communauté Economique Européenne," *Revue du Marché Commun*, VI, 1 (March, 1958), 6–14.

Robertson, A. H. "Legal Problems of European Integration," *Recueil des Cours*, XCI, 1 (1957), 105–211.

Valentine, D. G. "The Jurisdiction of the Court of Justice of the European Communities to Annul Executive Action," *British Yearbook of International Law*, XXXVI (1960), 174–222.

Van Vredenburch, H. E. Jonkheer. "European Co-operation, as Seen from The Hague," *International Relations* (London), I, 11 (April, 1959), 521–528.

Weil, Gordon. "The Merger of the Institutions of the European Communities," *American Journal of International Law*, LXI, 1 (January, 1967), 57–65.

Yondorf, Walter. "Monnet and the Action Committee: The Formative Period of the European Communities," *International Organization*, XIX, 4 (Autumn, 1965), 885–912.

F. EUROPEAN COURT OF HUMAN RIGHTS

Public Documents

Cassin, René. "La Cour Européenne des Droits de l'Homme," *Annuaire Européen*, VII (1959), 75–99. Published under the auspices of the Council of Europe.

Council of Europe. *European Convention on Human Rights: Collected Texts*. 2nd ed. Strasbourg. November, 1963.

Council of Europe, Directorate of Information. *Council of Europe News*. 1960–65.

———. *Forward in Europe*. 1960–68.

Council of Europe, Registry of the Court. Publications of the European Court of Human Rights (Series A: Judgments and Decisions 1966–67). *Case "Relating to Certain Aspects of the Laws on the Use of Languages in Education in Belgium"* (preliminary objection). Judgment of February 9, 1967.

"De Becker Case: Judgment," *Annuaire Européen*, X (1962), 633–643. Published under the auspices of the Council of Europe.

Germany, Federal Republic, Auswärtiges Amt, Forschungsinstitut der deutschen Gesellschaft für Auswärtige Politik E.V. "Beratende Versammlung [des Europarates] (3. Sitzungsperiode) 1951, Empfehlung betr. die Schaffung eines Europäischen Gerichtshofs," in *Europa: Dokumente zur Frage der Europäischen Einigung*. Bd. 17 (in drei Teilbänden). München: R. Oldenbourg Verlag, 1962, 502–503.

Ireland, Department of External Affairs. *Iris Sheachtainiúil na Roinne Gnóthai Eachtracha (Weekly Bulletin of the Department of External Affairs)*, VII, 536 (1961), 6–8.

"Lawless Case: Judgment," *Annuaire Européen*, VIII (1960), 409–433. Published under the auspices of the Council of Europe.

Modinos, Polys. "La Convention Européenne des Droits de l'Homme," *Annuaire Européen*, I (1953), 141–172. Published under the auspices of the Council of Europe.

"Summary of the Debates in the Consultative Assembly of the Council of Europe," *European Assembly*, I, 2, 3, and 4 (August 14–28, 1950). Published by authority of the Council of Europe by the Hansard Society.

Van Emde Boas, Menno J. "La Convention Européenne de Sauvegarde des Droits de l'Homme et des Libertés Fondementales dans la Jurisprudence Néerlandaise," *Annuaire Européen*, X (1962), 226–266. Published under the auspices of the Council of Europe.

Books

Lauterpacht, Hersch. *International Law and Human Rights*. New York: Frederick A. Praeger, 1950.

Luard, Evan (ed.). *The International Protection of Human Rights*. New York: Frederick A. Praeger, 1967.

McNair, Lord. *The Expansion of International Law*. Jerusalem: Magnes Press of Hebrew University, 1962.

Morrison, Clovis C. *The Developing European Law of Human Rights*. Leyden: A. W. Sijthoff, 1967.

Robertson, A. H. *European Institutions: Co-operation, Integration, Unification*. New York: Frederick A. Praeger, 1959.

————. *Human Rights in Europe*. Dobbs Ferry, N.Y.: Oceana Publications, Inc., 1963.

————. *The Law of International Institutions in Europe: Being an Account of Some Recent Developments in the Field of International Law*. New York: Oceana Publications, Inc., 1961.

Siegler, Heinrich. *Dokumentation der europäischen Integration*. Bonn: Siegler & Co. KG. Verlag für Zeitarchive, 1961.

Weil, Gordon. *The European Convention on Human Rights: Background, Development and Prospects*. Leyden: A. W. Sythoff, 1963.

Articles and Periodicals

"Council of Europe," *The Europa Year Book*, I (1966), 113–118.

"The European Commission of Human Rights and the European Court of Human Rights: Recent Developments," *Bulletin of the International Commission of Jurists*, No. 24 (December, 1965), 12–19.

Greenberg, Jack, and Anthony R. Shalit. "New Horizons for Human Rights: The European Convention, Court and Commission of Human Rights," *Columbia Law Review*, LXIII, 8 (December, 1963), 1384–1412.

Meyers, Denys P. "The European Commission on Human Rights," *American Journal of International Law*, L, 4 (October, 1956), 949–951.

Partch, Karl Joseph. "Die Entstehung der europäischen Menschheits-konvention," *Zeitschrift für ausländisches öffentliches Recht und Völkerrecht,* XV, 4 (September, 1954), 631–660.

Robertson, A. H. "The European Convention for the Protection of Human Rights," *British Yearbook of International Law,* XXVII (1950), 145–163.

————. "The First Case Before the European Court of Human Rights: *Lawless* v. *the Government of Ireland,*" *British Yearbook of International Law,* XXXVI (1960), 343–354.

Waldock, C. H. M. "The European Convention for the Protection of Human Rights and Fundamental Freedoms," *British Yearbook of International Law,* XXXIV (1958), 356–363.

Weil, Gordon. "The Evolution of the European Convention on Human Rights," *American Journal of International Law,* LVII, 4 (October, 1963), 804–827.

INDEX